British Writing, Propaganda and Cultural Diplomacy in the Second World War and Beyond

British Writing, Propaganda and Cultural Diplomacy in the Second World War and Beyond

Edited by
Beatriz Lopez, James Smith and
Guy Woodward

BLOOMSBURY ACADEMIC
LONDON • NEW YORK • OXFORD • NEW DELHI • SYDNEY

BLOOMSBURY ACADEMIC
Bloomsbury Publishing Plc, 50 Bedford Square, London, WC1B 3DP, UK
Bloomsbury Publishing Inc, 1359 Broadway, New York, NY 10018, USA
Bloomsbury Publishing Ireland, 29 Earlsfort Terrace, Dublin 2, D02 AY28, Ireland

BLOOMSBURY, BLOOMSBURY ACADEMIC and the Diana logo are trademarks of Bloomsbury Publishing Plc

First published in Great Britain 2024
This paperback edition publishd 2026

Copyright © Beatriz Lopez, James Smith and Guy Woodward, 2024

The editors and contributors have asserted their right under the Copyright, Designs and Patents Act, 1988, to be identified as Authors of this work.

For legal purposes the Acknowledgements on p. xi constitute an extension of this copyright page.

Cover design by Eleanor Rose
Cover image: British poet and writer Dylan Thomas (1914–1953) and British poet Patric Dickinson (1914–1944) in a BBC recording studio, August 1946 © Francis Reiss/ Picture Post/ Hulton Archive/ Getty Images

All rights reserved. No part of this publication may be: i) reproduced or transmitted in any form, electronic or mechanical, including photocopying, recording or by means of any information storage or retrieval system without prior permission in writing from the publishers; or ii) used or reproduced in any way for the training, development or operation of artificial intelligence (AI) technologies, including generative AI technologies. The rights holders expressly reserve this publication from the text and data mining exception as per Article 4(3) of the Digital Single Market Directive (EU) 2019/790.

Bloomsbury Publishing Plc does not have any control over, or responsibility for, any third-party websites referred to or in this book. All internet addresses given in this book were correct at the time of going to press. The author and publisher regret any inconvenience caused if addresses have changed or sites have ceased to exist, but can accept no responsibility for any such changes.

A catalogue record for this book is available from the British Library.

A catalog record for this book is available from the Library of Congress.

ISBN: HB: 978-1-3504-1213-2
PB: 978-1-3504-1217-0
ePDF: 978-1-3504-1214-9
eBook: 978-1-3504-1215-6

Typeset by Deanta Global Publishing Services, Chennai, India

For product safety related questions contact productsafety@bloomsbury.com.

To find out more about our authors and books visit www.bloomsbury.com and sign up for our newsletters.

Contents

List of illustrations	vii
Notes on contributors	viii
Acknowledgements	xi

Introduction: Literature, propaganda and the intellectual *Beatriz Lopez, James Smith and Guy Woodward* 1

Part I

1. Haw-Hawing Hitler: Radio comedy as propaganda *Debra Rae Cohen* 17
2. Radio pages, morale reading and the word war *Damien Keane* 32
3. Dylan Thomas at the microphone: The BBC's *Book of Verse* and imperial cultural propaganda *Daniel Ryan Morse* 48

Part II

4. PEN, refugee writers and propaganda *Katherine Cooper* 65
5. Visual storytelling in the Ministry of Information's wartime exhibitions *Harriet Atkinson* 82
6. Propaganda as elegy in the Ministry of Information's *Britain in Pictures* series *Megan Faragher* 101

Part III

7. Colonial insurgency, propaganda and the British 'soldier-aesthete': Maurice Cardiff, Lawrence Durrell, Patrick Leigh Fermor and Freya Stark in the Cyprus Revolt *Maria Hadjiathanasiou* 125
8. John Bankole Jones, *London Line* and the Central Office of Information in the era of cultural propaganda *Scott Anthony* 145
9. The British Council, *Writers and Their Work* and literature as cultural diplomacy *James Smith* 161

Part IV

10. Lynette Roberts's *Gods with Stainless Ears* and the poetics of propaganda *Adam Piette* 179

11	'Dialectical tight-rope acts of self-deception': Arthur Koestler's anti-communist propaganda *Annabel Williams*	196
12	Psychological warfare in Thomas Pynchon's *Gravity's Rainbow* *Kirk Robert Graham*	214
13	Dramatizing secrecy and propaganda: Sir David Hare in conversation *Guy Woodward*	233

Select Bibliography 249
Index 253

Illustrations

Figures

1.1	'Tommy Handley and Funf!', *Radio Fun*, 5 July 1941	24
5.1	'Specimen Exhibition Script' drawn up by exhibition scriptwriter Adrian Thomas to demonstrate the interplay between written and visual elements	85
5.2	Photomontage across the back wall of *London Pride*	87
5.3	Visitors to *London Pride*	93
6.1	Cover of Peter F. Anson's *British Sea-Fishermen*	103
6.2	Cover of Geoffrey Grigson's *Wild Flowers in Britain*	104
6.3	'Assembling a Hawker-Hurricane', by E. D. Hewland	118

Table

6.1	*Britain in Pictures* Books under Analysis	109

Contributors

Scott Anthony is Deputy Head of Research & Public History at the Science Museum Group, London. His books include *The Story of Propaganda Film* (2024), *Shell: Art and Advertising* (co-written with Oliver Green and Margaret Timmers, 2021), *Public Relations and the Making of Modern Britain* (2013) and *The Projection of Britain: A History of the GPO Film Unit* (co-edited with James Mansell, 2011).

Harriet Atkinson is Senior Lecturer at the Centre for Design History at the University of Brighton, UK. Her recent books include *Showing Resistance: Propaganda and Modernist Exhibitions in Britain, 1933-53* (2024) and, as co-editor, *Exhibitions Beyond Boundaries: Transnational Exchanges through Art, Architecture, and Design 1945-1985* (2022).

Debra Rae Cohen is Distinguished Professor of English Emerita at the University of South Carolina, United States. Her books include *Remapping the Home Front: Locating Citizenship in British Women's Great War Fiction* (2002) and, as co-editor, *Broadcasting Modernism* (2009) and *Teaching Representations of the First World War* (2017). She is completing a manuscript entitled *Sonic Citizenship: Intermedial Poetics and the BBC*.

Katherine Cooper is a writer, researcher and broadcaster based in Norwich, UK. A BBC/AHRC New Generation Thinker, she is the author of *War, Nation and Europe in the Novels of Storm Jameson* (2020) and is finishing a book about how British authors and English PEN helped European refugee writers during the Second World War.

Megan Faragher is Professor at Wright State University (Lake Campus), United States. She is the author of *Public Opinion Polling in Mid-Century British Literature: The Psychographic Turn* (2021).

Kirk Robert Graham is Honorary Research Associate at the University of Queensland, Australia, and the author of *British Subversive Propaganda during the Second World War: Germany, National Socialism and the Political Warfare Executive* (2021).

Maria Hadjiathanasiou is Research Fellow at the National Struggle Museum in Nicosia, Cyprus, and Adjunct Faculty at the University of Nicosia. She is the author of *Propaganda and the Cyprus Revolt: Rebellion, Counter-Insurgency and the Media, 1955-1959* (2020). In 2021 she completed a Marie Skłodowska-Curie Actions postdoctoral fellowship on British, Greek and Turkish cultural diplomacy in Cyprus (1945–74).

David Hare was described by the *Washington Post* as 'the premiere political dramatist writing in English'. He has written over thirty stage plays and thirty screenplays for film and television. In a millennial poll of the greatest plays of the twentieth century, 5 of the top 100 were his.

Damien Keane is Associate Professor of English at the State University of New York at Buffalo, United States. He is the author of *Ireland and the Problem of Information: Irish Writing, Radio, Late Modernist Communication* (2014), as well as articles on radio broadcasting, intelligence monitoring and literary recordings.

Beatriz Lopez completed a PhD on Muriel Spark and propaganda at Durham University, UK. Her journal article 'Muriel Spark and the Art of Deception: Constructing Plausibility with the Methods of WWII Black Propaganda' was published in *The Review of English Studies* (2020).

Daniel Ryan Morse is Associate Professor of English and Director of the Core Humanities program at the University of Nevada, Reno, United States. He is the author of *Radio Empire: The BBC's Eastern Service and the Emergence of the Global Anglophone Novel* (2020).

Adam Piette is Professor of Modern Literature at the University of Sheffield, UK. His books include *The Literary Cold War, 1945 to Vietnam* (2009), *Remembering and the Sound of Words: Mallarmé, Proust, Joyce, Beckett* (1996), *Imagination at War: British Fiction and Poetry, 1939-45* (1995) and, as co-editor, *The Edinburgh Companion to Twentieth-Century British and American War Literature* (2012).

James Smith is Professor of English Studies at Durham University, UK. He recently led the Leverhulme Trust-funded project 'The Political Warfare Executive, Covert Propaganda, and British Culture' (2018–22), and is currently leading a new Leverhulme Trust-funded project examining the cultural legacies of the Special Operations Executive (SOE). He is the editor of *The Cambridge Companion to British Literature of the 1930s* (2019) and the author of *British*

Writers and MI5 Surveillance, 1930-1960 (2013). He has published widely on censorship, surveillance and propaganda in British culture.

Annabel Williams is an independent scholar who has published on modernism, mid-twentieth-century literature, travel writing and war writing in journals such as *Modernist Cultures* and *Textual Practice*. Her *Twentieth-Century Literature* article 'Fantasias on national themes: Fantasy, Space and Imperialism in Rebecca West' won the Andrew J. Kappel Prize in Literary Criticism (2020). Her chapter 'Touring Political Berlin: Revolution, War, and Fascism' appeared in *Happy in Berlin? English Writers in the City* (2021).

Guy Woodward is a Research Associate in the Department of English Studies at Durham University, UK. He is the author of *Culture, Northern Ireland, and the Second World War* (2015) and has published '"Conducting his own Campaigns": Evelyn Waugh and Propaganda' in *The Review of English Studies* (2022). His next book examines Irish and British writers and Yugoslavia.

Acknowledgements

Most of the chapters in this volume evolved from presentations delivered as part of 'The Writer as Psychological Warrior: Intellectuals, Propaganda and Modern Conflict' online conference, hosted by Durham University in July 2021. We organized this event as part of 'The Political Warfare Executive, Covert Propaganda and British Culture' research project (2018–22), funded by the Leverhulme Trust.

We are grateful to Ben Doyle and Laura Cope at Bloomsbury Academic for their advice and guidance as we prepared this book for publication.

Introduction
Literature, propaganda and the intellectual

Beatriz Lopez, James Smith and Guy Woodward

Writing in 1943, George Orwell reflected upon the challenges posed for both governments and the intelligentsia by the rapid growth in wartime propaganda production. If the British government had begun the Second World War 'with the more or less openly declared intention of keeping the literary intelligentsia out of it', he suggested, it now faced the reality that 'after three years of war almost every writer, however undesirable his political history or opinions, has been sucked into the various Ministries or the BBC'.[1] As Orwell recognized, the recruitment of cultural actors by government information and psychological warfare departments changed both spheres, as the 'tone and even to some extent the content of official propaganda' were 'modified' by the new entrants, and, in turn, literary culture began to display the effects of wartime propaganda.

Orwell's own contentious role as a propagandist – from 1941 to 1943 he broadcast to India over the BBC's Eastern Service, famously likening it to the experience of being trodden on 'by a very dirty boot'[2] – shows how writers both volunteered and were recruited for service in propaganda, a field which assumed new importance in the Second World War, as emerging military and media technologies raised political warfare to the status of the 'Fourth Fighting Arm' of the state and established cultural figures as integral actors in modern warfare.[3] The later deployment of his work by the Information Research Department (IRD) during the Cold War further demonstrates that culture became a key component of the conflict. Indeed, the projection of British national interests and the battle for ideological legitimacy assumed new urgency in the post-war, post-imperial world order, as Britain's military and diplomatic pre-eminence was eclipsed by the emergence of the United States as a world power.

Using Orwell's contentions as starting points, this volume interrogates a series of interactions between literature, culture and propaganda. Its chapters chart an expansive constellation of British government propaganda and cultural diplomacy agencies, as well as non-governmental organizations such as PEN, analysing the involvement of cultural actors in political persuasion from the Second World War – a critical inflection point in the history of propaganda – to the Cold War. To do this, the volume presents case studies by leading and emerging literary scholars and cultural historians who provide new insights into the domestic and global deployment of British cultural propaganda and diplomacy, particularly in decolonizing theatres such as India, Cyprus and Sierra Leone. Chapters re-evaluate the propaganda work of prominent writers such as Dylan Thomas and Arthur Koestler in light of new research in propaganda archives and scrutinize the involvement of lesser-known writers such as Storm Jameson and Freya Stark in propaganda and cultural diplomacy.[4] Other chapters examine how propaganda agencies such as the Ministry of Information (MOI) and the Central Office of Information (COI) engaged with emerging media forms and formulated cultural campaigns, investigate the role of bodies such as the BBC and PEN as entities mediating state propaganda and study how British literature and culture was deployed and projected as a form of soft power which contributed to advancing policy objectives across the world, through case studies of book series such as the MOI's *Britain in Pictures* and the British Council's *Writers and Their Work*. A further important strand of chapters in this collection analyses cultural representations of propaganda service and considers how the themes and techniques of psychological warfare began to influence the fictional creations of authors, ranging from Second World War–era works such as the BBC radio comedy *It's That Man Again* (1939–49) and Lynette Roberts's long poem *Gods with Stainless Ears* (1951) through to works by later authors looking back on earlier British psychological warfare campaigns such as Thomas Pynchon's novel *Gravity's Rainbow* (1973) and David Hare's television film *Licking Hitler* (1978).

Orwell, of course, was not the only critic to notice this interaction. The symbiosis between culture and propaganda has occupied the attention of various distinct fields of scholarship, and this current volume situates its debates at the intersection of several bodies of research. Within literary studies, the involvement of writers in propaganda campaigns during the First and Second World Wars has received considerable attention. Peter Buitenhuis's *The Great War of Words* (1989) examined the secret recruitment of a range of prominent British writers during the First World War by the newly established War Propaganda Bureau (commonly known as Wellington House), which distributed material using covert arrangements with leading commercial publishers including Hodder & Stoughton, Macmillan and Methuen, a strategy returned to by British propagandists in the Second World War and Cold War.[5] Wellington House's targeting of elites (specifically in the United States) likewise established the rationale for future cultural operations during these later conflicts. Gesturing to the impact of propaganda on literary style and aesthetics, Buitenhuis also suggested that the involvement of writers in propaganda campaigns contributed to an interwar collapse of faith in a shared culture, resulting in the development of a more ironic idiom. Building on this work, Mark Wollaeger's *Modernism, Media, and Propaganda: British Narrative From 1900 to 1945* (2006) sought to chart a symbiotic relationship between propaganda and modernist writing and filmmaking, suggesting that both 'raise the problem of the separation of form from content; both try to make meaning effective through ambiguity'.[6] Similarly, scholarship on British literature of the Second World War has noted how 'an unprecedented number of authors were recruited into the realm of the British information agencies',[7] with the work of figures such as J. B. Priestley and Orwell at the BBC now standard features of British cultural histories of the Second World War.

Linked to this last point, a second area of significant ongoing scholarship has traced the intersections between literary history and the BBC, with recent studies by Melissa Dinsman, Daniel Ryan Morse, Vike Martina Plock and Ian Whittington exploring the wartime recruitment of writers and intellectuals to work on radio programming for domestic and international audiences.[8] Whittington notes that intellectuals' generalized dislike for radio during the early decades of the twentieth century evaporated with the coming of the Second World War, as 'participation in a total war against a Nazi government hostile to much cultural production made the convergence of political and aesthetic goals all but unavoidable'.[9] Dinsman suggests that radio work enabled writers to 'translate high modernist modes and aesthetic principles – artistic autonomy and individualism, the cosmopolitan and trans-historical imagination, exile and alienation, eclecticism – for distribution to a mass audience during 1940s wartime radio'.[10] Yet, as Whittington observes, they were propagandists to the extent that they regarded their radio work 'as a way of orienting listeners in a crowded media environment, a project most of them felt to be ethically defensible'.[11]

A third area of scholarship has tracked Cold War developments in literary culture as intellectual movements were recruited, diverted, corralled and funded by actors directing the battle for hearts and minds, and has given particular attention to covert government subsidies for publications and organizations. In *Who Paid the Piper? The CIA and the Cultural Cold War* (1999), Frances Stonor

Saunders examined the US intelligence agency's covert backing of a range of cultural publications, conferences and other events across the globe. Her account of the Congress for Cultural Freedom (CCF) shows that Britain remained a key battleground, with British agencies co-funding CCF operations and British intellectuals taking key leadership roles in CCF activities. This analysis was continued by scholars such as Hugh Wilford, who, in his work examining interactions between the CIA and Britain's Cold War left-wing intelligentsia, detailed how the IRD circulated editions of Koestler's *Darkness at Noon* (1940) and Orwell's *Animal Farm* (1945) and also commissioned a strip cartoon version of the latter novel for newspaper syndication in South America, the Middle East and the Far East.[12] Further scholarship in this vein has explored the role of Cold War state-private partnerships in promoting modernist literature and art and thereby demonstrating 'that these artistic achievements were possible only in a free, individualistic society';[13] other work has argued that the 'literatures of decolonization' needs to be understood as part of the 'literatures of the global cold war', shaped by pressures such as overt and covert 'cultural diplomacy programmes' by Soviet-bloc and Western agencies as well as 'increasingly severe sanctions, including surveillance, censorship, and imprisonment'.[14] And, in the wide field of propaganda studies and history, key surveys of British propaganda give increasing weight to the intellectual context and the deployment of British culture; indeed, the growing appreciation of this element was (as Philip M. Taylor noted in his pioneering work of 1981) one of the defining developments of modern propaganda studies, which has moved away from earlier histories that simply 'concentrate[d] upon the more blatant examples of state propaganda' during war.[15]

However, across these diverse and growing fields of scholarship, it is evident that certain limitations remain. One of the most basic but significant impediments is that of source materials: the archives of British propaganda agencies are often unruly entities, offering overwhelming paperwork on certain areas and silences in others, particularly where papers on sensitive campaigns are withheld or destroyed.[16] Combined with the fact that many individual authors who undertook propaganda work remained evasive about such work in their own published writing and private papers, untangling such histories often depends on patient scholarship working across different archives and sources. A further barrier has been the tendency towards historical periodization: when scholarship remains tied to particular moments (whether the MOI of the First World War or the CCF during the Cold War), it can seem that in each moment propaganda emerged *ex nihilo* rather than as part of an interlocked evolution of relationships, as evidenced by the transference of people and expertise from the Political Warfare Executive (PWE) to the IRD. Certain agencies – such as the PWE and British Council – have remained largely absent from modern literary history, despite being increasingly recognized as major actors in the employment of modern writers and in the dissemination of modern British literature, while other bodies such as PEN have not typically been studied in the context of propaganda, despite their undoubted roles in international advocacy and persuasion. Meanwhile, operational histories of such propaganda agencies rarely look at the specific techniques of campaigns and are more interested in navigating bureaucratic institutional structures, without considering how propaganda was actually crafted and conveyed, what made it effective (or not) and how it was received by its target populations (a particularly difficult topic of study).[17] One further long-standing – and understandable – tendency has been to focus on production at the expense of research, even though propaganda agencies were dependent on extensive and intensive programmes of intelligence gathering to craft successful campaigns – the archives of the MOI and PWE testify to this, and in this volume, Damien Keane's chapter highlights the literary significance of the BBC's monitoring operation.

Definitions and contexts

This collection therefore provides the first sustained analysis of these complicated interactions between British authors, propaganda and culture during and after the Second World War, with analysis that serves to illuminate more contemporary debates about the relationship between propaganda and the arts, as demonstrated by the concluding interview with Sir David Hare. But, before moving to the case studies of this collection, it is necessary to pause to elucidate a broader framework of the terms and definitions that shape what follows. The first basic question to grapple with is perhaps the most vexed: the question of what is meant by the term propaganda. It is often noted that propaganda is almost as old as art itself. A 1942 manual produced by the PWE observed that 'psychological warfare' was by no means a 'new device [and] has been practised at every stage in history', citing '[t]he war-paint of barbarous tribes, the "Trojan Horse," the Pyrrhic elephants, the "leaflets" and "whispers" employed by Richelieu to infiltrate and to destroy the morale of the besieged population at La Rochelle'.[18] But there is little doubt that the twentieth century saw an inflection point in this relationship: as David Welch puts it, 'propaganda came of age in the twentieth century', amid a wider and fundamental shift in the nature of propaganda and its deployment by state actors.[19] One of the most basic but significant shifts was in the understanding of the term propaganda itself. For centuries a neutral term merely describing a scheme 'for the propagation of a particular doctrine',[20] the early twentieth century increasingly saw the association of propagandizing with presenting information in a specifically negative or biased way – in its most extreme forms, propaganda began to stand for 'the enemy of independent thought and an intrusive and unwanted manipulator of the free flow of information'.[21] Concurrent with this linguistic shift gaining wide traction were technological, political and media developments: the emergence of cinema and radio as mediums of mass communication, and the rise of the aircraft and the bomber specifically allowing unprecedented dissemination of newspapers and leaflets into active conflict zones. This was an era in which state agencies began to speak of propaganda in terms of a form of 'political' or 'psychological' warfare, an 'indispensable component of Total War', when experts from psychology, advertising, publishing and other fields were harnessed for their expertise and when formal doctrines for integrated propaganda were developed as strategies for conflict.[22]

Across all this, propaganda took many forms. Jacques Ellul, one of the most influential modern theorists of propaganda, makes a useful explanation of the distinction between clandestine propaganda and those that operate more openly – the so-called distinction between 'black' and 'white' forms of propaganda:

> The former tends to hide its aims, identity, significance, and source. The people are not aware that someone is trying to influence them, and do not feel that they are being pushed in a certain direction. This is often called 'black propaganda.' It also makes use of mystery and silence. The other kind, 'white propaganda,' is open and aboveboard. There is a Ministry of Propaganda; one admits that propaganda is being made; its source is known; its aims and intentions are identified. The public knows that an attempt is being made to influence it.[23]

These basic assumptions have governed how the British state propaganda apparatus has evolved and operated over the past century. In wartime, much of the overt propaganda in Britain fell to the MOI which, after a short life during the First World War, was reinstituted in September 1939 at the outbreak of the Second World War, taking charge of domestic publicity, propaganda to neutral and Allied countries and censorship of Britain's post and media.[24] Although it officially remained independent of the government, the BBC was key to Britain's overt propaganda apparatus over most of the twentieth century, especially following its expansion in 1938 to offer programming in foreign language broadcasting. By the end of the Second World War, the Corporation 'had established an intimate if chequered working relationship with Whitehall and the murky world of the intelligence services, while at the same time building from scratch a reputation on the international stage for emphasising the truth'.[25]

The British black apparatus has been more secretive and is harder to study because its materials were disseminated unattributed and often appear to have been the first items to have met the incinerator when the archives were culled. In the late 1930s, with the prospect of war looming, a secretive body known as Department EH was founded (so-called due to its base in Electra House on Victoria Embankment in London), chaired by the veteran propagandist Sir Campbell Stuart and charged with preparing anti-German propaganda. Separately, other branches of the British state were also developing their own propaganda arms, which were in 1941 consolidated into a distinct, independent entity – the PWE – tasked with propaganda to enemy countries and occupied territories, and whose output ranged from policy direction for the BBC European Service to the faked 'black' radio broadcasts recorded at the organization's country headquarters in the small rural village of Milton Bryan in Bedfordshire. Although the PWE was wound up at the end of the war, many of its campaigns and personnel continued operating, whether in new, open forms of publicity devised by the COI, a post-war successor to the MOI which was mandated 'to produce information campaigns on issues that affected the lives of British citizens, from health and education to benefits, rights and welfare'[26] or in covert forms by Cold War entities such as the IRD, the secretive branch of the Foreign Office formed in 1948 and charged with leading Britain's anti-communist propaganda.[27]

If this taxonomy outlines the broad layers of responsibility and key organizations within it, it is also important to note that, in practice, during the twentieth century, the lines between agencies and types of propaganda were often blurred, and British propagandists increasingly conceptualized propaganda on a spectrum. For example, in the Second World War, Britain's clandestine propaganda guru Sefton Delmer claimed to have developed 'grey' propaganda as 'something new' – as something that the consumer realizes is fake to some degree, but nonetheless 'gratefully' consumes – and gestured towards the further gradation of PWE campaigns using the phrase 'dirty off-white' material.[28] The nuanced approach continued after the war as the IRD, founded with the aim of projecting Britain as a positive 'third force' in the global order, quickly became associated with grey and black campaigns.[29] The IRD was not the only branch of the Foreign Office concerned with propaganda: the FO's Cultural Relations Department liaised with bodies such as the British Council and UNESCO.[30]

If this sets out the blurry lines between overt and covert propaganda and the evolving British apparatus tasked with delivering this, a further tension this collection explores is that of the relationship between propaganda and cultural diplomacy. On first glance, at least in common usage, there seems to be an instinctive dividing line between the two concepts. Propaganda implies some form of communication that is forceful and immediate in its intent, conducted with clear policy aims and typically activated in times of war or crisis. On the other side, cultural diplomacy seems to convey a less direct way to spread influence, part of an ongoing process undertaken by states in peacetime, but without short-term instrumental ambitions – the exercise of 'soft power' rather than coercion. On closer examination, however, this neat distinction again starts to blur. As Smith notes in his chapter, the British Council was conceptualized from its foundation in the mid-1930s as a 'cultural propaganda' organization. More broadly, most British propaganda agencies, whether overt or covert, engaged in techniques such as educational book publishing that appear far more in the realm of cultural diplomacy than that of propaganda.[31] Therefore, following Menand's contention that 'cultural diplomacy just *is* propaganda. It puts a national brand on art and ideas',[32] one of the motivations of this volume is to analyse the commonalities between propaganda and cultural diplomacy in order to provide a more holistic understanding of British attempts to influence public opinion at home and abroad from the Second World War to the Cold War.

Finally, in a collection assessing the interactions between British writing and propaganda, there is the question of what 'writing' we mean and who qualifies as a 'writer' and possible subject of attention. Clearly, as this introduction already lays out, our dialogue (at least in one direction) is within the parameters and assumptions of literary history: in this understanding, a career bureaucrat who writes technical reports as part of their role would be unlikely to be considered a 'writer'. However, despite acknowledging this assumption, this collection has not sought to impose overly tight generic or formal restrictions upon who qualifies for attention, and we have seen our remit as one that encompasses any facet of Britain's public intelligentsia that crossed into the spheres of state propaganda. Of course, as Stefan Collini has argued, the concept of the intelligentsia is itself an unstable one – particularly in the context of Britain, a country often assessed to lack a tradition of 'public intellectuals' shaping national debates in the mode of France or other nations.[33] Yet this collection suggests that the British intelligentsia has in fact exerted power through its involvement in propaganda. Across the twentieth century, Britain was able to wield a formidable propaganda apparatus precisely because its culture had nurtured a cadre of skilled cultural workers with reputations for artistic and intellectual innovation and independence, who could be co-opted to produce persuasive literature, art and ideas for government-backed publications and broadcasts in ways that in many cases proved far more effective than comparable operations by career bureaucrats.

Structure of the volume

In light of these distinctions, this collection is structured to reflect the complex, evolving relationship between British propaganda and modern culture, as contributors explore varying facets of propaganda work and its effects across linked case studies. The opening sequence of chapters focuses on the crucial involvement of writers in radio broadcast propaganda during and after the Second World War. Debra Rae Cohen argues for the central role of radio comedy as a propaganda tool deployed by the BBC, and specifically looks at how the series *It's That Man Again* (*ITMA*) countered the notorious broadcasts of the Nazi collaborator William Joyce (better known as Lord Haw-Haw). It shows how *ITMA* 'provided a common reference point and a common vocabulary' for its immense listenership, which reached 40 per cent of the British population by 1944.[34] Damien Keane next explores the vast textual production of the BBC's monitoring service during the war and considers the significance of transcripts in political warfare, specifically addressing the role of narrative in shaping the disinformation, innuendo, half-truths and lies that constitute political warfare. Daniel Ryan Morse then traces this propaganda evolution beyond the war through an account of the BBC's literary programme *Book of Verse* (1944–50s), designed for Indian students and broadcast over the period when India gained independence, illuminating the role played by canonical Anglophone literature in BBC propaganda efforts which stressed the common culture of Britain and its colonies in the post-war era.

The next sequence of chapters presents a series of case studies showing how movements, book series and exhibitions were sponsored by propaganda and cultural diplomacy agencies as a key mechanism for projecting British soft power during and after the Second World War. Katherine Cooper explores how PEN's refugee writers were drawn into the Allied propaganda war, focusing on the 1941 PEN Congress in London and wartime BBC broadcasting to shed new light on the problematic repercussions of deploying such writers as part of official propaganda efforts. Studying the MOI's 1940 'civilian morale exhibition' *London Pride*, Harriet Atkinson describes how the ministry used exhibitions and displays of 'photogenic story-telling' as propaganda during the war, integrating the work of leading designers with scripts by authors such as Orwell and Louis MacNeice. Megan Faragher then addresses the MOI's widely disseminated *Britain in Pictures* series (1941–50), which commissioned works by authors such as Elizabeth Bowen, Rose Macaulay, Orwell, Vita Sackville-West and Edith Sitwell. Faragher argues that this series developed a particular elegiac rhetorical style to project the supposedly democratic qualities of British culture at home and abroad.

The third sequence of chapters examines British cultural propaganda and cultural diplomacy at the end of empire, and how Cyprus, West Africa and the Far East became targets as Britain attempted to counteract the waning of its global influence. Maria Hadjiathanasiou addresses the role of the British 'soldier-aesthete' in Cyprus during the anti-colonial Revolt in the 1950s and traces how a cluster of expatriate writers, including Lawrence Durrell, became involved in intelligence and propaganda activities at this time. Scott Anthony then examines British cultural propaganda to Africa during the 1960s through the 'telezine' *London Line* and the career of the British-Sierra Leonean presenter John Bankole Jones, showing how the outputs of agencies such as the COI and the BBC World Service reflected global societal changes occurring during the time of decolonization. Following this, James Smith considers how the British Council helped to shape the global post-war Anglophone literary canon through its long-running *Writers and Their Work* series, launched in the 1950s with the ambition of its books being 'emissaries' aimed at 'the university type of reader in the East', and which has gone on to become a ubiquitous presence in libraries and reading lists of post-war students around the world.

The final sequence of chapters considers the legacy of wartime propaganda agencies in writings by significant authors, tracing the extent to which the form and content of literary texts has been shaped by cultural awareness of propaganda techniques or personal involvement in propaganda campaigns. Adam Piette shows how the integration propaganda of the Second World War was registered in literature on the home front, harnessing F. C. Bartlett's seminal wartime study *Political Propaganda* (1940) as a means to re-read Lynette Roberts's long poem *Gods with Stainless Ears* (1951). Annabel Williams next examines the novels of Arthur Koestler, one of the leading anti-communist activists of the Cultural Cold War, using the issue of 'irrationality' in Koestler's writing to explore wider interactions between literature and propaganda. Turning to

Thomas Pynchon's landmark postmodernist novel *Gravity's Rainbow* (1973), Kirk Graham then sheds new light on the global post-war legacy of Britain's wartime black propaganda agency, revealing how the PWE generated specific source material for Pynchon, and considering more broadly how the legacies of psychological warfare campaigns enacted by such agencies inform the themes of Pynchon's work. Bringing this section up to the present moment, the collection closes with Guy Woodward's interview with Sir David Hare, arguably Britain's most influential contemporary political dramatist. Hare discusses his 1978 BBC film *Licking Hitler*, which depicts the work of the PWE, and considers how the agency's psychological warfare methods have influenced propaganda and creative art in contemporary British society.

The collection is certainly not the last word on British writing and propaganda. New archives will continue to be opened, and long-opened material will be revisited with new eyes and approaches. New authors, publications, agencies and regions will undoubtedly come into scholarly focus. Recent history suggests that future scholars of propaganda will find no shortage of twenty-first-century ideological battles to research, with the age of the internet (and, even more recently, the rise of deepfakes and AI) ushering in an entirely new frontier of psychological warfare. And yet, as the chapters in this volume attest, many of the fundamental techniques and debates concerning propaganda remain the same, and we hope that this collection will provide a pathway to connect with such future work.

Notes

1 George Orwell, 'Poetry and the Microphone', in *The Collected Essays, Journalism and Letters of George Orwell: Volume 2: My Country Right or Left 1940–1943*, ed. Sonia Orwell and Ian Angus (Harmondsworth: Penguin, 1970), 381.
2 George Orwell, letter to Rayner Heppenstall, 24 August 1943, in *Collected Essays: Volume 2*, 349.
3 This doctrine was most clearly articulated in the wartime manual, 'The Meaning, Techniques and Methods of Political Warfare', released by the Political Warfare Executive in 1942. A copy of this was transcribed on the now defunct website www.psywar.org and is available at https://www.psywar.org/psywar/reproductions/MeanTechMethod.pdf [accessed 13 November 2023]. The original can be found in the UK's National Archives, Kew, London (hereafter TNA), at FO 898/101.
4 It is worth noting that the roles of women writers in the secret services have often been overlooked, though there is an emerging body of scholarship that addresses

this lacuna. See, for example, Megan Faragher, 'The Form of Modernist Propaganda in Elizabeth Bowen's *The Heat of the Day*', *Textual Practice* 27, no. 1 (2013): 49–68; Beatriz Lopez, 'Muriel Spark and the Art of Deception: Constructing Plausibility with the Methods of WWII Black Propaganda', *The Review of English Studies* 71, no. 302 (2020): 969–86; and the special issue of *Modernist Cultures* on 'Women, Modernism and Intelligence Work', ed. Simon Cooke and Natalie Ferris (2021).

5   Peter Buitenhuis, *The Great War of Words: Literature as Propaganda 1914–18 and After* (London: Batsford, 1989), 16.
6   Mark Wollaeger, *Modernism, Media, and Propaganda: British Narrative from 1900 to 1945* (Princeton, NJ: Princeton University Press, 2006), xiv.
7   James Smith, 'Covert Legacies in Postwar British Fiction', in *British Literature in Transition, 1940–1960*, ed. Gill Plain (Cambridge: Cambridge University Press, 2019), 338.
8   See Melissa Dinsman, *Modernism at the Microphone: Radio, Propaganda, and Literary Aesthetics during World War II* (London: Bloomsbury Academic, 2015); Ian Whittington, *Writing the Radio War: Literature, Politics and the BBC, 1939–1945* (Edinburgh: Edinburgh University Press, 2018); Daniel Ryan Morse, *Radio Empire: The BBC's Eastern Service and the Emergence of the Global Anglophone Novel* (New York, NY: Columbia University Press, 2020); and Vike Martina Plock, *The BBC German Service during the Second World War: Broadcasting to the Enemy* (Cham: Palgrave Macmillan, 2021).
9   Whittington, *Writing the Radio War*, 5–6.
10 Dinsman, *Modernism at the Microphone*, 6.
11 Whittington, *Writing the Radio War*, 20.
12 Hugh Wilford, *The CIA, the British Left and the Cold War: Calling the Tune?* (London: Frank Cass, 2003), 58. John Jenks, in his *British Propaganda and News Media in the Cold War* (Edinburgh: Edinburgh University Press, 2006) suggests this was highly successful (71).
13 Greg Barnhisel, *Cold War Modernists: Art, Literature, and American Cultural Diplomacy* (New York, NY: Columbia University Press, 2015), 21.
14 Peter Kalliney, *The Aesthetic Cold War: Decolonization and Global Literature* (Princeton, NJ: Princeton University Press, 2022), 5, 7.
15 Philip M. Taylor, *The Projection of Britain: British Overseas Publicity and Propaganda, 1919–1939* (Cambridge: Cambridge University Press, 1981), vii.
16 For example, Ellic Howe speculates that only one in ten documents survives as part of the Political Warfare Executive Papers (The National Archives, UK). See *The Black Game: British Subversive Operations against the Germans during the Second World War* (London: Queen Anne Press, 1988), 7.
17 A case in point here is David Garnett's official history of the PWE. Despite being a noted Bloomsbury author in his own right and a key worker in the PWE's Secretariat during the war, Garnett's history reads more as an extended synthesis

of committee minutes than an engaging historical narrative. See David Garnett, *The Secret History of PWE: The Political Warfare Executive, 1939–1945* (London: St Ermin's Press, 2002).
18 'The Meaning, Techniques and Methods of Political Warfare', TNA, FO 898/101.
19 David Welch, '"Opening Pandora's Box": Propaganda, Power and Persuasion', in *Propaganda, Power and Persuasion: From World War I to Wikileaks*, ed. David Welch (London: I.B. Tauris, 2014), 3.
20 See the Oxford English Dictionary, which tracks such usage back to 1790, with this in turn having emerged from a seventeenth-century association of the term with a specific committee of the Vatican.
21 Philip M. Taylor, *Munitions of the Mind: A History of Propaganda from the Ancient World to the Present Day*, 3rd edn (Manchester: Manchester University Press, 2003), 1. The Oxford English Dictionary gives an example from 1929 of a use of propaganda associating it with 'sinister meaning'.
22 This is set out in 'The Meaning, Techniques and Methods of Political Warfare' document. While a distinction has occasionally been drawn between 'political' and 'psychological' warfare, in practice these terms came to be used interchangeably. The same document notes at its opening that: 'Political Warfare is referred to variously as "Psychological Warfare," "Morale Warfare," or "Ideological Warfare." More often it is regarded merely as "propaganda"' ('The Meaning, Techniques and Methods of Political Warfare', TNA, FO 898/101).
23 Jacques Ellul, *Propaganda: The Formation of Men's Attitudes*, trans. Konrad Kellen and Jean Lerner (New York, NY: Vintage Books, 1965), 15. As Megan Faragher notes in Chapter 6, the relative opacity of propaganda variants remains a central concept in propaganda studies, although the associations between white/black and truth/deception are increasingly problematic.
24 For the most recent scholarship on the MOI, see 'MOI Digital: A History of the Ministry of Information, 1939–46', at https://moidigital.ac.uk/, which carries materials of the AHRC-funded project 'A Publishing and Communications History of the Ministry of Information, 1939–46', including ongoing publications and a searchable database of MOI reports [accessed 13 November 2023].
25 David Hendy, *The BBC: A People's History* (London: Profile Books, 2022), 289.
26 This description is taken from the British Library's guide to the Central Office of Information archives and can be found at https://www.bl.uk/collection-guides/central-office-of-information-archive [accessed 27 August 2023].
27 On the PWE, see Garnett, *The Secret History of PWE*; Howe, *The Black Game*; and Kirk Robert Graham, *British Subversive Propaganda during the Second World War: Germany, National Socialism and the Political Warfare Executive* (Cham: Palgrave Macmillan, 2021). On the IRD, see Paul Lashmar and James Oliver, *Britain's Secret Propaganda War 1948–1977* (Stroud: Sutton Publishing, 1998); Wilford, *The CIA, the British Left and the Cold War*; Andrew Defty, *Britain, America and Anti-*

Communist Propaganda, 1945–53: The Information Research Department (Abingdon: Routledge, 2004); and Lowell H. Schwartz, *Political Warfare against the Kremlin: US and British Propaganda Policy at the Beginning of the Cold War* (Basingstoke: Palgrave Macmillan, 2009). Most recently, Rory Cormac has analysed new archival releases from the IRD and concluded that 'British Cold War black propaganda ... was more systemic, ambitious, and forceful than generally acknowledged'. See Rory Cormac, 'British "Black" Productions: Forgeries, Front Groups, and Propaganda, 1951–1977', *Journal of Cold War Studies* 24, no. 3 (2022): 5.

28 Sefton Delmer, *Black Boomerang* (London: Secker & Warburg, 1962), 118.

29 See Defty, *Britain, America and Anti-Communist Propaganda,* for discussion of how ideas of the 'third force' shaped the founding of the IRD.

30 It should be noted that, while this volume does not deal with post-war military propaganda or psychological operations, this omission is simply a marker of the fact that, as David Hare notes in this volume, such operations are now integrated within the permanent and professional military apparatus rather than relying on the more fluid boundaries that this volume tracks between authors and other government propaganda agencies.

31 Megan Faragher's chapter in this volume discusses the MOI's *Britain in Pictures* series, a type of publication also planned by the PWE for its 'Projection of Britain' campaign. In the Cold War, even the IRD, an agency often associated with covert anti-communist media briefings, dedicated a considerable range of its output towards textbooks published by 'front' presses such as Ampersand.

32 Louis Menand, *The Free World: Art and Thought in the Cold War* (London: Fourth Estate, 2021), 221.

33 See Stefan Collini, *Absent Minds: Intellectuals in Britain* (Oxford: Oxford University Press, 2006).

34 Hendy, *The BBC*, 201.

Part I

1

Haw-Hawing Hitler

Radio comedy as propaganda

Debra Rae Cohen

In *Lord Haw-Haw of Zeesen*, a quickie 'biography' of comic snippets and sketches published to capitalize on his fortuitous naming of the Nazi broadcaster, *Daily Express* radio critic Jonah Barrington alludes in passing to the panoply of mockery that has already (by late 1939), he says, resulted in the transformation of the radio traitor into 'a harmless (and widely popular) comedian'.[1] To Barrington's list – Arthur Askey's turn as 'Baron Hee-Haw' on the BBC's *Band Waggon* show, the Western Brothers' hit comic songs featuring 'Lord Haw-Haw, the Humbug of Hamburg' as a simperingly effete propagandist, and the touring act 'Lord Haw-Haw and Winnie the Whopper' – one could add *Haw-Haw*, George Black's successful revue at the Holborn Empire starring Max Miller, George Sumner's '"Nasti" News' parodies for British Pathé newsreels, and a host of other music hall turns, advertisements and newspaper cartoons in the first year of the Second World War. What these early representations have in common – not least Barrington's 'biography' itself, which conjures up a history tracing the career of 'the infant Haw-Haw'[2] all the way back to the bullying of his nurse at his fictional stately home in Hertfordshire – is that (unlike the brilliantly radiogenic BBC comedy show *ITMA*, the greatest Variety hit of the war, to which I will turn later in this chapter) they derive their humour from a lampoonery uncertainly grounded in Barrington's original coinage.

As is well known, the sobriquet had its birth in a casual remark in Barrington's column. On 14 September 1939, he observed, 'A gent I'd like to meet is moaning periodically from Zeesen. He speaks English of the haw-haw, damit-get-out-of-my-way variety, and his strong suit is gentlemanly indignation.'[3] A few days later, Barrington incorporated this figure into a pre-existing stable of less memorable parodies, as the 'follower' of the Breslau propagandist he had dubbed 'Winnie the Whopper', and enlarged upon his description: 'From his accent I imagine him as having a receding chin, a questing nose, thin yellow hair brushed back, a monocle, a vacant eye, a gardenia in his button-hole. Rather like P.G. Wodehouse's Bertie Wooster.'[4]

It was clear to a few observers from the outset that Barrington was responding, in fact, to a rotating stable of propagandists, and that the upper-class accent he initially discerned – 'by Cholmondeley-Plantagenet out of Christ Church',[5] wrote the drama critic Harold Hobson – was probably that of the former army officer Norman Baillie-Stewart. But squabbles in the press over the provenance of a single, unitary 'Haw-Haw' helped build-up the character even before the role was permanently cast. William Joyce inherited not only the mantle of 'Britain's most annoying invisible mosquito' and 'Number One traitor'[6] but an already vigorous legend, bolstered by what Charles J. Rolo called 'the most spectacular free publicity build-up that any broadcaster has ever enjoyed'.[7] In a response to Hobson, Rose Macaulay spotted the bootstrapping at work in the inflation of Haw-Haw's reputation: 'I should not call it "public school" English. Do any listeners really think it is, or is the legend merely derived from music-hall parodies . . . ?'[8] As M. A. Doherty has observed, '[t]he traditional British press practices of simplifying complexities and personalising policies composited a ragbag of non-entities into a super-propagandist, about whom the press and public could joke'.[9] Such jokes were inextricable from the figure Barrington had conjured, organized around the lampooning of an imagined aristocratic body,[10] a fascist 'peer' who, as Ian Whittington has noted, was ripe for conflation with more visible homegrown specimens such as Oswald Mosley[11] – lending credence to fears that the propagandist's attacks would hit with real effect on the working classes.[12] By December 1939, General Sir Frederick Pile, General Officer Commanding-in-Chief of Anti-Aircraft Command, was warning of Haw-Haw's 'attempt to foment a social revolution' – and its possible effects on his men and others with 'only a limited knowledge'.[13]

That such critiques were in circulation even as the hyping of the monocled, music-hall version of Haw-Haw was at its height complicates the accepted narrative of response and counter-propaganda, one in which humour gave way to seriousness, or 'the joke began to wear thin'.[14] One can indeed easily trace in the popular press the gradual transition from boosterism to excoriation (or perhaps more accurately, lampooning-as-publicity to paranoia-as-publicity, as Haw-Haw rumours proliferated[15]), with even the American *Life* magazine intoning that the British government, 'which laughed once, is no longer amused'.[16] But the 'joke' of Haw-Haw here is too often conflated with his early popularity with listeners – a popularity that as Jo Fox and others point out, was itself measured by often unreliable self-reporting.[17] Similarly, the early publicity boom has often been attributed to a single cause: 'Haw-Haw's initial popularity is easily explained', according to Rolo, who, writing during the war to galvanize an American audience, blames the 'total loss of faith' in the Chamberlain regime, a dissatisfaction that, he says, 'vanished overnight' with the advent of Churchill, along with Haw-Haw's appeal.[18] For Siân Nicholas and others, Haw-Haw's initial popularity stands as an indictment of the quality of BBC offerings early in the war; tired of 'official announcements, blandly delivered', listeners 'would seek out more colloquial assessments of the war wherever they might be found, including the enemy airwaves'.[19] Such BBC-centric explanations gain credence from the Corporation's own retrospective mea culpas, such as Antonia White's disingenuous rendering in a 1942 pamphlet:

> In the first days of the war everyone had expected that exciting events and news would follow hot foot on each other. Therefore the BBC had arranged for the maximum provision of news and had only prepared emergency programmes of gramophone records. What happened was exactly the opposite. There was a total lack of events and news, and what the listening public clamoured for was entertainment.[20]

One telling detail from White's depiction of the BBC Variety section cranking up operations in Bristol (to which it had been relocated at the outbreak of war) is the ostensibly overheard snippet, 'Yes . . . you can have jokes about Hitler now.'[21] Nicholas has deftly traced the BBC's own policing of its 'tonal boundaries' around the depiction of Hitler, and of Nazis more broadly, through a series of reversals in the first years of the war; after the grim depletion of programming in the first weeks, the return to 'entertainment' saw the reversal of the 'fundamental tenet of BBC Variety that world leaders were never to be joked about':

> Within the week comedian Tommy Handley could be heard on the new wartime BBC Home Service singing 'Who is this man who looks like Charlie Chaplin?'; shortly afterwards the BBC's greatest variety star, Arthur Askey, released an updated version of his popular novelty hit 'Run, Rabbit, Run', featuring the new verse 'Run, Adolf, run'. On 6 October 1939 the BBC broadcast a 'pantomime' written by James Dyrenforth and Max Kester and closely based on Lewis Carroll's *Alice in Wonderland*, entitled *Adolf in Blunderland*.[22]

This early dictate was reversed within months, the shifting policies on comic tone and their ineffective enforcement[23] also affecting and constraining – though this has not been sufficiently acknowledged – the debate over how to 'deal with' or 'counter' Haw-Haw. Though Asa Briggs's detailed institutional history attests to the fact that some within the BBC bureaucracy believed from the outset that 'the answer to Haw-Haw was better entertainment',[24] most often the Corporation's internal response is charted as a progression from weighty counterprogrammed talks by a series of stuffed shirts under the rubric 'Onlooker', to the more populist, 'broadbrow' 'Postscripts' of the Yorkshire novelist J. B. Priestley. These latter, immensely popular broadcasts are thus both credited with the effective marginalization of Haw-Haw and seen as emblematic, along with the creation of the light-entertainment-centred Forces Network, of the Corporation's 'greatest shift . . . since its inception', the increasing responsiveness to listener desires.[25]

But this narrative is incomplete. The BBC's official abandonment of direct lampoonery of Hitler – and the congruence of such comedy with the treatment of Haw-Haw across media – has in large part effaced the success *as counterpropaganda* of a different comic approach, one that eschewed physical, music-hall-style mockery in favour of acknowledging and engaging with the uncanny incorporeality of the radio propagandist. I would argue that in fact *It's That Man Again*, or *ITMA*, the iconic wartime Variety series, succeeded by acknowledging and troping on the occult intimacy of the radio medium. Not only did the show enable, as I've detailed elsewhere, a morale-building model of sociability, in which the exchange of catchphrases created a kind of imagined and performative national community both compatible with Blitz myth and retrospectively essential to it,[26] but its distinctively radiogenic mode of humour, its foregrounding of mediation, and above all, its exploitation of the uncertainties of the acousmatic voice allowed for the salutary deflation of anxieties surrounding both official wartime discourses and the claims of Haw-Haw himself.[27]

The enormous presence of *It's That Man Again* in the wartime zeitgeist has at times resulted in a peculiar critical distortion, with historians reading onto the programme in its earliest stages the cultural weight it assumed over the course of the war. Briggs actually connects the early 'popularity' of Haw-Haw to *ITMA* ('The opening words of his programmes – Germany calling, Germany calling, Germany calling – quickly became catchwords, like snatches of dialogue from *ITMA*') despite the fact that such *ITMA* catchphrases only emerged months later.[28] Martin Dibbs, similarly, discussing the rebound in programming after the first weeks of the war, cites as one cause the return of '[f]lagship programmes' such as *ITMA*.[29]

But in fact the first weeks of *ITMA* made little impact. The show was launched – in a very different form from the one that became familiar to wartime listeners –

a couple of months before the war. An attempt to reproduce the enormous success of Arthur Askey's *Band Waggon*, the first regularly scheduled BBC comedy show, this first version of the show substituted Lancashire comedian Tommy Handley (a 'handyman' of BBC comedy who had first broadcast in 1925) for Askey, and for that show's ostensible 'location' – a top-floor flat in Broadcasting House occupied by Askey, his partner 'Stinker' Murdoch, and a goat – a pirate broadcasting ship. For each show, the 'broadcasting' connection created a diegetic context for variety spots. But this pre-war instantiation – perhaps because it so clearly aped the *Band Waggon* formula – proved disappointing; producer Francis Worsley recalled it as a 'broadcasting flop'.[30] All that carried over to Bristol (where, wrote Worsley, 'the real life of *ITMA* began'[31]) was a miasma of the piratical attaching to Handley, and the series title – *It's That Man Again*.

Like Haw-Haw, *ITMA* was named by the *Daily Express*: 'It's that man again' was a recurrent headline that paper used to mock Hitler's territorial adventurism. To Worsley in July of 1939, this seemed like a suitable title – a 'familiar catch-phrase of the moment', 'topical and well-known', without being overtly political.[32] 'That man' became Handley, 'a swashbuckling, plausible, quick-witted rogue',[33] with, at the outset, something nevertheless more than a little Fuhrerish about him. 'Hello folks. It's That Man Again and what a man', began Handley's opening monologue of 12 December 1939. 'My name today is at the tip of everyone's tongue and the toe of everyone's boot. Why, I can't go out in the open these days without people shouting "Heil Itma"!'[34] Similar echoes – such as Handley's plan to promote the pamphlet he calls 'Mein Pampf'[35] – dotted the early scripts, before the Hitler-joke policy was once again reversed. But their frequency at the outset, even as Handley was being established in his new role as 'Minister of Aggravation and Mysteries' in 'the Office of Twerps, otherwise known as ITMA'[36] – allowed for the unsettling eliding of authorities. 'I'll sign everything that prohibits anything. That's what I'm here for', Handley boasts, in a mockery of the petty tyranny of wartime bureaucracy, and describes himself as 'ITMA, the Ministerial Menace': 'Every day my office of Twerps issues reams of restrictions and then proceeds to cancel them, in fact I'm thinking of appointing myself Lord Cancellor'.[37] Undermining distinctions and mocking the excesses of bureaucracy, these early shows gave voice to national dissatisfaction with the restrictions of the Phoney War (on 7 November 1939, Handley recorded 'the official confirmation of my appointment as controller of ridiculous rations . . . broadcasting all my latest restrictions to the British nation and to your conster-nation'[38]). But they also troped on the techniques of Haw-Haw himself, what Adam Piette has identified as his performative exaggeration of Ministry of Information (MOI) propaganda claims.[39] If Haw-Haw 'made propaganda itself a joke, a dismissible noise of pompous exaggerations', reducing MOI home front tales to 'comic fictions' and thereby rendering government defence measures equally 'flimsy and fantastic', Handley annexed that technique to demystify it, rendering Haw-Haw's mockery moot.[40]

But the early slippage between Handley and Hitler, and the ongoing slippage between Handley and Haw-Haw, also reflected the more generalized vertiginousness of *ITMA*'s comedy. Handley's character morphed over time from head of the Ministry of Twerps to mayor of a seaside town to head of a munitions factory; he floated schemes for farms, schools, manufacturing enterprises, hotels, spas, milk bars and a secret radio station. Throughout, though the core of the show remained the same – Handley in his office, interrupted by bizarre intruders[41] – that core was itself based on a suspension of time, space and the laws of physics that only radio could provide. With the limits of the office defined exclusively by sound – including the distinctive squeak and slam of the *ITMA* door, and the ringing of the office phone – Handley could open a cupboard to discover a horse, rescue a diver from the bottom of a bottle of rum, or cue musicians for music both diegetic and extradiegetic. His engagement with the eccentrics who inserted themselves into this acoustic space was high-speed and incessant (with an estimated 100 planned laughs in the eighteen and a half minutes of dialogue of each half-hour show[42]), a regimen of non-stop wordplay whose boomeranging 'quick-fire' form was borrowed from the American *Burns and Allen Show*,[43] but whose punning humour was emphatically British.[44] The mechanism of interruption-as-plot – with intruders advancing, derailing, or merely delaying through 'the triumph of non sequitur'[45] Handley's scheme of the week – made sound itself, and its ability to convey possibility, the subtextual driver of the show. In this sense, it was, as contemporary listeners and commentators acknowledged, the first truly radiogenic humour programme, 'born of the air, about the air, only for the air';[46] Tom Harrisson of Mass-Observation, who wrote wartime radio columns for the *New Statesman* and, later, the *Observer*, returned repeatedly and rhapsodically to the idea of *ITMA* as *sui generis*, 'the nearest the B.B.C. has ever got to surrealism'.[47]

The sheer *giddiness* of *ITMA* – the way in which associations multiplied through metonymic series, cascading meaning like an avalanche down a slope – both rewarded and tested the limits of radio listenership. If each bit of wordplay was gone in a flash, the *ne plus ultra* of radio ephemerality, unrecoverable and almost impossible to explain,[48] the self-referentiality of the show's catchphrases, systematically and deliberately repeated, week after week, to define characters and establish continuity, created an identifiable shape for the show and instantiated a covenant of listenership.[49] The bond was perhaps greater because of the sheer improbability of the phrases – 'I wish I had as many shillings', 'Can I do you now, sir?' 'I don't mind if I do', 'TTFN' or even the sonorous repetition of the single word 'Friday'. *ITMA*'s ungrounded and inflationary catchphrase economy gloried in exactly the qualities that James Agate, in the *Tatler*, used to deride the show: 'its jokes have no roots. They are fantastications of nothing'.[50] At the same time, it was supremely topical, 'skits on a nine-hours wonder – a headline of that day's paper, and dead the following week', recalled writer Ted Kavanagh, who admitted that he himself (in 1949) could no longer understand all the referents.[51]

While the show is often characterized – even by Worsley himself – as a 'safety valve' for wartime anxieties, *ITMA*'s humour was neither simply escapist, nor, *pace* Worsley, reliant on the direct and embodied lampooning characteristic of the early Haw-Haw and Hitler mockery.[52] Rather, the admixture of topical referent and fantastication – including invented terms, brands, and names that were denatured, scrambled and rendered elastic, repeated to the point of muscle exhaustion, when meaning collapses into sound effect – stripped away the pressures of the immediate and rendered it temporarily benign. Not the least of these terms was 'Itma' itself: Within the show, ITMA does not equate to the acronym of the title; it refers vaguely to Handley's ministry and office but is not equivalent to either. Sometimes a name – 'Mr. Itma' – sometimes a brand, sometimes a state of mind, its status as a floating signifier is emblematic of *ITMA*'s process.

These machinations were inextricably tied up with the medium of radio itself, something *ITMA* routinely acknowledged in its in-joke allusions to BBC programmes and practices – Handley as a recurrent 'broadcaster', 'BBC commentators' arriving to interview Handley about his various enterprises, or to do Outside Broadcasts from his factory – and most ingeniously, in the recurrent early featured spots from 'Radio Fakenburg', meta-broadcast parodies that included advertisements for Itma cheese, Itma cars and even 'ITMA All-Purpose Lard – it's dripping with personality'.[53]

If in 'Radio Fakenburg' *ITMA* alluded to the mechanism of Lord Haw-Haw's dissemination – the European radio frequencies such as Radio Luxembourg that before the war had become a popular alternative to the BBC[54] – it was in the character of the German spy 'Funf' that the show most directly commented on the anxieties surrounding his broadcasts. Introduced in the second show of the first wartime *ITMA* series, Funf made his entry as a voice on the telephone, hectoring and threatening Handley with calamity ('Beware – you have enemies whom you

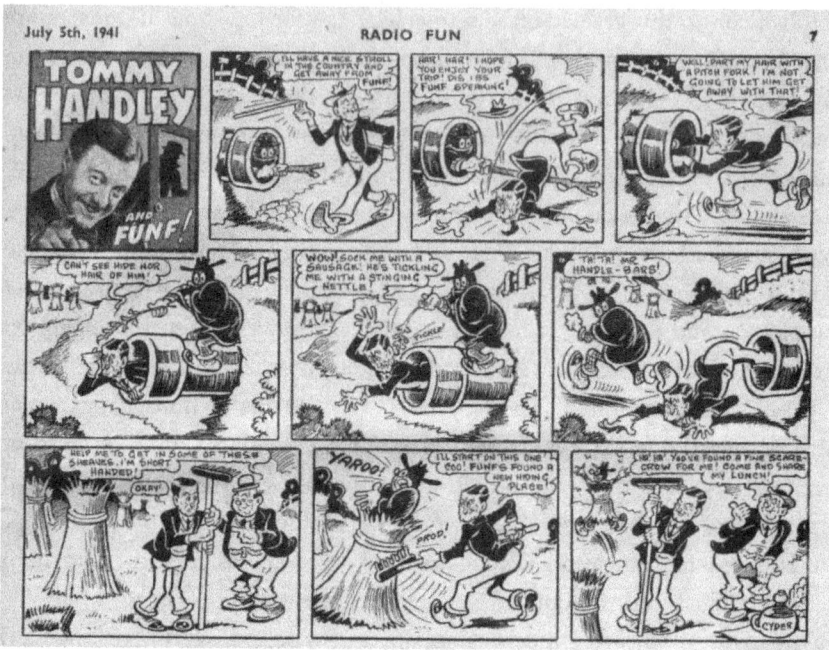

Figure 1.1 'Tommy Handley and Funf!', *Radio Fun*, 5 July 1941, 7. Reprinted by permission of Rebellion Publishing. Radio Fun © Copyright Rebellion Publishing IP Ltd. All rights reserved.

do not know!'[55]), and claiming to have 'found out everything'. Ubiquitous and persistent, his mediated tones echoing sonorously (an effect produced by the actor Jack Train speaking into a tumbler), he routinely announced his presence: 'This is Funf [*Foooonf*] speaking'. As distinctive as Haw-Haw's 'This is Germany calling', and as easy to repeat, this became the show's first popular catchphrase, exchanged in person and widely remediated (see, for instance, the *Radio Fun* comic in Figure 1.1). For Worsley, writing in 1948, this attested to a generalized defiance: 'Tommy's contempt for Funf expressed the people's contempt for the enemy, from Hitler himself down to Haw-haw'.[56] But this imaginative conflation of 'the enemy' has less in common with the actual mechanisms of *ITMA*, with its sliding and unstable referents, its imaginative conflation of authorities, stressors and threats, than with the retrospective codifications of the Blitz myth. In *It Was Different at the Time* (1941), which draws on her wartime journals, Inez Holden identifies a similar conflation as a means of bolstering Blitz morale:

> These men and women of work-town often speak of the enemy and even of a whole squadron of bombers as 'he'. Sometimes they mean 'Jerry', the collective name for all Germans in war-time, and sometimes they mean Hitler, but in either

case, this personification of the enemy as 'he' is a kind of gigantic debunk of the whole Nazi melodrama of bombs, paratroops, drawling Haw-Haw, screaming Hitler, limping Goebbels, and all the rest of it.[57]

This is not to understate Funf's morale-building appeal. Even as he positioned himself as Handley's nemesis, Funf allowed the show to deflate 'enemy within the gates' discourse; as Kavanagh put it: 'His name debunked every hair-raising spy story. . . . The insidious German secret service machine was reduced to a music hall – or rather, radio – joke'.[58] But that this was a *radio* joke was, of course, the larger point; though Funf's dire warnings of disaster were as baseless as Haw-Haw's rumours, and his plots were inevitably eventually foiled,[59] he also inevitably escaped, an uncontainable menace, as uncapturable as sound itself. The scripts acknowledge that he *is* fundamentally a voice – invisible, like all *ITMA* actors, but doubly (and, importantly, diegetically) so – with Handley deciding in one episode to use his Municipal Band as a 'Funf remover', drowning out the threat.[60] From series to series, he would threaten anew, his unsettling immediacy often intuited even when not directly audible: in the opening show of the fourth series, marking Tommy's triumphant return to his mayoral office in the seaside town of 'Foaming-at-the-Mouth', Funf – plotting with Handley's new Italian 'Foreign Secretary', Signor So-So, to kidnap the town's beauty queens – appears initially only as a minatory *presence* at the end of the line, who, despite the fact that 'He say nothing at all', is immediately recognizable to the audience.[61]

Though Funf's exaggerated accent was not Haw-Haw's – quite the reverse – it pointed up (in order to diffuse) the anxieties beneath all of the early discussion of the radio traitor's accent – reminding listeners that the acousmatic voice is *always* unverifiable, that radio can lie. It's useful in this context to think of how Rebecca West, covering the 1945 treason trial of William Joyce, was struck by the disjunction between the voice of 'Lord Haw-Haw' and Joyce's physical presence: 'His voice had suggested a large and flashy handsomeness. But he was a tiny little creature and, though not very ugly, was exhaustively so.'[62] West's shock may seem odd in light of the decade of anguished discussions about the sincerity or 'falseness' of the radio voice, explorations of the threats and possibilities opened up by the slippage between audible and incarnate self that dominated the pages of journals like the *Listener* in the 1930s. But here, with life and death at stake, the sensory shock of disjunction – the incongruity of the mismatch between sound and sight – stands in for a more fundamental ontological schism that renders tragically suspect the panoply of legal pomp at Joyce's trial. If, as Pamela Caughie has suggested, modern sound technologies create new, aural identities inseparable from those technologies,[63] is 'Lord Haw-Haw' present in the courtroom at all? Has he, in fact, been captured? Can he ever be contained?

It's telling that when West began her meditations on Joyce's trial, she did so by invoking 'something new in the history of the world':

> Never before have people known the voice of one they had never seen as well as if he had been a husband or a brother or a close friend; and if they had foreseen such a miracle they would not have imagined that the familiar unknown would speak to them only to prophesy their death and ruin. All of us in England had experienced that hideous novelty.[64]

West conflates the 'novelty' of betrayal with the 'miracle' of the intimacy of the acousmatic voice to render Joyce unprecedented – though the wireless 'miracle' was two decades old, dating long before William Joyce set foot in the Berlin offices of the Reichsrundfunk, and the 'novelty' of betrayal, whether as treason or simply as radio 'passing', was always inherent within it. In stressing the terrifying intimacy of the 'familiar unknown', of course, West is making an appeal to the uncanniness of the medium, what Jeffrey Sconce has termed its potential for the 'invasion and even dissolution of the private sphere',[65] its exposure of domestic vulnerability. That Haw-Haw made domestic vulnerability his explicit subject only makes this resonance more urgent.

Thus remediations like the long-running series of comic strips from *Radio Fun*, although indicative of the huge popularity of both *ITMA* and Funf, in particular,[66] get it exactly wrong (as indeed do most attempts to physically instantiate *ITMA* humour). The images of Funf hiding under a table, like a figure in a French farce, bopping Handley with his own sock samples or tickling him with a stinging nettle[67] – rather than lurking invisibly, instantiated by the telecommunications media that give him voice – return the figure to slapstick, to the lampoonery of the early Hitler and Haw-Haw comedy. Funf being turned into a scarecrow, as in Figure 1.1, or having his rear soaked with tea, renders him unmistakably *corporeal*, thus muting the particularity of his threat and mooting any future reappearance. Indeed, the essence of Funf is that, like Haw-Haw himself, he reactivates old anxieties about the radio: its ventriloquism, its invasiveness, its ability to penetrate and permeate private space, its persistence and presence, even in silence. *ITMA* stands as the most telling counter-propaganda to Lord Haw-Haw because only *ITMA* ever met Haw-Haw on his own turf; where the early comic interventions stressed the ludicrousness of an imagined physical self, *ITMA* recognized and successfully exploited the deep anxieties that attached to an ultimately unseeable threat.

Notes

1. Jonah Barrington, *Lord Haw-Haw of Zeesen* (London: Hutchinson), 9. The book is undated, but J. A. Cole dates a promotion party for it at Foyle's to January 1940; see J. A. Cole, *Lord Haw-Haw: The Full Story of William Joyce* (1964, Repr., London: Faber, 1987), 133.
2. Barrington, *Lord Haw-Haw*, 14.
3. Quoted in Cole, *Lord Haw-Haw*, 115.
4. Quoted in Cole, 115; see also Jonah Barrington, *And Master of None* (London: Walter Edwards, 1948), 223.
5. Quoted in Cole, *Lord Haw-Haw*, 132.
6. 'Radio: Haw-Haw on Haw-Haw', *Time*, 20 January 1941, 59; Harold Ettlinger, *The Axis on the Air* (Indianapolis, IN: Bobbs-Merrill, 1943), 39.
7. Charles J. Rolo, *Radio Goes to War: The 'Fourth Front'* (New York, NY: Putnam, 1942), 69.
8. Quoted in Cole, *Lord Haw-Haw*, 132.
9. M. A. Doherty, *Nazi Wireless Propaganda: Lord Haw-Haw and British Public Opinion in the Second World War* (Edinburgh: Edinburgh University Press, 2000), 90.
10. For instance, the Western Brothers, 'Lord Haw-Haw of Zeesen', Columbia D.B. 1883, 1939: 'My name is Cuthbert / And my name is Basil. / The Fuhrer has told us / Our monocles dazzle.'
11. Ian Whittington, 'Writing the Radio War: British Literature and the Politics of Broadcasting, 1939–1945' (PhD diss, McGill University, Montreal, 2013), 53–6.
12. As Harold Graves of the Princeton Listening Center indicated in 1940, Haw-Haw's attacks were scattershot, but tailored to provoke class antagonism: 'Haw-Haw laid an appalling list of grievances at the door of Governmental neglect and plutocratic indifference. For housewives and heads of families, he traced the rise in commodity prices. [...] For the labor-minded, he praised the trade unions as "the only organized body" of popular opinion opposing the Government. For the middle class, he condemned – not profits, to be sure – but "enormous profits." For the poor, he condemned niggardly pensions.' Harold N. Graves, 'Lord Haw-Haw of Hamburg: 1. The Campaign against Britain', *Public Opinion Quarterly* 4, no. 3 (1940): 431.
13. See Asa Briggs, *The History of Broadcasting in the United Kingdom, Vol. 3: The War of Words*, rev edn (Oxford: Oxford University Press, 1995), 131, and Doherty, *Nazi Wireless Propaganda*, 100–1.
14. Doherty, *Nazi Wireless Propaganda*, 91. See also Cole, *Lord Haw-Haw*, chapter 17, 'Joke Over'.
15. Jo Fox offers the most penetrating reading of the significance of Haw-Haw rumour in Jo Fox, 'Confronting Lord Haw-Haw: Rumour and Britain's Wartime Anti-Lies

Bureau', *Journal of Modern History* 91 (March 2019): 74–108. See also Doherty, *Nazi Wireless Propaganda*, 111–15; Cole, *Lord Haw-Haw*, 154–8.

16 'Radio Traitors', *Life*, 22 April 1940, 39.
17 Fox cites Mass–Observation reports that stressed the disjunction between citizens' private views and 'what they think the public thinks' (qtd. in 'Confronting', 84). Doherty points out that there were 'perfectly good and understandable reasons in the early period of the war for ordinary citizens to exaggerate the extent of their own listening to Haw-Haw, just as later on, when the war had taken a terrible and frightening turn, there were perfectly good and understandable reasons for doing exactly the reverse' (*Nazi Wireless Propaganda*, 95).
18 Rolo, *Radio Goes to War*, 73, 74.
19 Siân Nicholas, *The Echo of War: Home Front Propaganda and the Wartime BBC, 1939–45* (Manchester: Manchester University Press, 1996), 41; Ian Whittington, *Writing the Radio War: Literature, Politics and the BBC, 1939-1945* (Edinburgh: Edinburgh University Press, 2018), 44. See also Doherty, *Nazi Wireless Propaganda*, 88–9.
20 Antonia White, *BBC at War* (Wembley and London: British Broadcasting Corporation, 1942), 5.
21 Ibid.
22 Siân Nicholas, 'Policing Tonal Boundaries: Constructing the Nazi/German Enemy on the Wartime BBC', in *Political Languages in the Age of Extremes*, ed. Willibald Steinmetz (Oxford: Oxford University Press, 2011), 183. Handley's song, written by Max Kessler and John Watt, was released as the B-side of 'The Night that We Met in a Black-Out', Decca F.7246, 1939.
23 See Nicholas, 'Policing', 184.
24 Briggs, *War of Words*, 140.
25 Nicholas, *Echo*, 41; see in particular Whittington, *Writing the Radio War*, chapter one, '*Out of the People*: J. B. Priestley's Broadbrow Radicalism', 30–64. Whittington summarizes the shift away from strict Reithianism in this way: 'the BBC acknowledged that it could not simply give the public what it *ought* to want at the expense of what it *did* want' (*Writing the Radio War*, 44).
26 Debra Rae Cohen, 'Catchphrase Community: *ITMA* and Radiogenic Morale', in *Modernist Communities Across Cultures and Media*, ed. Caroline Pollentier and Sarah Wilson (Gainesville, FL: University Press of Florida, 2019). For 'sociability' see Paddy Scannell, *Radio, Television, and Modern Life* (Oxford: Blackwell, 1996), 22–57.
27 These very distinct approaches – one directly rebutting or undermining the propagandist, one focusing on the use of the broadcast medium – represent different modalities of counter-propaganda still operative today.
28 Briggs, *War of Words*, 128. See also Doherty, *Nazi Wireless Propaganda*, 95: 'to confess you did not listen [to Haw-Haw] was to place yourself outside the "knowing" social group, almost akin to confessing that you could not stand *ITMA* and that Tommy Handley wasn't funny.'

29 Martin Dibbs, *Radio Fun and the BBC Variety Department, 1922–67: Comedy and Popular Music on Air* (Cham: Palgrave Macmillan, 2019), 112. He also erroneously refers to the show as a 'proven pre-war [favourite]' (114).
30 Francis Worsley, *ITMA: 1939–1948* (London: Vox Mundi, 1948), 4.
31 Ibid., 5.
32 Ibid., 3.
33 Francis Worsley, 'Anatomy of *ITMA*', *Pilot Papers: Social Essays and Documents* 1, nos. 1–4 (1946): 45.
34 *ITMA* Second Series No. 13, 12 December 1939; qtd in *The ITMA Years* (London: Woburn, 1974), 21.
35 *ITMA* Second Series No. 1, 19 September 1939, BBC Written Archives Centre (hereafter BBC WAC).
36 *The ITMA Years*, 21.
37 *ITMA* Second Series No. 1; *ITMA* Second Series No. 6, 24 October 1939.
38 *ITMA* Second Series No. 8, 7 November 1939.
39 Adam Piette, *Imagination at War: British Fiction and Poetry, 1939–1945* (London: Papermac, 1995), 175.
40 Piette, *Imagination at War*, 175. If, as Piette claims, part of Haw-Haw's initial appeal was that of 'some star of radio comedy', Handley thus goes him one better (Piette, *Imagination at War*, 174).
41 Handley was the pivot point of the series, identifiable *as* 'himself' – 'Mother's pride and joy/Mrs. Handley's boy', as the words of the theme song had it – and surrounded by a troupe of veteran actors who usually played two or three recurring roles, differentiated by accent and catchphrases.
42 Worsley, *ITMA: 1939–1948*, 75.
43 Dibbs, *Radio Fun*, 70.
44 Notably, American troops seemed to dislike *ITMA* intensely, and, according to a report on reactions to the BBC's Allied Expeditionary Forces Programme, would often switch during it to 'German stations playing popular music'. R34/185, 21 December 1944, BBC Written Archive Centre. Many thanks to David Hendy for this reference. Francis Worsley defends *ITMA*'s use of 'pun-comedy' in 'Anatomy of *ITMA*', 51.
45 The phrase comes from the critic Caroline Lejeune; see 'The Films', *Observer*, 21 February 1943, 2.
46 This 1944 letter to the editor of the *Bournemouth Echo* went so far as to claim *ITMA* as 'the only purely radio entertainment probably in the world'; see Moy Howard, 'Letter to the Editor', *Bournemouth Echo*, n.d. 1944, *ITMA* Press Cuttings, P184, BBC WAC.
47 Tom Harrisson, 'Radio', *Observer*, 17 May 1942, 7. Harrisson here is somewhat sweeping, ignoring in his encomium early experimental shows like Lance

Sieveking's 'Kaleidoscope' – but as regards mainstream BBC programming, his point is well taken.

48 Key here is Harrisson's observation that 'Written down [*ITMA* humour] doesn't sound anything special. Perhaps that is the definition of first-class feature broadcasting – looking dead on paper. Yet I have listened to Itma in every surrounding . . . [and] never knew it to fail. All over Britain to-day you may hear people using Handleyisms' (Harrison, 'Radio', 7).

49 As I've written elsewhere, the deployment of catchphrases beyond their radio moment served as 'a citational act of sonic citizenship' that demonstrated listener cohesion. See Cohen, 'Catchphrase Community', 246.

50 James Agate, 'Myself at the Pictures: The Riddle of Itma', *Tatler*, 3 March 1943, *ITMA* Press Cuttings, P184, BBC WAC. Writer Ted Kavanagh, in his biography of Handley, uses 'senseless' as a term of approbation; see Ted Kavanagh, *Tommy Handley* (London: Hodder & Stoughton, 1949), 125.

51 Kavanagh, *Tommy Handley*, 114.

52 See Worsley, 'Anatomy of *ITMA*', 46.

53 *ITMA* Second Series No. 6, 24 October 1939.

54 Ironically, after this feature debuted, in May 1940, the Radio Luxembourg facilities were turned over to Großdeutscher Rundfunk, which used its frequencies to carry Lord Haw-Haw's broadcasts.

55 *ITMA* Second Series No. 2, 26 September 1939.

56 Worsley, *ITMA: 1939–1948*, 11.

57 Inez Holden, *It Was Different at the Time* in *Blitz Writing*, ed. Kristin Bluemel (1941, 1943; Reprint, Bath: Handheld Press, 2019), 161–2.

58 Kavanagh, *Tommy Handley*, 123.

59 Funf's plots were myriad: in Worsley's words, he was 'the Fairy Queen as well as the Demon King' of the early wartime *ITMA* series ('Anatomy of ITMA', 46). Among other things, he stole the plans for Tommy's radio station, waylaid his orchestra and, in one glorious episode, kidnapped the diver and pinched the Foaming-at-the-Mouth pier ('It only needs someone to purloin the promenade and we'll be the only inland seaside resort in the world', *ITMA* Fourth Series No. 10, 28 November 1941).

60 *ITMA* Fourth Series No. 6, 31 October 1941.

61 *ITMA* Fourth Series No. 1, 26 September 1941.

62 Rebecca West, *The Meaning of Treason* (New York, NY: Viking, 1947), 5. West's dispatches originally appeared, in slightly different form, in the *New Yorker*.

63 See Pamela Caughie, 'Audible Identities: Passing and Sound Technologies', *Humanities Research* 16, no. 1 (2010): 96–7.

64 West, *The Meaning of Treason*, 4.

65 Jeffrey Sconce, *Haunted Media: Electronic Presence from Telegraphy to Television* (Durham, NC: Duke University Press, 2000), 109.
66 Funf remained amazingly popular, even after fifth columnist scares had abated; says Kavanagh, 'To the very end people were writing to ask that Funf should come back when there was no reason to have a German spy lurking about the place even in a show as crazy [as] ITMA' (*Tommy Handley*, 110–11).
67 *Radio Fun*, 23 March 1940, 13; *Radio Fun*, 12 July 1941, 7.

2

Radio pages, morale reading and the word war

Damien Keane

Along with the grim distinction of being the deadliest conflict in modern times, the Second World War has often been called the 'wordiest war in history'.[1] This characteristic is in turn often attributed to the role broadcasting played in the prosecution of the war, as the ability of governments around the world to address combatants and non-combatants alike over the airwaves helped redefine the scale and intensity of warfare.[2] Whether sober or snarled, trustworthy or dissembling, words on the radio became necessary implements in the modern arsenal.[3] Even before the start of outright hostilities, states had sought political advantage with pro-active and self-interested radio programming, while also looking to devise defensive measures to respond to and counteract unfavourable transmissions; when the war did come, its wordiness was in large part realized within this feedback loop of rival propaganda campaigns. Yet the effects of this dynamic far exceeded the strictly radiogenic or technological aspects of broadcasting. While words on the radio certainly led to more words on the radio, they were likewise central to the generation of words in print *about* radio, a corpus of texts ranging from internal memoranda and production scripts to periodicals dedicated to broadcasting and programme schedules in the daily press. As with the transmissions to which they had a proximate relationship, the materials in this textual field existed along a continuum stretching between the confidential and covert to the openly accessible and actively promoted. In Britain, the war inaugurated little of this intermedial activity, but the strategic requirements drastically altered the motivations behind it, notably resulting in a series of institutional networks committed to managing and, where needed, manipulating this economy of words.

This chapter examines one strand of this wartime intermedial traffic, by tracing the relations of the typewritten pages made by the BBC Monitoring Service for departments of state to the pamphlets and books published to explain the medium as an instrument of war to a readership on the home front. After describing the working procedures of the Monitoring Service, it considers published texts from Antonia White and E. Tangye Lean that broach this wartime circuit. In doing so, the chapter argues that domestic readers, as the objects of this particular type of intermedial wordiness, were instructed through their reading to become more acute listeners. This was done in such texts by projecting a model of the individual listener at odds with the forms of corporate listening practiced at the Monitoring Service, but in sync with broader directives aimed at bolstering morale. Through this pedagogical subterfuge, readers on the British home front were taught to listen anew without fully recognizing they were doing so. Reading these printed works now, perhaps the most telling marker of this feint is the use of the heuristic figure of the singular listener – the first-person author, the second-person reader, the third-person employee of the BBC – to embody a way of listening that is nonetheless not possible with one pair of ears alone.[4] As a kind of reportage meant to humanize the war effort, this rhetorical technique is understandable and not ineffective, but it should not be mistaken for anything other than the propaganda it is. By harnessing embodied styles of radio listening that had become familiar in the previous two decades to the new conditions ushered in by the war, these publications hid the work of the Monitoring Service in plain sight. As the chapter will describe, the considerable repository of foreign broadcast propaganda created and maintained by the Monitoring Service allowed for a thorough analysis of transmissions both in the moment (by tracking claims and highlighting inconsistencies) and over time (by identifying patterns or departures from them), and its work was considered to be essential to the operations of its clientele in the military and intelligence branches of the British government. This 'radio archive' set the corporate listening procedures of the Monitoring Service apart from the habits of general listeners, but it was also what facilitated the conversion of enemy propaganda transmissions into home front morale reading. By emphasizing the informational value of the service's files over their evidential value, books about the radio could enumerate and parse the words heard on the airwaves without saying more than officially needed about the institutional means of their collection and analysis.[5] And the corollary to this retiring guile was silence about the link of home front morale to the control of words.

Evidential value: radio pages

During the war the BBC Monitoring Service existed to make documents. The British Foreign Office had begun listening to overseas broadcasts in the run-up to the Italian invasion of Ethiopia in 1935, although it was not until the German invasion of the Sudetenland in March 1939 that the BBC established a department dedicated to monitoring the airwaves. While the Corporation's slogans such as 'nation shall speak peace unto nation' and 'Britain calls the world' were to become synecdochally associated with its mission, the marked rise of international broadcasting in the second half of the 1930s had not resulted in a new broadcasting service per se – the Empire Service would be subsumed in the more broadly construed Overseas Service – but rather in the textual production of the Monitoring Service. To be sure, broadcasting services were greatly expanded and reorganized several times over in the three years after the declaration of war, and it is this development which has dominated both contemporaneous and subsequent accounts of the BBC during the period. Josephine Dolan has noted a fixation on the 'moment of transmission' and the bias towards sound over page in considerations of broadcasting agencies and their radio archives: 'the transmitted voices that are the focus of the sound archive cannot be isolated from the voices of the written policy statements about audition, selection criteria, scripts and performance standards that are anterior to the moment of transmission.'[6] In this context, the Monitoring Service is doubly noteworthy (and interesting) because of its singular concentration on received voices, on what was heard over the airwaves. The typewritten documents made there provide a means not only to think about the exigencies of maintaining a serviceable repository of wireless propaganda, but also, from there, to demonstrate how monitored broadcasts continued to circulate, often long after the moment of radiophonic transmission, among a set of official audiences with very different reasons for paying attention than average or imagined listeners to the radio. As the war stretched on, this interplay of holding and re-deployment proved uniquely important to British authorities, as the archive of broadcast propaganda became a vital resource for designing and conducting political warfare campaigns. Against the durable truism that radio is an ephemeral medium, one instead finds a volatile instance of what Dolan calls the 'relationship between continuing circulation and commission to the archives'.[7]

The typed sheets produced at the Monitoring Service took form as transcripts, digests and reports, documents that can be collectively grouped together and called radio pages.[8] Although largely derived from open-source information and used in turn to create open-source information, radio pages are themselves an example of what has been labelled 'grey literature', a class of 'near print' or 'half-published' documents made for a designated and limited readership and circulated outside (or at least on the margins of) more conventional means of publication.[9] Like other 'genres of internality', such as technical manuals, government documents, research and development reports and white papers, they existed to communicate information for a reason or set of reasons, but their distribution was institutionally regulated and circumscribed.[10] While no secret was made of the Monitoring Service and its remit, its output carried a confidential classification, a situation determined as much by its clientele as by the contents of the documents it produced.[11] In addition to the news sections of the home and external services at the BBC, the primary clients for radio pages were the War Office, Admiralty, Air Ministry, Foreign Office, Home Office, Ministry of Information (MOI) and the secret services that would eventually be subsumed into the Political Warfare Executive (PWE); they were also shared selectively with governments-in-exile in London and more comprehensively with American military and intelligence agencies.[12] Where references to documents the Monitoring Service produced are found beyond this official loop – usually in sponsored academic research – they are accompanied by acknowledgement of the special permission granted for use of restricted materials.[13] This form of delimited access is both an essential feature of radio pages and a marker of their strategic importance. Unlike the random access to voices transmitted over the air, which was contingent on tuning an appropriate receiver to the proper wavelength at the right time under favourable conditions, access to these documents depended on one factor: clearance. In this intermedial shift from loudspeaker or headphones to typescript, bureaucratic power 'refracted agency through its medium'.[14] With its access to radio pages, the British government gained considerable analytical control and political advantage in conducting the war of words.

The Monitoring Service instituted the 'increasing realisation that the study of what the enemy was saying would bring rich dividends'.[15] In an article on the service that appeared in the *BBC Handbook 1940*, its work is depicted as taking place on a new kind of battlefield:

> In the short space of a generation, the naked ear of the soldier, applied close to the ground, has been replaced by the antennae of dozens of receiving sets tuned to the transmitters of the world. A new medium of communication, broadcasting, has intervened, bringing with it, as one of its functions in war-

time, the monitoring service established by the BBC, at the request and charge of the Ministry of Information, as a branch of intelligence indispensable to modern war.[16]

This was war fought through the study of words. Having begun its efforts in London, the Monitoring Service was quietly moved just before the war to Evesham in Worcestershire – the *Handbook* profile gestures vaguely to a 'special base' where its work is carried out – before eventually and again quietly relocating in 1943 to Caversham in Berkshire (where it remained until returning to London in 2018). Six months into the war, the service's intelligence mandate required that 'something between 160 and 200 broadcasts in 25 different languages [be] monitored, recorded, translated, summarized, edited, and distributed daily by the BBC to all the Ministries of State engaged on the prosecution of the war'.[17] In another six months, the three-shift, round-the-clock operation was transcribing close to a million words a day.[18] By the time of the move to Caversham in early 1943, the Monitoring Service employed just over 500 people, not including engineering staff and support personnel.[19] Its M Unit listened to open-source 'voice' broadcasts (news, speeches and talks) from enemy, occupied and neutral stations; its Y Unit focused on a variety of transmissions (such as musical broadcasts and intercepted point-to-point communications), while also keeping tabs on German 'freedom stations' and other clandestine sources. These two units were administratively separate, with the latter more directly supplying information to military and political intelligence authorities.[20] Working with the materials the two units produced were the Editorial Section, which was responsible for compiling the Daily Digests (selected items from the previous day's broadcasts) and Monitoring Reports (evaluations of broadcasts from the same period), and the Research Section, which studied transcripts to report on propaganda trends in a weekly analysis for government agencies. Because of the high proportion of émigré and refugee intellectuals on its staff, Asa Briggs portrayed the wartime Monitoring Service as 'a genuine international centre, almost a kind of international university', although its very specific and client-oriented brief (and lack of 'students') suggests closer affinity to the think tanks that would thrive under the post-war national security state.[21]

Even as the work of the service expanded in scale, its procedures remained stable throughout the conflict. It began in front of receiver sets, where, depending on their listening assignments, monitors trawled through the wavelengths or tuned in to particular stations. Sound recordings of broadcasts were made on wax cylinders using Ediphone dictation machines; these served primarily as aids to written transcription and, as such, were rarely kept as objects of interest in their own right. For items anticipated to be of value for use in news reports and counter-broadcasts, recordings on gramophone discs were favoured because of the finer acoustic qualities and longer running-times of the format; otherwise, cylinders were more efficient and economical, for they could be mechanically shaved and re-used many times over in the production of transcripts.[22] However dependable, the format was not failsafe: 'cylinders were not always "shaved" very cleanly, and occasionally part-passages and odd words or sounds from previous recordings could be heard when monitors listened to subsequently recorded programmes. This intermingling could cause confusion and was fraught with danger.'[23] While seeking to furnish text that was as complete and as comprehensive as reception conditions allowed, monitors aimed for accuracy of sense and intent rather than verbatim accounts in their transcripts. Whether crude hectoring or wheedling casuistry or some amalgam of both, propaganda of all sorts was designed to play on the affective charge of words in context, and this relationship presented many impediments to the objective of accurate transcription. These issues were only exacerbated when translation was necessary for the monitoring process, as it so very often was. In cases of breaking and sensitive news that needed to be immediately relayed via teleprinter to broadcasting authorities or government ministries, something close to simultaneous translation was required of monitors.[24] General guidelines at the service set parameters within which staff were to work as they rendered foreign text into English, yet nothing could offset the fact that 'broadcast monitoring was a cross between translating and interpreting'.[25] This 'cross' was further borne in the complex bureaucratic handling of so-called raw transcripts in order to produce the aforementioned digests, reports and research analyses. Whatever routine complications and vexing contingencies might attend their creation, transcripts were at the very centre of the entire procedure because they were the only viable means of registering and storing the contents of such a massive number of monitored broadcasts. Owing to demands for their almost instantaneous processing and accession to the operational knowledge of the wartime state, these typescripts moreover constituted the most significant archive of radio propaganda made at the point of reception. Two years into the war, both the MOI and the PWE viewed the work of the Monitoring Service as integral to the war effort, with Asa Briggs later describing its activities as 'a linchpin of the whole BBC wartime organization'.[26] In all this, the service was effective not only because it 'listened' in a continuous present tense of urgent necessity, but because its system of making, refining and cataloguing documents provided the contextualizing frame needed to counterbalance that very urgency. In that activity lay a sense of future possibility.

Informational value: Morale reading

Their status as grey literature notwithstanding, radio pages proved very useful in fashioning open-source information about the course and conduct of the war. Their contents could be applied to a wide variety of informational activities, many of which aimed to counteract the (potential) effects of Axis propaganda and sustain morale. Early in the war, one unambiguous example was the programme 'Listening Post' for Anglophone listeners on the BBC Overseas Service, which drew on monitoring reports to debunk the claims of German transmissions by exposing patterns of inconsistencies and falsification. The systematic listening procedures at the Monitoring Service yielded exactly this material, although the programme was not always successful at conveying it, as one American researcher noted: 'It has brought out contradictions and analyzed propaganda tricks. But again the presentation and the analysis were more for the student than for the man on the street.'[27] One way to read this criticism of the programme's tone is that it suggests monitoring information remained too embedded in the evidential context of its institutional origin, without adequate attention to its reformatting and stylization for public reception: it sounded too much like a listening post and not enough like 'Listening Post'. For home listeners in Britain, this donnish cast exemplified the Reithian tenor of the prewar BBC, and as the war continued broadcasters and intelligence officials looked to mitigate this holdover. The need was for pedagogical description minus the pedantry, superiority or bluff advocacy. While it could most immediately be addressed through on-air adjustments to delivery, listener experience also became, in the context of wartime demands, something to explain and interpret in books and pamphlets about radio. The profile in the *BBC Handbook 1940* (also called 'Listening Post') is an early example of a kind of informational activity that peaked in the years that followed. In such texts, readers would learn of the institutional dynamics of waging a war of transmitted words, but be instructed in how to situate what they heard on the radio in this contentious and unprecedented context. Against the 'propaganda of events', morale reading secured its readers by encouraging them to identify their own listening habits with those of the state.[28]

The principal task of these print works was to rationalize this incommensurable identification. One of the most frequent and efficient ways to justify monitoring, as a method of listening to the radio in wartime, was to link it to modes that were already familiar. In *BBC at War* (1942), a booklet published by the Corporation, the writer and translator Antonia White walks readers through the transition from peace to belligerence as it was manifested in the workings of the institution. Perhaps best known for her novel *Frost in May* (1933), White worked at the BBC during the first half of the conflict (and at the Editorial Section of the PWE during the second), and her text provides a concrete sense of its trials and accomplishments in adapting to speak war unto nations. In the three pages (of twenty-seven total) dedicated to the Monitoring Service, she gives a vivid description of what listening to the airwaves at this institutional scale necessitated, even as her terms continually lapse into the singular: 'In peace-time the BBC had to talk. In war-time it has also to listen. Besides a mouth, it has had to develop ears – ears of extraordinary acuteness and intelligence – that can catch a significant whisper in the torrent of a million words poured out day and night in thirty different languages.'[29] For the next eight paragraphs, she presents the collective work of the monitoring staff, but focalized through the discrete actions of the individual 'monitor', who tunes in, takes notes and gets tired, before finalizing 'his' transcript and handing it off. In the last paragraph of the section, she details what she calls the 'less picturesque but even more strenuous' phases spent at the typewriter:

> Every twenty-four hours the notes of the monitors take down in shorthand or in some personal form of 'speedwriting', transcribe and translate, amount to something like a million words – the equivalent of ten full-length novels. It is the task of the editorial section of the service to condense that material to a clear and readable summary of from 50 to 60,000 words – about one-twentieth of the original. Think of précis-writing at school where you boiled down a thousand-word essay to a hundred words. Then think of ten long novels being boiled down to the length of one short one every twenty-four hours. That is the work of the thirty-odd sub-editors. During their twelve-hour shifts a continuous stream of closely typed pages blow down the tubes on to their desks and pile up in a mountain of paper. Redundant matter is deleted, long speeches are summarized, crossheads inserted, mistranslations queried, all at breakneck speed, and the corrected copy collated into one lucid document.[30]

With its dramatic vision of editorial skill and fortitude, of specialized labour measured in the knowable quantities of the everyday world, this passage is effective propaganda for the home front. It is no coincidence that in a direct address to the second-person reader, White invokes the school, that prototypical site of individual formation through collective (or social) reproduction: a common scene of primary instruction here serves as the vehicle for an allegorical lesson in sustaining morale. This collective work is coordinated and orchestrated, yet remains meaningful and compelling for those engaged in it, with no one person standing above another in this necessary, if taxing, endeavour. Rather than being lectured to, the reader ('you') is asked to identify as a student with fellow students in a scenario of peer-to-peer learning. The propagandistic ruse of the passage is the suggestion that these 'students' have authority over the classroom.

This point can be refined by way of White's specific reference to the listening routine of 'the' monitor. In an extract more akin in persuasive technique to the retreat sermon in Joyce's *A Portrait of the Artist as a Young Man* than to the usual BBC publication, she invites readers to grasp the undoable through the habitual:

> Have you ever tried reporting an ordinary BBC news bulletin as you get it with perfect reception on your own set? You'll find it a good deal harder than you think. Now, imagine yourself listening through earphones to a broadcast in a foreign language, often against a background of deliberate jamming. When reception is bad, the speaker can only be heard muttering away to a deafening accompaniment of shrieks, whistles and crackling. Picture yourself listening to that unintelligible din and reducing it to a clear and accurate précis for eight hours at a stretch and you know what the monitor is up against.[31]

White allows that, for the majority of readers, the answer to her initial question is 'no'. Yet the passage works because of the way it depicts the monitoring regimen as an amalgam of listening practices that had become familiar or at least recognizable to many people over the previous two decades. What Simon Potter has termed 'wireless internationalism' relied precisely on the kinds of 'distant listening' White gestures to, from the headphones and interference to the polyglot transmissions from afar: 'Distant listening exposed audiences to a very different soundscape [than domestic broadcasting]. Signals transmitted across national borders were often poor and unreliable. They carried foreign languages and music and other content that would have been unfamiliar to many listeners, and sometimes incomprehensible.'[32] For Potter, the interwar years brought a series of social, technological and political changes to how people listened to foreign broadcasting, as the solitary (and often male) enthusiast of the 1920s gave way to more communal forms of radio listening in the 1930s.[33] These individual and collective listening techniques continued to co-exist during the war, and it is this fact that permits White to couch monitoring as a habit already ingrained in the experience of listeners, even if they still need to imagine the actual stages of 'reporting' what they tune in. The knowing point here is that the production of radio pages exceeds this analogy both in scale and intent. As a corporate practice achieved through the work of many ears, many eyes and many hands, monitoring had less to do with embodied familiarity or affective association than with national security.

By way of conclusion, it is worth asking what motivated such evasiveness about the Monitoring Service. No more striking use of radio pages is made in a book about wartime radio than in Edward Tangye Lean's *Voices in the Darkness* (1943), which sets out to examine the role broadcast propaganda had played in the evolution and course of hostilities. When he presented the manuscript for publication, Lean was the Associate Director of the BBC's French Service, which operated under stricter government supervision than other overseas services owing to the complicated status of occupied France in the Allied war effort.[34] Subtitled 'The Story of the European Radio War', the book narrates the conflict from its 'opening sounds' to the occupation of the continent by the Axis powers, along the way delivering a mix of technical description and propaganda analysis to suggest how Britain might escape the fate of its continental neighbours. In telling this 'story', Lean gives three pages (of 240) to the Monitoring Service, in which he too channels his sketch through the work of a singularized 'monitor': 'I cannot give you a close description of him because he is sometimes a Russian girl who speaks Chinese, an anglophile Pole, a forlorn and brilliant Jew, a Greek, Roumanian, Dane, even an Englishman. But he is an exceptional person if only because of the number of languages he knows.'[35] Yet the first appearance of this type of individualized listener comes in the book's foreword, where Lean introduces himself to readers:

> This is not a guidebook, handbook or Official History of the War. I have been too much involved in it to be impartial. I wanted as far as possible to write only of what I heard with my own ears, choosing Germany's offensive against France instead of her attack on Jugoslavia, reporting speakers on whom I had my own notes, and where my languages gave out and my ignorance of different audiences set in, it did not worry me that the treatment became sketchy. The German radio stood no chance of a fair hearing from me who listened to it as a counsel for the prosecution, and the news-service from London, which made up nine-tenths of the B.B.C. output, is represented only by a few inadequate paragraphs.[36]

In this opening scenario, Lean establishes an analogy between radio listening and judicial hearing as a way to demonstrate his position as author. He does not try to hide his bias or adopt a posture of disinterestedness, instead arguing through this figural connection that active critical judgement is a necessary part of wartime listening. In this propaganda trial, Lean appoints himself as both judge ('no chance of a fair hearing from me') and 'counsel for the prosecution', in doing so suggesting that his book has a case to make against the 'German radio' and to the British public about the stakes of the war of words. As an author writing about this struggle, he assigns himself the additional role of court reporter, a figure responsible for listening to oral proceedings in order to transcribe and provide a textual record of them. Even with his languages and notepad and 'involved' status, this last is remarkable. Despite claiming he 'wanted as far as possible to write only of what I heard with my own ears', it would have been more accurate to state that *Voices in the Darkness* is based on what he read with his own eyes, for the radio pages produced at the Monitoring Service underwrite the book.

This misrepresentation is most apparent in 'Political Warfare Documentary', the forty-page chapter at the centre of the book that chronicles the invasion of the Low Countries, the evacuation from Dunkirk and the fall of France as they sounded on the airwaves. As its title indicates, the chapter links the military timeline of defeats and surrenders to the half-truths, innuendo and disinformation that accompanied German advances, in this way asserting a strong correlation between the two. Under a succession of dated headings, it arranges short items broadcast from a number of stations about the fighting; organized in this manner, the items reveal the patterns of distortion and contradiction meant to confuse listeners, destabilize opinion and erode morale. The chapter includes material from eight nations and several clandestine 'freedom stations', broadcasting in seven languages and translated, when needed, into readable English, and items list station of origin, time of transmission, language of address and intended audience. In places, Lean inserts italicized interpolations to provide context, sometimes laterally by expanding on a detail, sometimes proleptically by linking a detail to future events and sometimes editorially by presenting an opposing account of events. This technique renders competing and calculated appeals to grievance, pride, affiliation and contempt with exceptional force, as the flat and mostly unadorned reproduction of transmitted words preserves both their intensity and premeditation. Here are two items from German radio, with Lean's gloss:

> (*In Flemish*): Flemings, Soldiers! In the Belgian State you have always been citizens of inferior status. In the Belgian Army you are treated in the same way as the French and English treat their black colonial troops, as cannon fodder and nothing more. Thousands of your officers do not even understand your language; they despise you, and now you are to die for a pro-French clique which wants

to sacrifice the Fleming for England and France. Are you going to be fooled? . . . Throw down your arms! When you come over to us, we shall treat you as the sons of a kindred Germanic nation.

(*To Walloons*): If you help the Germans now, they will help you later to develop your country. . . . Belgium doesn't care a damn for you. She only expects Walloons workers to die for her.

Separatist appeals to Flemings and Walloons had been made sporadically since March 1939; they increased with the invasion and continued daily and sometimes hourly until after King Leopold's capitulation. The importance Germany put on them could be seen from the fact that they were transmitted over the highest powered stations, at first on Deutschlandsender *interrupting other programmes, and then on the captured transmitters of Brussels and Luxembourg. A similar campaign was carried out in April 1941 against the Serbs and Croats.*[37]

'Political Warfare Documentary' does not present any one person's listening experience, but is instead an example of what could be achieved from the work of the Monitoring Service. On the page, the chapter looks like the near facsimile of a monitoring report, but reset from typescript for trade publication, and Lean's 'documentary' is indeed just this. While contemporaneous listeners would have been familiar with hearing something approaching the cacophony of voices that is on display in this section of the book, it is important to remember the chapter is designed for readers. With its arrangement of disparate items to tell a clear – and persuasive – 'story', the note it accentuates is less one about good ears than the bibliographic control of documents. 'Political Warfare Documentary' is one product of the archival function of radio pages.

A last turn remains to be made. Nothing in the chapter indicates the provenance of its contents, and Lean only admits later in *Voices in the Darkness* to having used monitoring transcripts for it: 'Germany's radio offensive in 1940 appalled some of the hardiest monitors, and a Dutch girl, who took down some of the sentences I have reprinted in "Political Warfare Documentary," collapsed.'[38] Deflected through its focal attention to an individualized monitor, this mumbled acknowledgement still confirms a critical point about motivation. Even though it 'reprints' monitoring reports, 'Political Warfare Documentary' reproduces on the page only their informational value, with hints of their evidential value dispersed elsewhere in the book or left out. In his review of the book, George Orwell singled out 'Political Warfare Documentary' as 'probably [its] most useful section' for the patient examination of German tactics of mixing truth and insinuation, rumour and fact.[39] He concludes with a suggestion about the book's value to potential readers, when he states that 'it would be a good thing if more books like Mr Tangye Lean's describing the B.B.C. and other organs of propaganda from the inside, were available to the general public. . . . This book should help towards a better understanding, though about half a dozen others along roughly the same lines are needed'.[40] Yet 'more' information is only half the issue. For the intermedial relationship of radio pages and morale reading, it is worth recalling Josephine Dolan's sharp comment that 'an absence of lies does not necessarily equate to the reproduction of transparent truths'.[41] One lesson of the wordiest war in history is how understanding is manipulated by providing information, but not giving evidence.

Notes

1. The quoted phrase is from Harold Graves, *War on the Short Wave* (New York, NY: Foreign Policy Association, 1941), 7. Many other versions of this 'wordiness' could be cited, but one need look no further than Asa Briggs, *The History of Broadcasting in the United Kingdom, Volume 3: The War of Words* rev. edn (Oxford: Oxford University Press, 1995). In the present context, it is worth noting Kenneth Burke's unfinished study of the rhetoric of militarism, which was written in the immediate aftermath of the war and whose manuscript also bears the title 'The War of Words'. It was recently published as *The War of Words*, ed. Anthony Burke, Kyle Jensen, and Jack Selzer (Oakland, CA: University of California Press, 2018).
2. For a helpful recent account of conceptions of total war in this period (and since), see Paul Saint-Amour, *Tense Future: Modernism, Total War, Encyclopedic Form* (New York, NY: Oxford University Press, 2015), esp. 55–70.
3. One document of the increasing prominence of 'verbal warfare in the ether' (7), published weeks before the start of the war, is Thomas Grandin, *The Political Use of the Radio* (Geneva: Geneva Research Centre, 1939).
4. Oddly enough, in a booklet published online to mark the seventieth anniversary of the founding of the Monitoring Service, Brian Rotheray adopts this mode while describing the challenges radio posed: 'Radio monitoring needed more system than press monitoring. You had to know who broadcast on what frequency and in what language. You needed people who could understand the broadcasts, pick out what was significant and report it objectively, consistently and clearly.' Brian Rotheray, *A History of BBC Monitoring* (Caversham Park: BBC Monitoring, 2009), 7.
5. The terms 'informational' and 'evidential' are taken from T. R. Schellenberg, *The Appraisal of Modern Public Records* (Washington, DC: U.S. Government Printing Office, 1956). For him, records have informational value due to the information (about 'persons, or things, or phenomena') they contain, while their evidential value

derives from the evidence they provide of the 'organization and function' of 'the agency that produced the records' (6–7).

6   Josephine Dolan, 'The Voice that Cannot Be Heard: Radio/Broadcasting and "The Archive"', *Radio Journal: International Studies in Broadcast and Audio Media* 1, no. 1 (2003): 69.

7   Dolan, 'Voice that Cannot Be Heard', 68.

8   On radio pages and their implications in related circumstances, see Damien Keane, 'An Ear Toward Security: The Princeton Listening Center', *Princeton University Library Chronicle* 71, no. 1 (Autumn 2009): 45–61; and *Ireland and the Problem of Information: Irish Writing, Radio, Late Modernist Communication* (University Park, PA: Pennsylvania State University Press, 2014), 108–40.

9   On grey literature, see C. P. Auger, *Information Sources in Grey Literature*, 4th edn (London: Bowker-Saur, 1998), esp. 1–36. The inaugural work on 'grey literature' (or 'reports literature') is Charles Auger, ed., *Use of Reports Literature* (London: Butterworth, 1975). It should be noted that the use of 'grey' in this context does not correspond to the white-grey-black spectrum used to describe propaganda.

10 Lisa Gitelman, *Paper Knowledge: Toward a Media History of Documents* (Durham, NC: Duke University Press, 2014), 69–70, 115–16.

11 This point is noted in David Garnett, *The Secret History of PWE: The Political Warfare Executive, 1939–1945* (London: St. Ermin's Press, 2002), 228. Written just after the war, this text also observes that the News Digest issued by the PWE (and its pre-cursors) had no security mark, although the organization was a secret service.

12 See Briggs, *War of Words*, esp. 379–442; Garnett, *Secret History of PWE*, xxiii–xxiv, 361–3; and Olive Renier and Vladimir Rubinstein, *Assigned to Listen: The Evesham Experience 1939–43* (London: British Broadcasting Corporation, 1986), 40–1.

13 One prominent example is Hans Speier and Ernst Kris, *German Radio Propaganda: Report on Home Broadcasting during the War* (London: Oxford University Press, 1944), which heavily relies on Monitoring Service daily digests (v–vi). They co-directed the Rockefeller Foundation-funded Research Project on Totalitarian Communication in War Time at the New School for Social Research in New York. Before going to the United States, Kris had worked at the Monitoring Service, where he ran its Research Department while Speier worked at the Foreign Broadcast Intelligence Service, the American monitoring agency, during most of the composition of the book. Even with these connections, they still note having access only to the digests, not to the more selective reports and analyses.

14 Ben Kafka, *The Demon of Writing: Powers and Failures of Paperwork* (New York, NY: Zone Books, 2012), 74.

15 Gerard Mansell, *Let Truth Be Told: 50 Years of BBC External Broadcasting* (London: Weidenfeld and Nicolson, 1982), 99.

16 E. A. Harding, 'Listening Post 1939', *BBC Handbook 1940* (London: British Broadcasting Corporation, 1940), 84.

17 Ibid., 85.
18 Asa Briggs, *The History of Broadcasting in the United Kingdom, Volume 2: The Golden Age of Wireless* (London: Oxford University Press, 1965), 653.
19 Renier and Rubinstein, *Assigned to Listen*, 144.
20 The basic division of labour was established between 'voice' and other forms of monitoring early in the war, but it gradually lessened as more transmissions required tracking. On this point, see Renier and Rubinstein, *Assigned to Listen*, 39–43; and Briggs, *War of Words*, 441. On wireless signals detection units more generally, see Hugh Skillen, *Spies of the Airwaves: A History of Y Sections during the Second World War* (Pinner: H. Skillen, 1989).
21 Briggs, *War of Words*, 171.
22 In the *BBC Handbook 1940*, for example, there are photographs of both of these sound recording formats in use. The first shows four monitors, each at a desk with a radio on it, all wearing headphones and writing on notepads; between the second and third of them are two Ediphone machines (image between pages 80 and 81). In the second, Laurence Gilliam and Maurice Brown lean over a row of turntables, on one of which is a gramophone disc; the caption notes they are 'marking a passage from the recording of a speech by Herr Hitler' (image between pages 96 and 97).
23 Renier and Rubinstein, *Assigned to Listen*, 65.
24 While different modes of translation (including early forms of simultaneous translation) were in use at the League of Nations in the interwar years, its contemporary form is often dated to the International Military Tribunal trials at Nuremberg: see Francesca Gaiba, *The Origins of Simultaneous Interpretation: The Nuremberg Trial* (Ottawa, ON: University of Ottawa Press, 1998), esp. 25–32. Broadcast monitoring seems never to have been considered in this context, although it falls along the same practical continuum.
25 Laura Johnson, 'Translation and Open-Source Intelligence: BBC Monitoring', in *The Palgrave Handbook of Languages and Conflict*, ed. Michael Kelly, Hilary Footitt, and Myriam Salama-Carr (Cham: Palgrave Macmillan, 2019), 259–60.
26 Briggs, *War of Words*, 440–1.
27 Daniel Katz, 'Britain Speaks', in *Propaganda by Short Wave*, ed. Harwood Childs and John Whitton (Princeton, NJ: Princeton University Press, 1942), 114.
28 The quoted phrase appears several times in Ian McLaine, *Ministry of Morale: Home Front Morale and the Ministry of Information in World War II* (London: George Allen & Unwin, 1979).
29 White, *BBC at War*, 27.
30 Ibid., 29.
31 Ibid., 27–8.
32 Simon Potter, *Wireless Internationalism and Distant Listening: Britain, Propaganda, and the Invention of Global Radio, 1920–1939* (Oxford: Oxford University Press, 2020), 202.

33 Ibid., 203–5.
34 Simon Potter, *Broadcasting Empire: The BBC and the British World, 1922–1970* (Oxford: Oxford University Press, 2012), 117. In addition, see Briggs, *War of Words*, 401–17.
35 E. Tangye Lean, *Voices in the Darkness: The Story of the European Radio War* (London: Secker and Warburg, 1943), 181.
36 Ibid., 3.
37 Ibid., 113–14, ellipses in original.
38 Ibid., 181.
39 George Orwell, 'Review of *Voices in the Darkness* by Tangye Lean', in *The Complete Works of George Orwell, Vol. 15: Two Wasted Years, 1943*, ed. Peter Davison (London: Secker and Warburg, 1998), 85.
40 Ibid., 86.
41 Dolan, 'Voice that Cannot Be Heard', 70.

3

Dylan Thomas at the microphone

The BBC's *Book of Verse* and imperial cultural propaganda

Daniel Ryan Morse

Dylan Thomas has long been a curiosity of the literary world. The 2014 centenary of his birth was accompanied by an inundation of 'state-approved imagery' of Thomas as a popular writer and performer, a 'wide-eyed figurehead of approved creative activity'.[1] On the other hand, some of Thomas's output remains stubbornly gnostic and opaque, with Thomas accused of favouring form (or sound) over meaning. Joining these two sides of the writer, one early reviewer found in Thomas an 'imaginative abandonment that is both his strength and his weakness'.[2] Missing from all three of these versions, however, is Thomas the propagandist. This is in no small part because the radio broadcasts in which Thomas took part advanced an image of Anglophone literature as a field above the coarse realities of geopolitical positioning. Thomas was subject to 'mid-term canon formation', particularly in BBC propaganda broadcasts to India.[3] Though subsequently neglected, Thomas's Indian broadcasts underline the confluence of modern literature, psychological warfare and imperialism. One of the least researched elements of Thomas's enduring fame is his popularity with Indian readers and writers, even though, as Ankhi Mukerjee reminds us, 'the invention of modern classics is sustained by a dynamic and variable conversation . . . as that conversation goes from being specifically Western to being worldwide'.[4] When Louis MacNeice arrived in India shortly before Independence, he was greeted by a crowd of 'young men . . . hoping to meet another poet': Thomas, their beloved broadcaster.[5] Despite the BBC's institutional support and Thomas's willing participation in what amounted to political propaganda to India – the majority of Thomas's broadcast output – he is best remembered as the author of the radio drama *Under Milk Wood* (1954). Edward Allen has written most extensively about Thomas's work on the Eastern Service, where he 'attempt[ed] to repurpose the verse of others, and so to think of the recording studio as a kind of reception area, soundproofed but not at all impervious to the latest in foreign affairs'.[6] But whereas Allen focuses on Thomas's scripts promoting the work of Welsh poets, I turn here to the lionization of Thomas himself. After an examination of the BBC's *Book of Verse* programme (1944 to 1950s) and its role in canon formation, this chapter takes a closer look at Thomas's work for the BBC's Eastern Service to recapture some of the complexity of Thomas's self-positioning in the context of late imperial cultural propaganda.[7]

For decades following the Second World War, the BBC's Eastern Service (founded in 1940 and directed to the Indian subcontinent) was reduced to a footnote in accounts of the career of George Orwell, Talks Producer at the Eastern Service from 1941 to 1943. The disproportionate attention granted to Orwell has severely distorted our understanding of the far-reaching and long-lasting impacts of the Eastern Service on late imperial cultural propaganda. Literary broadcasts served a pedagogical purpose (helping university students in India prepare for exams), but they also sought to reinforce cultural links between Britain and Anglophone Indians, many of whom were centrally involved in the nationalist, anti-colonial movement. Given that only the wealthiest, Western-educated Indians were likely to possess short-wave radios, the Eastern Service was free to cater to their highbrow tastes. As Thomas quipped, he may have enjoyed 'an audience of perhaps three' on the Eastern Service, but its focus on reaching an educated Indian audience meant that it could commission and cover unabashedly literary writing at a time when the BBC Home Service – tasked with lifting spirits – jettisoned serious literary talks.[8] As one British novelist at the time complained, 'the best literary talks' are not on the Home Service, but rather 'on the Eastern Service, audible to Indians but not to us'.[9] Recently, a handful of scholars have begun to recover the eclectic cast of figures who contributed to the Eastern Service, including a wide range of British writers (T. S. Eliot, E. M. Forster and Cyril Connolly) as well as several prominent Indian novelists such as Mulk Raj Anand, Ahmed Ali, Venu Chitale, G. V. Desani and Attia Hosain.[10] While this necessary correction has allowed for a more nuanced understanding of transnational broadcasting, intercultural friendships and the intermedial relationship between print and radio, it has privileged the *innovative* work of Indian and English writers at the BBC.

This chapter, on the other hand, examines the work of well-known British writers who participated in the formation of a revised canon of English Literature in the Eastern Service's *Book of Verse* series, part of the BBC's long-standing attempt to use literature as a form of propaganda. Given the British inability to cite Indian Independence or even fair treatment – Gandhi and a host of his followers were jailed during the war and famine was widespread and long-lasting in Bengal, killing 'as many as 3 million residents' – propaganda to India was largely reduced to stressing common culture, particularly literary culture.[11] Eastern Service programmes in the 1940s such as *The Development of the Novel, Books and People, Masterpieces of English Literature, Landmarks in American Literature, Calling All Students* and *Book of Verse* were all aimed at preparing students for literature exams.[12] Nonetheless, *Book of Verse* stands out for its longevity and its thoroughness: broadcast in thirty-minute instalments typically dedicated to a single work or writer, the programme offered more detailed treatments of literary works than was typical, even for the Eastern Service, whose serious approach to literature and cultivation of authors did much to prepare the way for the later BBC Third Programme (1946–70), the BBC's high cultural channel.[13]

As Gauri Viswanathan (echoed by later post-colonial critics) put it, 'the Western literary canon evolved out of a position of vulnerability, not of strength'.[14] This is particularly true in the case of *Book of Verse*, since the context of India's impending Independence shaped its educational broadcasts. Featuring many of the poets of the 1930s, including Thomas, Stephen Spender and Cecil Day Lewis, the series is remarkable for swinging dramatically between canonical texts well represented on university exam lists and more contemporary fare. It was also something of an outlier in Eastern Service literary programming for ignoring Indian Anglophone writing and writers, who were otherwise featured regularly as part of contemporary writing in English.[15] By returning to the staffing, organization and approach of the Eastern Service's *Book of Verse* programme, this chapter intends to add nuance to our understanding of the role of canonical English literature in BBC propaganda efforts that stressed the common culture of Britain and its colonies. *Book of Verse* is part of a larger wartime pattern identified by Damien Keane wherein 'the meaning of cultural work assumed new weight . . . as the manipulation and redirection of literary expression came to reflect not only the immense totality of total war, but also literature's increasingly explicit position among – rather than above or apart from – technological media of transmission and reception'.[16] Here I will consider the remediation of the literary anthology, by which I mean its refashioning 'to answer the challenges of new media' (broadcasting in this instance), as well as its simultaneous and inextricable impact on the new medium of short-wave broadcasting.[17] Alongside these twin processes, I consider the jockeying among players on the cultural field, all against the backdrop of the waning years of the British Empire. Thomas was one of its most effective propagandists, not least because he was seen as exemplifying aesthetic autonomy.[18] The case of Dylan Thomas reveals how the seemingly apolitical discussion and reading of poetry was in fact central to wartime propaganda aimed at India. Further, the seemingly neutral attention to the canon of English literature allowed the writers associated with *Book of Verse* to push their aesthetic preferences and boost their favourite contemporary poets. Taken together, these efforts demonstrate that India was central to the emerging post-war Anglophone literary consensus, the testing ground for the later Third Programme.

Book of Verse

As the literary anthology is remediated over the Eastern Service, particularly in *Book of Verse*, it retains much of its conservatism. The great majority of instalments cover the canonical British writers that are still found on English syllabi in India and throughout the Anglophone world: Blake, Wordsworth, Coleridge, Shelley, Keats, Tennyson, Browning and so on. Yet, remediated as a broadcast, it also offered contemporary context, both a sense of unfolding in real time and a vision of English verse shot through with the cultural positioning of its creators. It aimed to both close the temporal gap between London and India and reduce the historical distance of the literature included on the series. However, *Book of Verse* was of its moment in another sense as well; it argued for an apolitical approach to literary criticism that remained ascendent well through the 1950s, based on the voice of Eastern Service critics such as Empson and Eliot, who were so influential in critical trends such as New Criticism.[19]

As a broadcast radio programme, *Book of Verse* was not a book at all: it had no cover, spine or pages. At the same time, its title was far from arbitrary: in instalments resembling book chapters dedicated to individual authors, it presented an overview of English literature with a strong preference for verse, though the occasional episode discussed prose, Chinese poetry in translation and even 'modern radio drama'.[20] Originally produced by the writer, dramatist and music critic Edward Sackville-West, the programme switched hands to poet and cricket commentator John Arlott shortly thereafter. At a time of paper rationing, not to mention the difficulty of shipping printed material to India, the programme was on the one hand a broadcast book by historical necessity. On the other, the remediation of the book over short-wave radio wrestled with both the affordances and limitations of the broadcast medium. The typescripts for the programmes were dutifully maintained in the BBC archives, but the broadcasts were not recorded for posterity (only for repeat transmissions, then scrapped), nor were they regularly reprinted for the Indian audience. Like so much BBC radio programming until well after the war, they dissipated after their moment of transmission. At the same time, the affordances of the radio medium meant that *Book of Verse* was able to bypass many of the limitations of the literary anthology in print. At a minimum, it was never stale: most instalments were written shortly before transmission, quickly censored, rehearsed and broadcast. And the human voice reading the material reduced some of its historical distance: William Blake was presented and discussed as an eighteenth-century writer, yet the poems were read aloud as performed texts and unfolded in real time. One Indian listener remembers the reading 'made one's hair stand on end', signalling the audience's immediate physiological response.[21] The sense of contemporaneity produced by the radio anthology was further extended by its placement in the flow of programming, bracketed by current news. The arrival of voices from London in radio receivers in India in near instantaneity also went some way in closing the gaps of space and time, not to mention the Eastern Service's mélange of voices: not only British and Indian voices, but also a wide swath of Indian languages. The BBC also sent British writers from the Eastern Service on promotional tours to India: E. M. Forster in 1945 and Louis MacNeice in time for Independence and the violence of Partition in 1947.[22] And many books made the reverse journey, from India to BBC studios: Forster's *Some Books* programme regularly reviewed contemporary Indian writing.[23] Taken together, these elements combined to make the literary anthology for schools (in print form, the Methuselah of the literary world) a vibrant, live genre.

What is so fascinating about *Book of Verse* is that it both participates in the perpetuation of fixed exam lists (most noticeably in its thorough coverage of the works of William Shakespeare, which were explored in thirty-eight consecutive instalments) while at other times pushing the aesthetic interests of its practitioners.[24] In other words, while the programme claimed to be 'based on the poems which are being studied at Universities in India', this was subject to a good deal of mission drift.[25] In the first quarter of 1945, Arlott's bosses warned him to rein things in: 'I think we ought to concentrate on the compulsory English for B. A. pass degrees. Inevitably, the emphasis in all the syllabuses is on Shakespeare, with other poets second and prose a long way third.'[26] In practice, however, this meant that after dispensing with Shakespeare's plays and the major works of a handful of other central literary figures, the series was free to widen its focus.

This is precisely where the aesthetic and networking interests of the participants emerge. As Lionel Fielden, who helped establish the Eastern Service, put it, because of the incessant need for new content, the people 'who make the programmes (generally underpaid) sway the crowd: the administrators and authorities (usually overpaid) do not'.[27] Under Arlott, the programme's introduction was tellingly modified to the claim that it was 'based *in general* on the poems being studied at universities in India'.[28] *Book of Verse*, largely neglected in literary history, was a crucial source of support for Dylan Thomas. As Glyne Griffith makes clear, the later *Caribbean Voices* radio programme (based on the Eastern Service programme *Voice*) provided institutional and financial support to a core group of West Indian writers including V. S. Naipaul, Sam Selvon and Derek Walcott.[29] *Book of Verse* – particularly under Arlott – favoured the 1930s poets Thomas (often employed as a reader even when he was not the presenter), Vita Sackville-West, Louis MacNeice, Cecil Day Lewis and Stephen Spender, all of whom both presented programmes on other writers and were themselves the subjects of instalments covering their works. As Arlott's biographer admits, 'the programme became a little incestuous'.[30] Vita Sackville-West, cousin of *Book of Verse* producer Edward Sackville-West, is lauded as 'one of the most honoured figures in present-day writing'.[31] MacNeice claims that 'W. H. Auden – at the age of thirty-nine – is a legend'.[32] The other writers in and around *Book of Verse* were treated to equally exuberant appreciation.

But *Book of Verse* was more than an established poet's club, distributing institutional support among the already well regarded: it helped cement together apolitical literary-critical approaches with anti-communist sentiment, a compound central to the Cold War academy. John Lehmann's instalment on the work of Stephen Spender is a telling example, reading like a rehearsal and summation of Spender's contribution to Richard Crossman's *The God That Failed* (1949), a collection of six essays by writers who had recanted communism.[33] In Lehmann's telling, Spender is 'a Shelley who has eaten of the tree of knowledge of Freud and Marx'.[34] But whereas in Spender's early work 'a political, a revolutionary enthusiasm played', out of his experiences during the Spanish Civil War 'came some of his very best poems, but they were hardly poems to stiffen the morale of a Marxist warrior'.[35] In Spender's recent work, argues Lehmann:

> The prophet in him knows now, I think, that he cannot lead the way to the promised land, though – by a kind of hypnosis of habit rather than in true hope

– he will not give up the search; but when the prophet is silent, the artist who is concerned with truth and penetration of poetic vision, can sometimes tear the scales from our eyes, and can substitute symbols of beauty for the false and ugly symbols with which contemporary civilization surrounds our everyday life. And that, after all, is what poets are for.[36]

In other words, poetry is an antidote to the evils of 'contemporary civilization', and, tracing its 'symbols of beauty' the shared work of its readers. Similarly, in a programme on Cecil Day Lewis, the presenter is relieved that Lewis 'has resolved some of his earlier emotional and political conflicts' and turned to writing poems that 'yield something new at every reading'.[37] This line of presentation helps *Book of Verse* prepare India's literature students to write essays agreeable to the post-war hegemony of the New Critics, thus fulfilling its pedagogical aim. But uttered after the cessation of hostilities, it also serves as an implicit warning to the emerging nation against forging ties with the Soviet Union, Britain's erstwhile ally.

Dylan Thomas

Whereas the literary canon of the nineteenth century and earlier was relatively stable, when it comes to the unsettled waters of the twentieth century, *Book of Verse* favoured new authors skilled in mediation, who worked for the BBC and composed for the microphone in addition to the printed page. Dylan Thomas published poems in print, wrote film scripts for the Ministry of Information (MOI), radio scripts for the Eastern Service and – later – probably the best-known radio play, *Under Milk Wood* (1954). Douglas Cleverdon, who produced Thomas's features for the BBC, argued that 'Dylan knew exactly how to create a work of permanent value from the fluid medium of radio.'[38] Revivals of *Under Milk Wood* bear this out: it was produced for radio broadcast by the BBC in 1954, 1963 and 2003; for television in 1957, 1964 and 2014; and for film in 1972. It has also been adapted for theatre on several occasions, including a production directed by Lyndsey Turner at the National Theatre in the summer of 2021.[39] Audio recordings have been packaged and sold by the BBC and Caedmon records and it was published in print form by J. M. Dent in London and New Directions in the United States.

But if Thomas is remembered primarily for writing a radio feature for a domestic channel, he nonetheless made more regular appearances on the BBC

Eastern Service. Thomas first read poems for *Book of Verse* in September 1945 and appeared regularly thereafter, recording nearly forty instalments until December 1950.[40] Of these, Thomas wrote 'Welsh Poetry' (5 January 1946) and 'Wilfred Owen' (27 July 1946) with an additional script on Augustus John commissioned in 1945 but not delivered. As a regular reader for *Book of Verse* – Edward Allen identifies *Book of Verse* as 'by far the most frequent of Thomas's radio stints' – Thomas was forced to attend to the acoustic properties of poetry.[41] Even with Thomas's background in acting and broadcasting, his approach to reading poetry continually evolved. As Thomas explained to an American audience: 'At first I thought it enough to leave an impression of sound and feeling and let the meaning seep in later, but since I've been giving these broadcasts and reading other men's poetry as well as my own, I find it better to have more meaning at first reading.'[42] Opinions varied, with some critics accusing Thomas of exaggerating before the microphone and others defending his approach. Either way, Arlott was clearly satisfied, and Thomas's Indian audience grew.

Nonetheless, these debates about the suitability of Thomas's readings are deeply intertwined with perceptions of Thomas's poetics. In several cases, Thomas's Indian colleagues at the BBC defended Thomas's modernist aesthetics, part of a longer tradition traced by Peter Kalliney of 'late colonial and early postcolonial intellectuals . . . attracted to the modernist idea of aesthetic autonomy'.[43] Narayana Menon, a scholar of Indian music and regular contributor to the Eastern Service, remembers disagreeing with Orwell over the inclusion of 'A grief ago' in a programme they were assembling:

> We discussed what he should read. 'Light breaks where no sun shines' was his first choice. And then, 'A grief ago.' Orwell hesitated. Orwell was a prose man. A little obscure perhaps, he ventured. I myself didn't think it mattered and said so. It has a fine clear-cut structure and some moving, towering, highly concentrated phrases and images, and I was anxious to hear what else he would bring out. Let me read it out to you, just listen, said Dylan. That settled it.[44]

Menon, who wrote a book on Yeats during his employment at the BBC, was much less concerned about immediate intelligibility than Orwell. In this sense, Menon echoes his Eastern Service colleague Mulk Raj Anand, who defended Thomas's 'After the Funeral (In Memory of Ann Jones)' in another Orwell programme.[45] Thomas had a larger influence on Anand than is revealed in this one broadcast; Anand based one of his talks, 'London as I See It' on Thomas's 'Prologue to an Adventure'.[46] And Orwell was not as indifferent towards Thomas as Menon's anecdote implies. In fact, Orwell hired Thomas to read on the Eastern Service, and encouraged Desmond Hawkins to discuss Thomas's work in a series Orwell organized on modern verse, to be broadcast in instalments and then collected and 'printed in India as pamphlets'.[47] In the aggregate, these moments point towards a pattern of Thomas's writing receiving a significant – and regular – boost on the Eastern Service.

No programme on the Eastern Service worked towards the inclusion of Thomas in the literary canon more than one dedicated to his oeuvre in December of 1946, including poems Thomas published earlier that same year. The commentary was written and delivered by Terence Delaney, with Thomas reading his own work: 'Poem in October', 'After the Funeral (In Memory of Ann Jones)', a passage from *Portrait of the Artist as a Young Dog* (1940), 'On the Marriage of a Virgin', 'The force that through the green fuse drives the flower', 'This Bread I Break' and 'Vision and Prayer'.[48] Thomas's ability to write and read verse for the microphone led Delaney to argue:

> it is evident immediately that this is not the kind of poetry in which one follows the link of a narrative, or examines an argument, word by word. It is a flow of sounds and pictures, images, associations and changing rhythms, and you must put nothing in its way. You must be wide open, like a man leaning back listening to music with his eyes closed . . . Music first, then colour, movement and heat.[49]

Over and above defending Thomas's difficult poetics, Delaney uses the metaphor of music to highlight Thomas's intermedial aesthetic. Orwell, in 'Poetry and the Microphone', suggests that the significance of spoken poetry emerged from the affordances of radio.[50] Instead, *Book of Verse* clarifies that spoken poetry was a pre-existing form that received a significant boost at mid-century, with long-lasting implications for literary history. These effects are better appreciated by writers and scholars of Caribbean literature, who regularly cite the BBC in their origin stories, but the case of Thomas suggests a much wider impact.[51]

While we can readily see the appearances of Spender, Day Lewis and Sackville-West as a perpetuation or consolidation of prestige rather than a granting of it, with Thomas this is less clear.[52] In the programme dedicated to Thomas's work, Delaney almost apologizes for Thomas's inclusion:

> It is less possible to pass anything approaching a final verdict on Mr. Thomas than on any other poet in this series. Not only is he the youngest of them, but he is the poet who is most certainly changing and developing so ceaselessly and unmistakeably that we can attempt only an interim judgment. The critics of James Joyce once issued an examination of work in progress, and this programme must necessarily be of that nature.[53]

This is an apt comparison, not simply because *Our Exagmination Round His Factification for Incamination of Work in Progress* (1929) preceded – by a decade – the publication of *Finnegans Wake* (1939) in book form, but also because *Our Exagmination* was issued by the publisher of *Ulysses* (1922), Shakespeare and Company (with many of the essays appearing earlier, in the little magazine *transition*, when Joyce was unable to fill enough of its pages with his own writing). Further, Joyce was not simply the subject of *Our Exagmination*; he helped to put it together (choosing contributors and planning material for inclusion) and the same is true here, with Thomas reading his own work in the broadcast celebrating him as poet. For Joyce and Thomas alike, their 'surplus of elite cultural authority is, in fact, dependent on a legion of generative promotional and otherwise literary labors', literary broadcasts on the Eastern Service included.[54]

The broadcast on Thomas is also interesting in light of its historical moment because Delaney bemoans the Orientalism through which Welsh and Irish poets are read in England (with a not-so-subtle hint to Indian listeners subject to the same ideology):

> Welsh and Irish poets have brought out the worst in many critics, and we have heard so much sentimentality about the melancholy and mysticism of the Celt, that one is tempted to avoid the subject altogether. In this case it is not possible to ignore it. To the English, Wales is a foreign country, traditionally associated with singing, oratory, and evangelical religion. Behind the speech and writing of the Welsh there is always the music of their ancient Welsh language.[55]

This relationship between the ancient and modern is one that Thomas navigates throughout his career, argues Delaney. Many listeners would relate, given the prejudices faced by Indian writers in English, particularly those – like Raja Rao – who infused their English with other languages.[56] Yet part of what Delaney is after here, too, is a more general recovery of Thomas's reputation, linking Thomas's Welsh background with the recurring theme of religion; notably absent, as well, is any discussion of Thomas's famously bad behaviour.

Poetry as propaganda

At first glance, broadcasting Thomas's poetry across the British Empire may seem a curious choice for a nation at war. The necessity of refuting German and Japanese propaganda to India (which painted the British as uncultured barbarians) formed part of the background to the Eastern Service's commitment to high culture. But the more significant reason for its inclusion was precisely that it did not at first hearing sound political. English literature's supposed autonomy was mobilized to suggest that – despite the very real suffering of India at the hands of the British – the two were ultimately linked by a shared culture of literary study and appreciation, one that could be furthered after the war. Donald Stephenson, the Director of Eastern Services, wrote in a 1945 memo praising an elite private school for establishing Listening Societies among its students that 'there seems considerable advantage in encouraging direct interest among youngsters who are, potentially, the future leaders of India'.[57] More recent critics of English Studies in India found that this was all too successful: the economically privileged ensured that Indian education in English focused on literature rather than *literacy*.[58] But ultimately, what emerges from a closer consideration of *Book of Verse* is a picture of a writer who was both savvy about writing in various media and one attuned to – and eager to take advantage of – the relationship between cultural capital and imperial politics. Thomas's largely unheeded contributions to the Eastern Service speak volumes about our failure to properly wrestle with the history of writers as psychological warriors as well as the media in which they worked.

Notes

1 Rhian Barfoot and Kieron Smith, 'Introduction: [A] Writer of Words and Nothing Else', in *New Theoretical Perspectives on Dylan Thomas: A Writer of Words and Nothing Else?*, ed. Rhian Barfoot and Kieron Smith (Cardiff: University of Wales Press, 2020), 2.
2 Hugh I'Anson Fausset, 'Poet's Fantasies', review of Dylan Thomas, *The Map of Love*, *Times Literary Supplement*, 26 August 1939, 499.
3 Claire Squires, *Marketing Literature: The Making of Contemporary Writing in Britain* (Basingstoke: Palgrave Macmillan, 2007), 2.
4 Ankhi Mukherjee, *What is a Classic? Postcolonial Rewriting and Invention of the Canon* (Stanford, CA: Stanford University Press, 2014), 8.
5 Barbara Coulton, *Louis MacNeice in the BBC* (London: Faber and Faber, 1980), 100. MacNeice's work was also covered in an instalment of *Book of Verse* on 2 November 1946.
6 Edward Allen, 'Dylan Thomas on the BBC Eastern Service', in *Reading Dylan Thomas*, ed. Edward Allen (Edinburgh: Edinburgh University Press, 2019), 132.
7 Before Thomas became a fixture on the BBC's Eastern Service, he wrote features for the Latin American Service and appeared sporadically on the Home Service, the Welsh Home Service and the General Overseas Service. For an overview of these

broadcasts, see Peter Lewis, 'Before the Years of Broadcasting Fame: Dylan Thomas and the BBC, 1932–45', *The Durham University Journal* 86–87, no. 1 (1995): 129–37.

8   Thomas quoted in Lewis, 'Before the Years of Broadcasting Fame', 136. This trend is covered in more detail in Siân Nicholas, *The Echo of War: Home Front: Propaganda and the Wartime BBC, 1939–1945* (Manchester: Manchester University Press, 1996).

9   Anonymous, quoted in Mansell, *Let Truth Be Told*, 208.

10 See, in addition to the works cited herein, Jessica Berman, 'Re-routing Community: Colonial Broadcasting and the Aesthetics of Relation', in *Modernist Communities across Cultures and Media*, ed. Caroline Pollentier and Sarah Wilson (Gainesville, FL: University Press of Florida, 2019), 251–69; Julie Cyzewski, 'Making Friends: The Geopolitics of the Interview on the BBC's Eastern Service', *Biography* 41, no. 2 (2018): 322–43; Susheila Nasta, 'Sealing a Friendship: George Orwell and Mulk Raj Anand at the BBC (1941–43)', *Wasafiri* 26, no. 4 (2011): 14–18; Sejal Sutaria, 'From Punjab Trilogy to the Eastern Service: The Cultural Critiques and Cultural Mediations of Mulk Raj Anand', in *Indian Sound Cultures, Indian Citizenship*, ed. Laura Brueck, Jacob Smith, and Neil Verma (Ann Arbor, MI: University of Michigan Press, 2020), 201–25.

11 Janam Mukherjee, *Hungry Bengal: War, Famine and the End of Empire* (New York, NY: Oxford University Press, 2015), 11–16, 83; Babli Sinha, 'The BBC Eastern Service and the Crisis of Cosmopolitanism', *Historical Journal of Film, Radio and Television* 39, no. 2 (2019): 309–21.

12 Thomas first appeared on the Eastern Service reading 'A saint about to fall' for an instalment of *Calling All Students* dedicated to 'The Apocalyptic Poets' on 8 August 1943.

13 Daniel Ryan Morse, *Radio Empire: The BBC's Eastern Service and the Emergence of the Global Anglophone Novel* (New York: Columbia University Press, 2020), 189–90.

14 Gauri Viswanathan, *Masks of Conquest: Literary Study and British Rule in India* (New York, NY: Columbia University Press, 1989).

15 The Eastern Service received mixed reviews of its efforts to include Indian writers in its broadcasts and to transmit in local languages. One memo reported: 'the more I meet people and talk to them about our broadcasts, I find that most of our listeners, indeed a good majority of them, know English and take interest in our English programme. I have come across some who even refuse to take interest in the Hindustani programmes' (T. Pande to Director of the Eastern Service, December 19, 1945, typescript, E1 / 891, BBC Written Archives Centre, Caversham (hereafter BBC WAC). BBC copyright content reproduced courtesy of the British Broadcasting Corporation. All rights reserved.).

16 Damien Keane, *Ireland and the Problem of Information: Irish Writing, Radio, Late Modernist Communication* (University Park, PA: Pennsylvania State University Press, 2014), 7–8.

17 Jay Bolter and Richard Grusin, *Remediation: Understanding New Media* (Cambridge, MA: MIT Press, 1999), 15.

18 The image of the literary field derives from Pierre Bourdieu, *The Rules of Art: Genesis and Structure of the Literary Field*, trans. Susan Emanuel (Stanford, CA: Stanford University Press, 1995).
19 'The American New Criticism ... was deeply marked' by the doctrines of Richards (Terry Eagleton, *Literary Theory: An Introduction* (Malden, MA: Blackwell, 2008), 40). Robert Douglas-Fairhurst argues against conflating the two movements but also points to the presence of Eastern Service broadcasters William Empson and T. S. Eliot in the audience of Richards's 1925 lectures in 'I. A. Richards's Practical Criticism', *Essays in Criticism* 54, no. 4 (2004): 377.
20 Arthur Waley, 'From the Chinese', *Book of Verse* No. 78, BBC Eastern Service, 8 April 1946, typescript, BBC WAC; V. S. Pritchett, 'Modern Radio Drama', *Book of Verse* No. 64, BBC Eastern Service, 29 December 1945, typescript, BBC WAC.
21 Narayana Menon, 'Memories of Dylan Thomas', in *Literary Studies: Homage to Dr A. Sivaramasubramonia Aiyer*, ed. K. P. K. Menon, M. Manuel, and K. Ayyappa Paniker (Trivandrum: Dr A. Sivaramasubramonia Aiyer Memorial Committee, 1973), 45.
22 Aasiya Lodhi, 'Countries in the Air: Travel and Geomodernism in Louis MacNeice's BBC Features', *Media History* 24, no. 2 (2018): 232.
23 Morse, *Radio Empire*, 77–113.
24 *Book of Verse*, Numbers 117–55, typescripts, BBC WAC.
25 Daniel George, 'Lewis Carroll and Edward Lear', *Book of Verse* no. 49, BBC Eastern Service, 8 September 1945, script, BBC WAC, 1.
26 C. Lawson-Reece to DES, 15 November 1945, E1 / 891, BBC WAC, 1.
27 Lionel Fielden, *The Natural Bent* (London: Andre Deutsch, 1960), 104–5.
28 Dylan Thomas, 'Welsh Poetry', *Book of Verse*, BBC Eastern Service, January 1946, script, BBC WAC, 1. Emphasis added.
29 Glyne Griffith, *The BBC and the Development of Anglophone Caribbean Literature, 1943–1958* (Cham: Palgrave Macmillan, 2016).
30 David Rayvern Allen, *Arlott: The Authorised Biography* (London: HarperCollins, 1994), 85.
31 Viola Meynell, 'V. Sackville-West & Ruth Pitter', *Book of Verse* No. 112, BBC Eastern Service, 30 November 1946, typescript, BBC WAC, 6.
32 Louis MacNeice, 'W. H. Auden', *Book of Verse* No. 110, BBC Eastern Service, 16 November 1946, typescript, BBC WAC, 1.
33 Identifying the cultural and intellectual effect of the volume as 'baleful', Edward Said sums it up as part of the 'battle for the hearts and minds of people all over the world' and 'the triumph of unthinking Manicheanism over rational as well as self-critical analysis' (Edward Said, *Representations of the Intellectual* (New York, NY: Vintage, 1994), 110–12).
34 John Lehmann, 'Stephen Spender', *Book of Verse*, BBC Eastern Service, typescript, BBC WAC, 2.

35 Ibid., 1, 5.
36 Lehmann, 'Stephen Spender', 13.
37 Denis [illegible], 'Cecil Day Lewis', *Book of Verse*, no. 109, BBC Eastern Service, 9 November 1946, typescript, BBC WAC, 4; 12.
38 Douglas Cleverdon, quoted in Walford Davies, *Dylan Thomas* (Cardiff: University of Wales Press, 2014), 105.
39 Dylan Thomas, *Under Milk Wood*, additional material by Siân Owen, National Theatre, 16 June–24 July 2021.
40 For a full list of Thomas's BBC broadcasts, see Ralph Maud, ed., *On the Air with Dylan Thomas: The Broadcasts* (New York, NY: New Directions, 1991), 283–305.
41 Allen, 'Dylan Thomas on the BBC Eastern Service', 119.
42 Thomas, quoted in Davies, *Dylan Thomas*, 106.
43 Peter Kalliney, *Commonwealth of Letters: British Literary Culture and the Emergence of Postcolonial Aesthetics* (New York, NY: Oxford University Press, 2013), 6.
44 Menon, 'Memories of Dylan Thomas', 45. I have not been able to locate this broadcast, but Thomas read 'A saint about to fall' for Orwell's Eastern Service series *Calling All Students* on 31 July 1943 (Thomas, *On the Air with Dylan Thomas*, 284).
45 Mulk Raj Anand, quoted in George Orwell, *All Propaganda Is Lies: 1941–1942*, vol. 13 of *The Complete Works of George Orwell*, ed. Peter Davison (London: Secker & Warburg, 1998), 464.
46 Mulk Raj Anand, 'London as I See It', BBC Eastern Service, 14 February 1945, typescript, BBC WAC; Morse, *Radio Empire*, 114–50.
47 George Orwell to Desmond Hawkins, 13 April 1943, reprinted in *Two Wasted Years: 1943*, vol. 15 of *The Complete Works of George Orwell*, ed. Peter Davison (London: Secker & Warburg, 1998), 62.
48 A passage from Thomas's short story 'The Mouse and the Woman' was cut in the interest of time, but also likely because it was not in verse. It would have preceded 'On the Marriage of a Virgin' (Terence Delaney, 'Dylan Thomas', *Book of Verse*, BBC Eastern Service, 21 December 1946, typescript, BBC WAC, 9–10).
49 Delaney, 'Dylan Thomas', 4.
50 George Orwell, 'Poetry and the Microphone' (1945), in George Orwell, *Essays*, ed. Peter Davison (New York, NY: Knopf, 2002), 857–65.
51 See, for instance, Edward Kamau Brathwaite, *History of the Voice: The Development of Nation Language in Anglophone Caribbean Poetry* (London: New Beacon Books, 1984) and James Procter, 'Wireless Writing, World War II and the West Indian Literary Imagination', in *Postwar: British Literature in Transition 1940–60*, ed. Gill Plain (Cambridge: Cambridge University Press, 2019), 117–35.
52 Philip Larkin, for one, agreed with the BBC's assessment of Thomas's significance, writing upon hearing of Thomas's death: 'I can't believe D. T. is truly dead. It seems

absurd. Three people [Eliot, Auden and Thomas] who've altered the face of poetry, and the youngest has to die' (Larkin, quoted in Davies, *Dylan Thomas*, 165).

53 Delaney, 'Dylan Thomas', 4.
54 Aaron Jaffe, *Modernism and the Culture of Celebrity* (Cambridge: Cambridge University Press, 2005), 201.
55 Delaney, 'Dylan Thomas', 6–7. Joseph Lennon traces 'The Semiotic Connection between the Celt and the Oriental', in *Irish Orientalism: A Literary and Intellectual History* (Syracuse, NY: Syracuse University Press, 2004), 2.
56 Ruvani Ranasinha, 'Talking to India: The Literary Production and Consumption of Selected South Asian Anglophone Writers in Britain and the USA (1940s–1950s)', in *Books without Borders, Volume 2: Perspectives from South Asia*, ed. Robert Fraser and Mary Hammond (Basingstoke: Palgrave Macmillan, 2008), 170–80.
57 Donald Stephenson to Controller Overseas, 'Discussion with Headmaster of the Doon School', 4 September 1945, E1 / 891, BBC WAC, 1.
58 For a more nuanced view that considers the everyday use of English across social classes, see Akshya Saxena, *Vernacular English: Reading the Anglophone in Postcolonial India* (Princeton, NJ: Princeton University Press, 2022).

Part II

4

PEN, refugee writers and propaganda

Katherine Cooper

Writing in 1960, John Lehmann described the 1941 PEN Congress as 'a demonstration against the Axis',[1] not merely because it was held in Blitz-battered London and attended by so many distinguished writers, but also because the refugee writers from occupied Europe who were by then settled in England used it to send out what he called 'their challenge to the military masters of their homelands'.[2] As Lehmann testifies, the Congress marked a crucial call to solidarity but also demonstrated that there was significant resistance to fascism in Europe and that it was coalescing in and around London. Storm Jameson, President of English PEN (Poets, Essayists and Novelists club) joked that the event had offered delegates 'the chance of being bombed, and three days of uncensored discussion of writers' problems and duties in the post-war world', and yet it turned out to be one of PEN's biggest congresses, attracting more than 400 delegates from as far-afield as Mexico.[3] This show of solidarity was seized upon by the British government, who took the opportunity of using the familiar voices of occupied countries' intelligentsia-in-exile to address populations in Europe. The co-option of refugee voices for British propaganda purposes was a tactic already being deployed elsewhere in cultural institutions and organizations. Examining this phenomenon, this chapter traces the ebb and flow of refugee writers between governmental and non-governmental sectors in Britain during the Second World War. While a number of studies have addressed wartime BBC work by specific national groups or the presence and work of particular refugee groups in Britain, this chapter focuses on the co-option of refugees by PEN (as a Non-Governmental Organization operating internationally at this time) and the BBC (as a government-funded independent cultural institution) and their direct use by British propaganda and intelligence agencies for operations in Europe.[4] It demonstrates that the activities of these separate organizations were similarly inflected by two narratives at play around refugees during this period: of refugees as crucial witnesses of events in Europe but also as potentially untrustworthy sources exploiting those same experiences for personal gain in wartime Britain. In doing so, I want to consider here both parallels and inconsistencies in these organizations' approaches to refugee voices and what their responses might tell us about the deployment and understanding of refugee voices up to the present day.

PEN, refugees and the 1941 Conference

PEN had been founded in 1921 by Catharine Amy Dawson Scott, a playwright, poet and key member of London's literary and artistic circles, to countermand the divisive and destructive politics of the First World War, to reunite European writers around shared values and interests and to encourage 'nations to draw together in peace'.[5] By the outbreak of the Second World War, PEN had forty-six centres worldwide, including in Bolivia, China and Mexico, and counted writers such as Thomas Mann, Rabindranath Tagore, H. G. Wells and Rebecca West as members. PEN hosted – and continues to host – yearly congresses as an opportunity for writers to meet, exchange ideas and discuss the challenges, literary and non-literary, facing the world. These annual events also operate as a setting for regular AGMs at which writers debate PEN's stances on a range of issues from war to nuclear disarmament, which causes or writers to support and how the organization as a whole will respond to key global challenges. However, these events have since their inception also been exercises in statecraft, bankrolled by governments, often infiltrated by spies and secret police watching dissident writers in exile, and have frequently been the settings of clandestine plots to recapture and imprison outspoken writers by repressive regimes across the world. In short, PEN's congresses have never been simply social or literary events for writers and publishers and have always been imbued with the politics of the time. The 1941 Congress in London was no exception.

The proliferation of conferences, meetings and gatherings during the interwar years was connected to the rise of international organizations like PEN at the end of the nineteenth century and in the early decades of the twentieth. As Akira Iriye notes in his definitive study of the growth of international organizations, these 'associations that are established by private individuals and groups' began to spring up as a result of progressive political and social movements and advances in transport and communications.[6] These developments gave rise to a connected wave of international conferences and congresses, gatherings and events aimed at tackling international ills, run by organizations such as the League of Nations, the Peace Pledge Union or the Women's International League. Many of them, like the American Anti-Imperialist League and the Berlin-based Workers International Relief organization, were tied implicitly to communism, fascism or other political causes. Unlike some of these early NGOs, PEN had always strived to be politically impartial.[7] However, throughout the twentieth century, events and gatherings organized by supposedly impartial organizations were vulnerable to being hijacked by prevailing political agendas and interests, particularly if they had taken advantage of generous funding offered by governments or political groups. PEN itself explicitly exploited political interests at its Czechoslovakia Congress in 1938, which was funded by President Edvard Beneš's government as a 'propagandistic forum' to encourage writers to persuade other European countries to defend and support Czechoslovakia in the event of further Nazi aggression.[8] The power of these sorts of gatherings and organizations reached its pinnacle in the Cold War with the foundation of the Congress for Cultural Freedom (CCF), a CIA-backed initiative which infiltrated a number of events and congresses, including those organized by PEN.[9] PEN's wartime involvement with the British government and the British Establishment was therefore unremarkable at the time.

The London Congress took place from 10 to 13 September 1941 in a city which had until recently been ravaged by nightly bombings. As well as offering 'the chance of being bombed', as Jameson had joked, the event functioned as both a last hurrah in London for those destined for more distant shores such as America, and the opportunity to revel in all of the qualities which Nazi fascism apparently detested: multiculturalism, gender equality, art, free thought and just a whiff of extravagance, courtesy of Jameson's lavish hospitality. It also had a captive audience, as London was already home to a good proportion of Europe's intelligentsia, all eager for an opportunity to reconnect with each other, re-build their professional lives and, of course, enjoy a good party. However, there was far more at stake than many delegates imagined. Jameson cynically plotted that 'what we need is a list of patrons so eminently respectable that the Government will be ashamed to do nothing for us',[10] and a list of exiled politicians was drawn up, including Beneš (by then President of the Czechoslovak government-in-exile), Jan Masaryk (Foreign Minister of Czechoslovakia), Władysław Sikorski (Prime Minister of the Polish government-in-exile) and the exiled King Haakon of Norway, as well as the writers Phyllis Bentley, Arthur Koestler, Denis Saurat, Desmond McCarthy, Erika Mann and H. G. Wells. PEN thereby placed itself and its writers at the forefront of a wider political game to influence and befriend those who would lead and transform post-war Europe. These sorts of strategic social events afforded opportunities for the organization to raise its political profile, allowing it to lobby the British government for visas and financial support for refugees, and to put writers in dialogue with those who would be forming national and international policy after the war.

PEN was so preoccupied with its own intentions for the Congress and with the practical considerations of organizing such an event that it almost neglected to notice the way that the British government, in the form of the Foreign Office and the intelligence services as well as branches of the British propaganda machine, had begun to insert itself in proceedings. Shortfalls in finances, difficulties with visa and travel arrangements and restricted access to central London venues meant that generous offers from the Foreign Office, the BBC and even the United States government were snapped up, with little thought or care for the motivations of such magnanimity. In fact, the British government could already see the possibilities presented by such a prestigious gathering of writers, which offered an opportunity to speak to inhabitants of enemy and occupied countries such as Germany, Czechoslovakia, France and Poland through an apparently impartial organization and through the familiar and renowned voices of their own writers living in exile. It also offered a brilliant recruiting ground for individuals new to Britain and in dire need of employment who had language skills and direct experience of the continent at war. These skills were essential for governmental and non-governmental intelligence-gathering, listening operations and, of course, propaganda.

The conference's social offering was extensive and lavish, and included tea at *The Times* offices, a Foreign Office wine reception and a function hosted by the Free French at the Dorchester hotel. Each of these events marked the staking of a claim to writers, and particularly *refugee* writers, by different groups. *The Times* wished to cement its status as an elite British institution, the Foreign Office wished to gain intelligence by forging connections with intellectuals from the continent, and the Free French sought, perhaps, to use some of these voices in its own propaganda campaigns. The invasion of France the previous year had led to a new influx of French refugees and exiles to London, figures who were beginning to find their way onto influential platforms to promote their cause and to further that of the Allies. The inaugural Congress luncheon was held at the Savoy hotel on the strand, at which the surprised organizers found themselves with more than 470 guests, including 'four heads of government in exile, thirteen ambassadors and ministers [and] six High Commissioners'.[11] A speech was given by John Winant, the American

Ambassador, with J. B. Priestley leading the toasts.¹² Three months before Pearl Harbor and the US entry into the war, Winant's attendance is significant, affording him an opportunity to address influential British and European writers, and to reassure them that America would defend Europe and European literature and culture.

The theme of the Congress was 'Literature and the World After the War', tying the interests of free expression and of literary and cultural advancement firmly to the progressive politics of the Allied side.¹³ The advert for the conference sent to PEN members and to national and international news outlets explained that '[a]mong the subjects discussed will be: the duty of the writer to the world after the war, authorship and propaganda, ideas of nationalism and internationalism so far as they affect the writer, writers without language [a reference to refugee and writers displaced from their linguistic and literary homelands], will there be literature from young Germans after the war?'¹⁴ The tone was defiant and implied that an Allied victory was expected, with a full return to pre-war literary and political freedoms. Speeches were given by Bentley, Priestley, Wells and West, all examining the future of Europe and of literature itself. Refugee writers such as Erika Mann, Antoni Słonimski and Robert Neumann (who was already working with PEN to help to match refugee writers up with opportunities to work in Britain) also featured in the programme. Collaborative panels featured refugee writers alongside their counterparts from Britain, India and China, who discussed the ongoing conflict in Europe and how the continent might be rebuilt after the war, culturally and politically.¹⁵

The final session of the Congress featured a reception by the directors of the Free French journal *La France Libre*. What follows this is particularly interesting, being obliquely described in the Congress running order as '[a] feature programme by the French Section of the BBC English, Polish and Czechoslovak Artists'.¹⁶ This suggests that the Corporation's French Section wished to present an example of the types of programmes that refugees were already working on at the BBC, perhaps in the hope of recruiting more interested parties from the gathered writers. Also present were Priestley, who had worked extensively for the Corporation earlier in the war, and Herberth Herlitschka, the Austrian refugee who, with his wife Marlys, had translated works by Virginia Woolf and Charles Morgan, and had taken up work 'translating and transmitting German radio broadcasts for the BBC' on the advice of Storm Jameson herself.¹⁷ Herlitschka had received a stipend from the PEN Refugee Fund when he first arrived in Britain and had good contacts both within and beyond PEN.¹⁸ This BBC presence seems designed not only to show support but, potentially, to take advantage of this large group of talented writers and translators, who had assembled in London to showcase the work of the BBC European services. While these refugees had been silenced in their own countries and robbed again of their agency and voices as they tried to leave, here they were encouraged to speak as part of a collaborative effort to plan and shape a new Europe. As writers, they were asked to lend their voices not only to a new literary and cultural Europe, but to a new political vision for the continent, underpinned by liberal values and the growing language of rights.

The connections between literature and freedom and between writers and rights had been well established by 1941. As Rachel Potter argues, the 1948 Universal Declaration of Human Rights 'would have been impossible without the political and cultural shifts towards both an internationalist and individually based "universal" human rights agenda in the two decades preceding the Second World War'.[19] PEN and its writers played an important role in this 'cultural shift', and could draw direct connections between their literary freedoms and more basic human rights, as fascist and communist governments attacked first books and writing and then human populations. Lyndsey Stonebridge examines the relationship between human rights and the literary arts more closely in *Writing and Righting* (2021), in which she argues that the literary community is one 'that identifies with the forms of being human made possible by the arts of writing' and that 'the human capacities, perceptions, relationships, and interpretations disclosed by literature exceed the art itself'.[20] While Stonebridge rightly problematizes such assumptions in the contemporary moment when the concept of human rights is under sustained attack, it is easy to see the impact that these ideas had on writers – and particularly refugee writers – during the war, for whom 'the connections between the self-evident humanity of books and the bigger project of securing humanity seemed obvious'.[21] For PEN, defending writing had become by this time synonymous with defending humanity itself. Writers in Europe at this time thus came to look at PEN's literary community as offering a blueprint for the type of global cooperation that they hoped for in the post-war world.

Overlapping networks between PEN and war work

Partly as a result of this association between literature, free speech and human rights, writers were easily convinced to lend their skills to British institutions – such as the BBC – which sought to promote the Allied campaign. In their view, they were defending fellow writers, literature itself and promoting the ideals of freedom and democracy; as one refugee, the Austrian-born art historian Ernst Gombrich, commented later, 'we could not have sustained the effort if we had not hoped to contribute to Hitler's ultimate downfall' – though many would have been reluctant to acknowledge their work as propaganda.[22] Jameson, who served throughout the war as President of English PEN, fiercely denied any complicity in Foreign Office affairs, writing in her autobiography of a furious argument with H. G. Wells, who had accused her of wanting 'to make [English PEN] an instrument of Foreign Office propaganda'.[23] However, she was pragmatic, as many in PEN were, particularly when it came to the *quid pro quo* of gaining government help for PEN's refugees. Of course, during this time, other writers operated outside the orbit of progressive politics: from Ezra Pound's fascistic fantasies to W. B. Yeats's flirtation with Eoin O'Duffy's Blueshirts, literary circles were not always anti-fascist in sentiment. Moreover, as Mark Wollaeger writes, 'propaganda itself was the alter-ego of modernist distanciation', or was frequently seen as such by both practitioners and critics alike.[24] Wollaeger notes that for writers like Virginia Woolf and the Bloomsbury group, government work might have sounded the death knell of artistic freedom, but for others it offered an opportunity to defend this. Writers and PEN stalwarts of this period such as Bentley, E. M. Forster, Lehmann, Priestley, Stephen Spender and Wells all took part in war work of one kind or another. Among these, Bentley and Mary Agnes Hamilton worked at the MOI, while Arnold Bennett served as the ministry's first Director of Propaganda for France. Lehmann was a regular broadcaster for the BBC's Austrian Service, but was blocked from intelligence and other information work as James Smith has described.[25] Countless others lent their pens and their voices on formal and informal terms, either in government positions or at the BBC.

The BBC offers an interesting counterpoint to PEN's work as an NGO: as a public service broadcaster, the Corporation had been paid for by a licence fee since 1928. This licence fee was overseen and distributed by the General Post Office (GPO), tying the BBC financially and politically to the British government and to organizations such as the Political Warfare Executive (PWE), the secret service established just before the 1941 Congress to produce and coordinate British propaganda to enemy and occupied Europe. The BBC's situation does, however, mirror some of the issues and inconsistencies faced by PEN in cooperating with government strategies and in the way that it treated and understood its refugee employees. British writers were being deployed by the BBC to galvanize the nation even before the war, and as Ian Whittington describes, '[t]he existential threat that Nazi Germany posed to Britain – and to the tenets of liberal humanism and artistic freedom that subtended much of its literary culture – compounded the urgency of this intermedial imperative'.[26] PEN did have connections to the BBC in its own right, mainly through some of its most illustrious figures: Priestley, himself a former President of English PEN, became, through his BBC radio shows, 'a leader second in importance only to Mr Churchill' and was almost as recognizable a voice on the air waves during the early years of the war.[27] This comparison is almost certainly part of the reason why Priestley was removed from the airwaves, with memos by Churchill criticizing his anti-government on-air stances indicative of establishment displeasure at the broadcasts.[28] This heavy-handedness demonstrates just how important a tool the radio had become, in British as in European politics. Just as pre-war 'domestic wartime programming became a means of interpellating British listeners into the nation,'[29] the wider European operations of the BBC became a way of bringing them into contact with the continent and, eventually, of uniting Europe under a banner of common progressive values. The accounts of those who had experienced life on the continent were crucial not only to writers and audiences at home, but, as we have already seen in the PEN Congress, to those abroad. Their words carried an authenticity of experience which those on the British home front could not approach. This was a valuable asset in the propaganda war.

Since its launch as a constituent part of the GPO in 1922, the BBC had fought for its independence but remained subject to a measure of government control, in large part due to its funding model. As an institution, it nevertheless retained a bullish attachment to self-governance, thanks to the political connections and eccentricities of its founding fathers John Reith, Arthur Burrows and Cecil Lewis. The Corporation also sought to reach beyond the metropole, establishing stations in Manchester, Glasgow and Cardiff, which broadcast regional programming. In the following decade, as technology evolved, its services began to expand internationally. The BBC became the voice of Britain abroad, with the Empire Service launched in 1932 mimicking imperialist processes to try to maintain control over British colonies and to '"project" Britain' to the rest of the world.[30] These broadcasts set London at their centre and British language and culture as the product and selling point.[31] During the Second World War, this became a different mission in which Britain sought to promote itself as the de facto leader of the Allied nations, broadcasting in a range of European languages designed to speak to different territories and perspectives.

A key moment in this mobilization of the radio and of the BBC was, as David Hendy describes in his remarkable history of the organization, the broadcast of Chamberlain's speech on 27 September 1938. This took place at the height of the political crisis over Hitler's invasion of the Sudetenland and, at the behest of the Foreign Office, was broadcast in French, German and Italian in an effort to reach audiences across Europe – as well as refugees who had already arrived in Britain – to persuade them of the anti-fascist cause and version of events. From autumn 1938, there were daily broadcasts of fifteen minutes per day in these three key European languages. By May 1944, the European Service, as it was known, was broadcasting programmes in German, French and Italian, as well as in 'Polish, Czech, Slovak, Romanian, Hungarian, Serbo-Croatian, Greek, Dutch, Danish, Flemish, Swedish, Spanish and Portuguese'.[32] This was chiefly organized around a central desk where news was scripted by British-born staff in English. Scripts were then distributed to foreign language speakers – mostly refugees – who translated them into their native tongue and liaised with supervisors also familiar with that country or territory.

As the Corporation sought not only to promote Allied news and perspectives to enemy and occupied territories but also to develop a comprehensive programme for monitoring continental broadcasts, refugees became even more central to its mission; in Hendy's words, '[t]he wartime BBC was a cosmopolitan enterprise'.[33] Hendy also suggests that 'ministers and civil servants had accepted that any attempt at spreading official propaganda would most likely succeed if done though a trusted source such as the BBC. This meant the state accepting some loss of control over the process'; in fact, the BBC's 'credibility depended on audiences continuing to believe in its complete editorial independence'.[34] In this, perhaps unsurprisingly, refugee voices became indispensable. They conveyed, even when unacknowledged, authenticity and familiarity to audiences abroad and even to producers working with them directly, as well as crucial language skills and expertise on the wider cultural and political temper of their respective home countries. Their work was highly varied and 'as the threat of invasion receded and the focus shifted to the liberation of Europe, it was the largely hidden and sometimes totally secret work with which these men and women were engaged that would lay the foundations for the BBC's reputation as an international broadcaster – and contribute materially to the defeat of Nazism'.[35] Refugees and exiles used their language skills and cultural understanding to monitor propaganda broadcasts in occupied Europe, to write and translate scripts and to work with producers to shape material into languages and formats suitable for broadcast in different countries across Europe. They even monitored pilots' radios and provided translations of broadcasts from European stations to ensure that the BBC – and, of course, the Foreign Office – remained abreast of developments across Europe.[36]

These operations at the BBC were incredibly complex, with the additional wartime imposition of policy direction from the MOI and PWE to ensure that the BBC's wartime output did not conflict with the objectives of other branches of the wartime state. Teams were established for each country or language group, with the German and French sections unsurprisingly being the biggest. The German section was overseen by the fastidious Hugh Carleton Greene, correspondent for the *Daily Telegraph* in Berlin during the 1930s, and employed refugees such as the lawyer Carl Brinitzer, the theatre director Julius Gellner, the expressionist writer Karl Otten and the actor and director Walter Rilla. The French Service was overseen by Darsie Gillie – briefly *Manchester Guardian* correspondent in Paris at the beginning of the war – and many of its correspondents were anonymized to protect family members who had remained in France. They were spared the supervision of an Englishman as they fell beyond suspicion of collusion and espionage. Even André Philip, Free French leader Charles De Gaulle's Commissioner for the Interior, admitted that '[t]he underground resistance movement was built up by the BBC'.[37]

Operating across most of Europe, 'for each and every language service, the BBC needed to recruit – and get security clearance for – a sizeable pool of writers, translators, supervisors and announcers'.[38] Some of these were PEN writers or had been brought into the country as a result of PEN's work with refugees; others had entered by other means. Sheer Ganor describes how refugee script-readers in the German Service 'whose all-too native Germanness exposed them, so it was feared, as undesirables to listeners in Germany, necessarily remained anonymous voices' – anonymity which certainly made it difficult to trace their path through or to PEN.[39] Nevertheless, Storm Jameson, who had taken a small flat near the BBC – alluringly cheap because 'no one wanted to live a few yards away from Portland Place, thought a German target' – described how 'several of our exiles were now working for the B.B.C.', complaining, characteristically, that too many of them called in on their way to Broadcasting House and disturbed her writing.[40] Jameson even writes of a 'Czech exile' whom she had helped at PEN through the Refugee Fund dedicating his BBC slot on the 14 May 1941 to telling viewers about her new novel *Europe to Let* (1940) and its section which paid homage to Czechoslovakia, 'The Hour of Prague'.[41] So it seems likely that whether through an alignment of political vision, or through financial necessity, there was some movement between members of PEN or refugees helped by PEN and the BBC. Moreover, the processes through which refugees were recruited and then used by both organizations highlights some important ethical problems around the use of refugees for this type of work.

It was not too long before this work edged across into the more clandestine operations of the intelligence services with the so-called 'Eavesdroppers', based at Wood Norton at Evesham in Worcestershire, where '[t]he entire operation, though largely overseen by British-born staff, depended, once again, on a teeming community of highly skilled immigrants'.[42] These monitoring staff included the Austrians George Weidenfeld (who later founded the publishing firm Weidenfeld & Nicolson) and the aforementioned Gombrich, as well as the Hungarian Martin Esslin, who went on to an illustrious career in broadcasting and academia. All three were Jewish. There was some overlap between these staff and those who translated or wrote copy for the European Service. The Listening Service – as it was more formally called – was ostensibly part of the BBC's news operation but was actually gathering intelligence for Allied operations across Europe by listening not only to civilian frequencies but to military transmissions as well. Similarly, as the war rumbled on, refugees' skills were utilized to receive information from Europe but also to signal covertly to Allied agents abroad. Hendy notes that '[b]y the end of August 1941, coded messages to British agents or resistance fighters had been transmitted in French, Serbo-Croat, Dutch, Czech, Norwegian and Greek' at the behest of the PWE, as code words and signals were inserted into news broadcasts.[43] Clear connections existed between the PWE, SOE and BBC, most notably through figures such as Ivone Kirkpatrick, who worked for both the BBC and the PWE. However, although all three organizations made extensive use of refugee labour, no clear connection can be drawn between PEN and the two secret services. Much as it later concealed its occasional interactions with the CIA and CCF during the Cold War, PEN may have sought to disguise and hide these connections internally in order to safeguard the organization's commitment to political impartiality. Certainly, Wells's ongoing presence at meetings and functions would have prevented even the pragmatic Jameson from attempting to make such involvement more formal.

Refugees and war work: Loyalty and suspicions

The qualities which suited refugees to these roles and increased demand for their skills often made them suspicious in the eyes of the British state. German-speaking refugees, as discussed earlier, were given access to the BBC's microphone only when they were delivering news as anonymous announcers or when they appeared as nameless voices in features – partly to avoid allegations of bias towards certain nations or politics, but also 'lest the Nazis accused the BBC of being a mouthpiece for disgruntled exiles'.[44] All translators were overseen by English producers with a background in the language and culture of the service, who were asked to ensure that refugees listening daily to Nazi broadcasts were not swayed by these. This distrust characterized the BBC's dealings with refugees during this period: the Corporation and some of its employees refused to take refugee loyalty for granted and it seems likely that many refugees – quite rightly in light of their experiences with the manoeuvrings of governmental apparatuses in their home countries – also viewed the British state and the BBC with a certain degree of suspicion. Both took wary advantage of each other, with the historian Alan Bullock claiming that 'the foreign refugees, though distinguished in their own fields "regarded themselves as helots, and, on the whole, we regarded them as that, too"'.[45] Ultimately, of course, power lay as always with the British state and with British institutions. Refugee voices were trusted insofar as they were useful, but despite their extensive contributions were not accepted in the same terms as the British heroes of the information war, and many faced internment and unemployment during and after the war. Writing to the PEN Refugee Fund from Onchan internment camp on the Isle of Man in March 1941, one such refugee, the German journalist Carl Wehner, noted that he had contributed to a BBC feature entitled 'Under Nazi Rule' in March 1940, and asked if this might go some way towards securing his release.[46] Replying to PEN, who were assisting with his appeal, the Home Office ignored this contribution and rejected Wehner's objections.[47] Wehner was finally released in January 1944, but his case clearly demonstrates the hypocrisy of a system which deployed refugee voices in the war effort but also distrusted and imprisoned these same 'enemy aliens' in the interests of national security.[48] By supporting the British government, PEN was complicit in these systems and emulated some of these practices in their own processes and dealings with refugees, even while the NGO worked hard to secure the release of many refugee writers who were interned.

The interplay observable here between the desires to amplify and to silence refugee voices is emblematic of a wider historical struggle in which refugee testimony is simultaneously prized and distrusted. Referring to the international structures erected before and after the Second World War, which were designed to aid and inform asylum claims and processes, Liisa H. Malkki observes that 'humanitarian practices tend to silence refugees'.[49] She argues that instead of being empowered, refugees actually suffer 'from a peculiar kind of speechlessness in the face of national and international organizations whose object of care and control they are'.[50] This is because an explicit part of gaining refugee status is to declare oneself a refugee and to present a testimony to confirm this status.

To the international organizations and governments charged with helping them, refugees were 'frequently regarded as simply unreliable informants', and there was even a tendency among some administrators 'to characterize the refugees as dishonest, prone to exaggeration, even crafty and untrustworthy' in their pursuit of safety.[51] Countless refugees provided such testimonies to PEN in hundreds of letters sent prior to and during the Second World War. German refugee writers such as Wehner, Joanna Schwartz, Dr Jonas Leszczer and his wife Serafine pleaded with PEN's administrators for financial support, help with visas and travel arrangements and even assistance in finding work in Britain, but all were subject to rigorous checks and had to provide third-party testimonials to ascertain their trustworthiness and literary standing. PEN, then, like the BBC, was complicit in the creation of a hostile environment, even while these organizations sought to amplify refugee voices at events such as their 1941 Congress or over the airwaves.

For some refugee writers and broadcasters such as Esslin, their early experiences of broadcasting did help them to build successful careers and lives in Britain and elsewhere. Originally named Julius Pereszlényi, Esslin monitored German radio broadcasts for the BBC during the war and went on to forge a successful post-war career as a producer and writer of drama programmes, eventually becoming Professor of Drama at Stanford University in the United States.[52] While success stories of this kind are rare, the BBC offered many others who arrived penniless a potentially life-saving opportunity as well as the chance, as Plock describes, to 'play a part in the fight against Hitler'.[53] Refugees working on other services also benefitted. The actor and dramatist Richard Duschinsky, another refugee who received help from PEN and who was introduced into BBC circles through his work translating Priestley's plays into German,[54] wrote and produced material for the Austrian service with his countryman Gellner.[55] Duschinsky also left Europe for the United States after the war and continued to make a living as a writer and dramatist. Notwithstanding these success stories though, it seems that there were countless others like Wehner who were deployed in propaganda and listening operations but who were also interned, distrusted and dropped at various points in the war and thereafter.

Although PEN was not itself officially involved with British propaganda, the channels of communication and flows of talent between English PEN, the BBC and the British government were rich and mutually sustaining. PEN was asked by the Home Office to provide information on refugee writers, from their literary standing to their skills and aptitude for different kinds of work, and its cooperation became a condition of the government funding that they got towards their fund for refugee writers in need.[56] It is clear that, for liberal and anti-fascist

NGOs such as PEN, for institutions such as the BBC, and indeed, for the British government, refugees offered a rich vein of talent to exploit for propaganda purposes. They provided the language skills to communicate to wider Europe and the cultural wherewithal to advise on how to approach different populations and formulate the Allied message. The presence of refugees at the heart of the propaganda operation endeared both the BBC and the British more generally to sympathetic audiences in their home countries and added authenticity, familiarity and prestige to propaganda broadcasts. Nonetheless, refugees were still distrusted, as exemplified by the significant supervision of their work and the requirement to provide third-party references to support their stories. The government also sought to protect itself from the supposed financial risk posed by refugees: Priestley himself had stood as guarantor for Duschinsky before the latter was admitted to Britain.[57] Furthermore, and as we have seen, even those working directly for the BBC were not immune to the British government's brutal internment sweeps. The conflicts of interest between the BBC and the refugees that they employed during the war, between the BBC and its overseers at the PWE and in the security services, and between PEN and the refugees it supported illuminate ongoing debates around the ways in which we seek to use refugee stories and experiences. They demonstrate that all of these organizations sought to benefit from refugee stories and refugee voices while at the same time doubting and underplaying those voices in other areas of their work in ways which echo our appropriation of refugee narratives today. Just as a bureaucracy of suspicion is created in camps at the edges of Europe, as refugees are forced to recount and testify repeatedly to trauma and suffering in order to secure passage or refugee status, so too NGOs, governments and elements of the media seek to appropriate the struggles of refugees for their own ends, whether in the case of the Refugee Olympic team, documentaries about *kindertransport* survivors or MPs' photo opportunities. Refugees' stories and testimonies have a currency in our culture still, and one which often benefits not the refugees themselves, but those structures which would often seek to deny them their status and their rights.

Notes

1 This chapter was produced in part through work on the AHRC-funded project *Non-Governmental Writers Organisations and Free Expression* based at the University of East Anglia and led by Rachel Potter, which sought to unearth the connections between PEN and the evolution of free expression, in law and attitudes, throughout the twentieth and twenty-first centuries. My work as part of this has

focused specifically on PEN's work with refugees and the evolution of its Writers in Exile Centres. I am very grateful to Dr Samantha Schnee, Daniel Gorman and English PEN for access to their additional research on the PEN Refugee Fund, which was invaluable in the writing of this chapter. Special thanks to Joan Sibley and the team at the Harry Ransom Center at the University of Texas at Austin and particularly for their help in locating documents in the newly re-catalogued PEN Archive. Thanks to the Harry Ransom Humanities Research Center and to English PEN for their permission to reproduce material from their archives here.

2   John Lehmann, *I am My Brother* (New York, NY: Longman, 1960), 8.
3   Storm Jameson, *Journey From the North: Volume II* (London: Collins & Harvill Press, 1970), 103.
4   There have been a number of significant studies produced lately which have examined the contribution of the BBC to propaganda during the Second World War, notably Ian Whittington's *Writing the Radio War: Literature, Politics and the BBC, 1939-45* (Edinburgh: Edinburgh University Press, 2018), and David Hendy's expansive history of the Corporation, *The BBC: A People's History* (London: Profile Books, 2022), published during its centenary year. Furthermore, a number of studies have examined the contribution of individual national groups to British propaganda operations such as J. F. Slattery, '"Oskar Zuversichtlich": A German's Response to British Radio Propaganda during World War II', *Historical Journal of Film, Radio and Television* 12, no. 1 (1992): 69–85; Charmian Brinson and Richard Dove, eds., *Stimme Der Wahrheit! German Language Broadcasting by the BBC* (Amsterdam and New York, NY: Rodopi, 2003); Alban Webb, *London Calling: Britain, the BBC World Service and the Cold War* (London: Bloomsbury Academic, 2014); Sheer Ganor, 'Forbidden Words, Banished Voices: Jewish Refugees at the Service of BBC Propaganda to Wartime Germany', *Journal of Contemporary History* 55, no. 1 (2020): 97–119; Vike Plock's *The BBC German Service during the Second World War* (Cham: Palgrave Macmillan, 2021). Examinations of espionage communities monitoring or employing refugees and exiles include Brinson and Dove's *A Matter of Intelligence: MI5 and the Surveillance of Anti-Nazi Refugees, 1933–50* (Manchester: Manchester University Press, 2014) and Marie Gillespie and Alban Webb, eds., *Diasporas and Diplomacy: Cosmopolitan Contact Zones at the BBC World Service (1932–2012)* (London and New York, NY: Routledge, 2013). This chapter brings this body of research together to examine the role of PEN in these operations.
5   C. A. Dawson Scott, 'Address to the Berlin Congress, 1926 in May 1926', PEN III International Congress: Berlin, Series III, 3:1: International PEN Congresses, PEN Archive, Harry Ransom Center, University of Texas at Austin.
6   Akira Iriye, *Global Community: The Role of International Organisations in the Making of the Modern World* (Berkeley, CA: University of California Press, 2004), 2.
7   Rachel Potter, 'International PEN: Writers, Free Expression, Organisations', in *A History of 1930s British Literature*, ed. Benjamin Kohlmann and Matthew Taunton (Cambridge: Cambridge University Press, 2019), 120.

8   Andrea Orzoff, *Battle for the Castle: The Myth of Czechoslovakia in Europe, 1914–18* (Oxford: Oxford University Press, 2009), 19.
9   Work around this is forthcoming from a number of scholars, notably Rachel Potter – see for now *PEN International: An Illustrated History*, ed. Carles Torner et al. (Brussels: PEN International-MGIP, 2021).
10 Jameson, *Journey II*, 104.
11 Ibid.
12 'Proceedings', PEN XVII International Congress: London, Series I, 86:1 in PEN Archive.
13 Ibid.
14 Ibid.
15 Ibid.
16 'Programme', in PEN XVII International Congress London, Series I, 86:2 in PEN Archive.
17 Emily Hayman, 'English Modernism in German: Herberth and Marlys Herlitschka, Translators of Virginia Woolf', *Translation and Literature* 21, no. 3 (Autumn 2012): 386.
18 Ibid.
19 Rachel Potter, 'Literature and Human Rights', in *British Literature in Transition 1920–1940*, ed. Charles Ferrall and Dougal McNeill (Cambridge: Cambridge University Press, 2018), 109.
20 Lyndsey Stonebridge, *Writing and Righting: Literature in the Age of Human Rights* (Oxford: Oxford University Press, 2021), 9.
21 Ibid., 1.
22 Quoted in Hendy, *The BBC: A People's History*, 239.
23 Jameson, *Journey II*, 24.
24 Mark Wollaeger, *Modernism, Media and Propaganda* (Princeton, NJ: Princeton University Press, 2006), xii.
25 James Smith, 'Surveillance, Security and Wartime Propaganda: John Lehmann at the BBC', *Modernist Cultures* 17, nos. 3–4 (November 2022): 319–43.
26 Whittington, *Writing the Radio War*, 4.
27 Graham Greene, quoted in Whittington, 45.
28 See Peter Buitenhuis, 'J. B. Priestley: The BBC's Star Propagandist in World War Two (Censorship and Left-Wing Views)', *ESC: English Studies in Canada* 26, no. 4 (December 2000): 445–72.
29 Whittington, *Writing the Radio War*, 8.
30 Hendy, *The BBC: A People's History*, 222.
31 James Procter's book *Scripting Empire: Broadcasting, the BBC, and the Black Atlantic* (Oxford: Oxford University Press, 2024) discusses the shifts in these relationships into the post-war period.

32 Hendy, *The BBC: A People's History*, 223–4.
33 Ibid., 218.
34 Ibid., 223.
35 Ibid., 218.
36 Ibid., 236.
37 Ibid., 235.
38 Ibid., 224.
39 Ganor, 'Forbidden Words', 99.
40 Jameson, *Journey II*, 111.
41 Ibid., 56.
42 Hendy, *The BBC: A People's History*, 236.
43 Ibid., 252.
44 Plock, *The BBC German Service during the Second World War*, xi; Hendy, *The BBC: A People's History*, 226.
45 Quoted in Hendy, *The BBC: A People's History*, 226. Helots here meaning serf, usually connected to the ancient Spartan caste system.
46 Carl Wehner to Hermon Ould, 14 March 1941, in 'Correspondence Wagner-Whittaker', *PEN Refugee Fund*, Series III, 98.2, English PEN Archive, Harry Ransom Center, University of Texas at Austin.
47 Home Office to Hermon Ould, 21 May 1941, in 'Correspondence Wagner-Whittaker', English PEN Archive.
48 Carl Wehner to Hermon Ould, 27 January 1944, in 'Correspondence Wagner-Whittaker', English PEN Archive.
49 Liisa H. Malkki, 'Speechless Emissaries: Refugees, Humanitarianism, and Dehistoricization', *Cultural Anthropology* 11, no. 3 (August 1996): 378.
50 Ibid., 386.
51 Ibid., 384.
52 Plock, *The BBC German Service during the Second World War*, 219.
53 Ibid., xi.
54 'A.D. Peters to Janet Chance 25th October 1939', in 'Refugee Fund: Pullach-Salpeter-Priestley', Correspondence, P-S, *PEN Refugee Fund*, Series III.25, 96.3, English PEN Archive.
55 Richard Dove, '"It Tickles My Viennese Humour": Feature Programmes in the BBC Austrian Service, 1943–1945', in *'Stimme der Wahrheit': German-Language Broadcasting by the BBC: Yearbook of the Research Centre for German and Austrian Exile Studies, Volume: 5* (Amsterdam: Brill, 2003), 59.
56 'Claims to the Central Committee for Refugees and Records of Payments (1941–50)', *PEN Refugee Fund*, Series III.27, 91.16, English PEN Archive.
57 Janet Chance to J. B. Priestley, 20 October 1939 in 'Refugee Fund: Pullach-Salpeter-Priestley', Correspondence, P-S, *PEN Refugee Fund*, Series III.25, 96.3, English PEN Archive.

5

Visual storytelling in the Ministry of Information's wartime exhibitions

Harriet Atkinson

During the Second World War the British government mounted a series of exhibitions, one of several forms of media deployed for propaganda purposes.[1] Intended to communicate practical information and to inspire pride in home audiences, these exhibitions were staged in public places across the country from underground stations to parks and bombsites.[2] They covered a multitude of subjects, from how to rear livestock at home to the military campaign in Japan. Observing how they combined photographs with written scripts, the *Architectural Review* magazine characterized the exhibitions as 'photogenic' storytelling, 'mainly literary in character'.[3] This chapter analyses the hybrid form of these exhibitions, focusing on one example: the 'civilian morale exhibition' *London Pride*, mounted at Charing Cross Station in the capital in December 1940. It considers the significance of the Ministry of Information's (MOI's) inclusion of such 'literary' exhibitions within its armoury and analyses how such exhibitions operated as propaganda.[4]

The MOI designed the exhibitions to be encountered in public spaces from libraries to shop windows, parks, factory canteens, village halls and station ticket halls. They were accordingly conceived as infinitely reproducible forms, constructed from photographs selected from picture libraries, with text amplifying their messages and set within temporary, moveable wooden structures. Photographic exhibition sets were produced in multiples, to be sent around the country. Six exhibition subjects were planned for each year, to be circulated every two months, as their organizers explained.[5] These were exhibitions for the machine age, shaped by contemporary modernist preoccupations with ideal form and mass-production. Taking a three-dimensional 'documentary' form, the exhibitions elucidated aspects of everyday life in contemporary Britain by combining visual, textual and spatial elements, working in tandem or '*relay*', as Roland Barthes described a mutually reinforcing image-text relationship in his 1967 essay 'The Rhetoric of the Image'.[6] The MOI appointed designers to articulate campaigns led by other Whitehall departments on a plethora of subjects, from 'Make Do and Mend' to the might of the British Army. These were mounted on many scales, from tiny window displays to large-scale exhibitions on city-centre bombsites.

How did the British government come to use this form? Soon after the outbreak of war, retailers started creating shop window displays as propaganda, identifying their potential to amplify government messages to a passing public, inspired by their successful use in Nazi Germany. This was endorsed by the display press and taken up by the MOI, which announced a non-commercial shop window display scheme in July 1940.[7] The intention, the shop scheme's director explained, was 'to bring pictorially to the public mind some important national fact – sometimes it may be an instruction – that hitherto may have been only an impression gained from radio or newspaper, thus driving home the point concerned and fixing it indelibly on the public mind'.[8] While the public might absorb guidance that they had read or heard on the radio, it was thought that seeing visual representations in photographs and pictograms would reinforce and supplement these other forms, creating a more vivid and immediate sense of a war that might otherwise seem removed and abstracted. By late 1940 a new programme of propaganda exhibitions was added to the MOI's expanding communications programme, which by now included radio, press, film, posters and booklets, deployed in tandem for each campaign. The addition of exhibitions was likely influenced by Frank Pick, Director-General of the MOI from 1940 to 1941, who had pioneered exhibitions for promotion in previous roles at the London Passenger Transport Board (LPTB) and the Design and Industries Association (DIA).[9] Pick's identification of exhibitions as suitable publicity vehicles was in keeping with the wider culture of persuasion being honed in the emerging profession of public relations and dispersed across a range of media.[10]

A report justifying the inclusion of exhibitions among the MOI's communications was written by civil servant A. G. Highet, whose background was in public relations for the General Post Office (GPO), an organization for which exhibitions were also a key form of promotional media. Highet's report focused on what exhibitions could achieve in a wartime context to amplify campaigns being mounted by MOI through other media, working with a range of departments.[11] Exhibitions could, he thought, 'compel' the examination of a theme even by the most 'disinterested spectators'. When used well, they could 'permit the designer' to tell a story 'chapter by chapter' as the visitors walked into or out of the display.¹² Highet's description of exhibitions telling 'stories' in 'chapters', underlined the MOI's conception of exhibitions as visual amplifications of existing literary propaganda forms.

Under the Nazis, exhibitions had been used as potent and affective media in Germany for several years. The most notorious of these, the *Degenerate Art Exhibition,* first staged at Munich's Archaeological Institute from July to November 1937, was one of many Nazi *Schandausstellungen* (exhibitions of shame) mounted to mock artworks, cultures, religions and races considered shameful.¹³ Many prominent artists whose work had been ridiculed at *Degenerate Art,* such as painter Oskar Kokoschka, spent the war in Britain as refugees and showed their understanding of the power of exhibitions to influence public opinion by mounting exhibitions as anti-Nazi propaganda in and from Britain.¹⁴

Commercial designer Milner Gray was appointed as head of MOI's exhibitions branch in 1940. Gray, a highly experienced designer and pioneer of the formation of collaborative practice in Britain, had led a series of practices including the Bassett-Gray Group of Artists and Writers in 1921, reorganized in 1935 as the Industrial Design Partnership.¹⁵ Gray requested that the MOI appoint his long-term collaborator, the designer Misha Black, to join him as 'constructive architect', citing Black's extensive technical knowledge of creating exhibitions and deep 'knowledge of propaganda requirements'.¹⁶ Black, a highly skilled exhibition designer, could create an engaging spectacle with limited materials and on almost any subject, quipping that he was happy to use exhibitions to 'sell a new line of tea-pots or a plan for the regeneration of Western civilisation'.¹⁷ Together Black and Gray brought their knowledge of commercial publicity design to the MOI, adroitly turning their knowledge of selling *things* towards selling *ideas,* a process they believed shared many similarities, in the sense that the visual, material and textual qualities of the exhibition were subordinate to the presentation of ideas.

Given the focus of MOI exhibitions on communicating ideas, scripts were integral, their planners describing them as 'photographic documentaries, linked together by captions, arranged and numbered so as to tell a consecutive story ... the captions to be devised by first-class caption writers'.¹⁸ Scriptwriter Adrian Thomas, who worked on government exhibitions, explained the interplay between scriptwriter and designer as close to writing for other commercial forms: 'the exhibition script writer must', he said, 'have the feature writer's capacity for research, the scenarist's ability to visualize the dramatic possibilities of the story he is telling and the advertising copywriter's ruthlessness when it comes to the condensation and editing of his text'.¹⁹ Words took space in MOI exhibitions as explanations, exhortations, narratives and labels. Thomas set out in table form a specimen exhibition script, showing how 'visual' and 'text' elements worked together (Figure 5.1). After researching the topic, the writer created a first draft, which they passed to the designer 'for translation into visual form, section by section'.[20] The designer then developed a visual plan, passing the draft back to the scriptwriter to create a more precise text, which then prompted the accumulation of drawings, exhibitions and photographs that precipitated a final draft and captions, which should not be 'visually obvious'.[21] Thomas's description of the typical scriptwriting process indicated the symbiosis and lack of hierarchy between these different elements.

The MOI developed two main types of exhibitions: 'instructional or utility' exhibitions, which were used for communicating practical information such as how to grow vegetables in your backyard, cook economically or mend clothing and 'inspirational or prestige' exhibitions, which were focused on inspiring confidence in the war effort. *London Pride* was of the latter kind, being a

Section	Code	Visual	Text
1. Special Purpose Lamps.	SP/1/1	Lighthouse lamp and bronchoscope lamp compared.	THE LARGEST LAMP AND THE SMALLEST LAMP. 10,000 watts, this lighthouse lamp
	SP/1/2	Heading.	
	SP/1/3	Lighthouse lamp.	goes through 118 separate tests in manufacture. An ordinary lighthouse using this lamp would have a beam of 1,000,000 candle power

Figure 5.1 'Specimen Exhibition Script' drawn up by exhibition scriptwriter Adrian Thomas to demonstrate the interplay between written and visual elements, from *Exhibition Design*, ed. Misha Black (London: Architectural Press, 1950), p. 119.

'civilian morale exhibition', intended, as its organizers explained, to 'establish the fact that "London can take it"', celebrating the endurance of Londoners in the face of the adversity of the Blitz.[22] The name *London Pride* made a double reference to pride felt in London and to the pretty pink flower London Pride (also known as saxifrage) that in taking seed even on bombsites was inspiring hope of renewal. A stylized image of the flower flanked the exhibition's entrance with the declaration: 'LONDON PRIDE. SMALL EMBLEM OF A GREAT DETERMINATION'.[23] Just as flowers, displaced from parks and gardens, were blooming on unpromising wartime sites, exhibitions mounted in ordinary public places, from workers' canteens, to bombsites, to small station spaces such as this, were intended to inspire hope and courage in a passing public.[24]

The exhibition's opening at Charing Cross Station was marked by a ceremony attended by the Home Secretary, Herbert Morrison, and his Parliamentary Secretary, Ellen Wilkinson MP. Clad in a heavy overcoat to protect him from the bitterly cold night, Morrison reassured the assembled company that the government's shelter-building programme was well underway, following the start of the Blitz a few weeks earlier.[25] Despite the exhibition's modest size and unassuming site in the ticket hall of the station, the presence of senior politicians indicated its perceived significance to the government's programme. Morrison, who was working with Wilkinson to ameliorate the worst impacts of the Blitz, was seen by the press as someone with the drive to make good on early deficiencies in civil defence. As former leader of London County Council (LCC), he was considered a suitable person to open the exhibition, which provided a photogenic opportunity for the government to attempt to restore public confidence and was attended by many press representatives.

The position of the exhibition on a bustling thoroughfare in the station was carefully calculated.[26] Being situated in an ordinary place 'where the public normally meets', in the words of its organizers, was considered crucial for allowing passing commuters to visit while going about their other duties.[27] This siting was a continuation of the interwar move by artists' campaigns – led by groups such as the Artists International Association – to take art out of the studio and the gallery, to speak to people going about their ordinary lives. However, far from reaching a mass audience, the small station space discouraged large crowds from gathering, which was in any case undesirable given the threat of air raids. Being in a liminal space between work and home, the Charing Cross exhibition site inhabited an ambiguous place for its visitors, set between labour and leisure, between daily work and the time outside work, an ambiguity mirrored in its subject-matter, positioned as it was between affecting private domestic actions and public life.

Like other MOI exhibitions, *London Pride* was structured around images drawn from MOI's in-house Photograph Library, which collected and organized photographs from agencies and official MOI photographers for use in official propaganda and in the press.²⁸

A photomontage along the exhibition's back walls gave 'a panoramic composite view of life in the blitz', as *Display* magazine described it (Figure 5.2). Each panel was displayed flat at the bottom and angled down at the top to meet the gaze of the public. Viewers were encouraged to relate these scenes to their own daily experiences, to identify with them. Such visual presentation had its legacy in earlier immersive photographic exhibition installations. These included didactic experiments from the late 1920s carried out by Soviet artist El Lissitzky, who had used enlarged photomontage environments to striking effect. In the Soviet section of the *International Press Exhibition* (or *Pressa*), held in Cologne in 1928, Lissitzky used text as a central element, with lettering in a range of bold, dominating sans serif fonts from tiny to human height, demanding attention and unsettling the viewer, following and reinforcing the structural elements. These were shown alongside powerful enlarged photographs on the horizontal

Figure 5.2 Photomontage across the back wall of *London Pride* (photograph by Topical Press). © TfL from the London Transport Museum collection.

and vertical axes over viewers' heads, producing rapid changes in rhythm and mood that disorientated and stimulated audiences.[29]

Bauhaus faculty members had also carried out notable experiments with the impact of photographic constructions on spectators.[30] Herbert Bayer's idea of the extended vision, set out in his essay 'Diagram of Field of Vision', considered the impact of immersive environments on exhibition spectators.[31] The German section of the *Building Workers' Union Exhibition* in Berlin 1931, designed by Bayer in collaboration with Marcel Breuer, Walter Gropius and László Moholy-Nagy, was constructed from photomontages and didactic texts set within a complex spatial environment, creating opportunities for visitors to climb above ground level. This and other such experiments had been much admired in the British design press for their ability to tell stories through spatial narratives that audiences followed.[32] Moholy-Nagy's visual programme, interest in modes of modern communication and in the impact of integrating text and image in what he described as 'typophotos', a 'visually . . . exact rendering of communication', were also known in Britain through the translation of his writings into English.[33] In addition, Moholy-Nagy and Gropius had spent time living as refugees in Britain during the mid-1930s, working on exhibitions and displays for shops alongside designers later employed by the MOI, such as Misha Black.[34]

Like other MOI exhibitions, *London Pride* was designed to tour: its structure could be dismounted and recreated across different sites, built as it was around a central island made up of panels each hung in cross shapes, with photographs mounted on one side and descriptive captions facing them. Its visual impact came partly from recent advances in photographic technologies that allowed the images to be enlarged by Photostat reproductions to life-size or even larger, giving them a great impact and intensity.[35] This was enhanced by the use of strong reflector, angled lighting illuminating every element of the pictures – made possible within Charing Cross's underground space despite blackout specifications – and by now familiar display techniques such as port-hole windows, which enabled a playful way of glimpsing information.[36]

The quality of *Aktualität* or contemporaneity – the ability to address what was happening in that moment, as a kind of temporal layering or densification – was crucial to the *London Pride*'s attempted direct and popular appeal.[37] This was realized through the exhibition's expanded photographic elements and script, which reinforced the unfaltering focus on what was happening in that moment by combining topical news photographs with textual use of the present tense. The exhibition's subtitle, announced on the advertising poster, was '*a photographic record of how London carries on through the blitz*', with the use of the present tense crucial to its direct appeal.[38] A giant, enlarged photograph of Prime Minister Winston Churchill with the capitalized caption 'CARRY ON LONDON' amplifying its impact loomed over the right side of the entrance. On the left, a crowd scene captioned 'LONDON CARRIES ON' promoted Londoners' supposed hardiness. The crowd, pictured in a bombed area, was described by *Display* magazine as 'a study of London's Pride – her triumphant citizenship'.[39]

Viewed together from the entrance to the Charing Cross space, the collage of black and white images crowding into the exhibition with the prime minister at the other end waving across to the crowd gave a strong sense of simultaneity. They brought passers-by into a collaborative act with the photographs' subjects, reinforcing and inspiring their citizenry in concert. This was a story about London and Londoners' resilience, played out urgently in the present.[40] With its title of *London Pride*, there was an ambiguity as to who felt pride in London and who, or what, was the pride of London, with its long and important history; its buildings, bricks and mortar largely immutable despite being under siege and subject to further destruction at any moment. London was presented in the exhibition as having significance for the whole 'family' of the United Kingdom, being the site of 'a brave and cheerful family party', as the exhibition's text put it. London's resilience, even in the face of destruction, was part of this serious and sincere narrative. London was shown not only through its people and buildings, but as an abstraction through the presence of a wall-mounted map next to Churchill. Parallel lines led the eye from the enlarged photograph of the prime minister into the map, giving visitors a sense both of being on the ground and above it, a multi-perspectival vision in, of and with London.

The exhibition's organizers attempted to democratize its subjects by seemingly presenting a broad and authentic social mix, diverse and yet in unity, a form of synecdochic presentation whereby part of the population stood in for the whole.[41] *Display* magazine described this as 'a complete cross-section of London life', from 'fire watcher down to the shelterer', and 'from the King and Queen to the humblest resident of Stepney'.[42] The Londoners pictured were intended to create recognizable 'types' with whom viewers could identify; photographs of 'typical Londoners who have been bombed', as *The Times* described them. These included ARP workers, firemen, nurses, police and postal workers pictured in around fifty or sixty photographs, again creating a direct sense of relevance.[43] This idea of showing what was 'typical', which *Display* echoed in its admiration for the 'typical character studies of Londoners', was repeated many times in the exhibition's text: 'here are typical Londoners' one caption read,[44] as life-sized photographs showed London 'characters' going about ordinary tasks to create a sense of what was typical or usual.[45] A woman doing her washing at home was pictured scrubbing her clothes using a washboard with accompanying text in the present tense:

> Its [sic] washing day as usual.
> The house next door has been bombed.
> Still . . . its [sic] washing day as usual.

This text created impact through a looping quality: a reassuringly humdrum normality contrasting with the abnormality of the Blitz, emphasized by repetition. Such integration of text and image relationships created a filmic quality to the exhibition, with its clamour of characters united within narrative, as the text worked to advance the action – since the images were not in themselves expressive enough of the intended message of Londoners' resilience, determination and normality in the face of the upheaval and catastrophe of war.

The 'voice' of *London Pride*, conveyed through the captions, was intended to appeal to a mass audience by communicating unity in class and regional difference, in the spirit of the wartime BBC.[46] However, this attempt also pointed to class difference, reinforced through image and text, a feature that was picked up by the press. Photographs in *London Pride* pictured the royal family leaving their protected spaces to engage with the wider populace; one image of the King visiting a bombsite was shown with the caption '"We have been bombed too", says the King, who goes amongst the people'. This image and caption were singled out by *The Times* who observed that a 'companion picture showed "Arry [sic] and Bill"', a pair of rescue workers, 'telling her Majesty all about it'.[47] The mocked accent of Harry and Bill, a familiar trope of wartime popular culture, pointed to a kind of informality and irreverence, suggesting proximity and collaboration across classes while also reinforcing rigid class structures.

Photographs conveyed immediacy, showing people settling down for the night in bomb shelters or buildings still smoking after recent bombings, suggesting that despite all the disruption, people were continuing with ordinary life. What was in view was deeply affecting, calculated to shift attitudes to those around them: to feel connection and to deepen feeling. While the exhibition was consistently upbeat and focused on the congenial, what was happening out of sight, beyond the exhibition, was crucial to viewers' engagement: the very real horror of a catastrophic war, in the process of wreaking havoc on the lives of ordinary people, mainly hidden from view except through glimpses of bombsites and armaments.[48]

Increasing the force and sense of the text, fonts were carefully chosen. Above the entrance, the title fascia 'London Pride' was mounted in a playbill slab serif, while the typeface chosen for the central storyboards was a friendly sans serif, creating an informal, conversational appeal. Lettering reinforced the atmosphere of the exhibition, a slogan by the exhibition's entrance declaring with alliteration, 'Citizens of no mean City: they stand to their posts that liberty may live'.[49] The complementary and mutually reinforcing textual and visual elements acted as filmic interplay, with dialogue functioning not only as elucidation, but advancing action in its own right. *London Pride* also used the spatial dimension to reinforce its message. Visitors were directed to follow a prescribed circulation route, bringing a filmic quality to the exhibition and creating onward momentum, propelling them through the didactic, unfolding narrative, realized through viewers' onward motion. If *London Pride* shared qualities with film in its structure and sequencing, it also shared the theme of the GPO film made in the same year entitled *London Can Take It*, which documented and paid tribute to the spirit of Londoners following the Blitz.[50] However, while *London Pride* spoke direct to a local audience who found themselves passing through Charing Cross Station, *London Can Take It* spoke to a US audience through its US narrator, created for international cinema distribution.

It is unclear who scripted *London Pride*, but the many professional writers from a range of literary backgrounds employed to work across MOI campaigns included the poets Cecil Day Lewis, Dylan Thomas (who wrote a commentary for the 1942 documentary *New Towns for Old*) and Louis MacNeice (who wrote the script for an Albert Hall pageant in 1943), as well as the novelists Eric Knight (who had collaborated on a script for the documentary *World of Plenty* (1943)) and Arthur Koestler (who wrote the script for documentary *Lift Your Head, Comrade* (1942)).[51] Writer Robert Sinclair contributed text to the exhibitions *How to Fight the Fire-Bomb* (on behalf of Ministry of Home Security) and *The March of the Nation* (the story of the growth of American aid to Britain). The novelist George Orwell wrote text for the 1941 exhibition *Free Europe's Forces*, 'the story of the men of our allies who are fighting with us for freedom' and writer Gavin Starey scripted *Women at War* exhibition.[52] *Shelf Appeal* magazine enthused that '[a]ll these writers and artists prepare their stories in close touch with the Government Departments and MOI officers concerned, and MOI Exhibitions Branch keeps a firm hand on the preparation of script and design at every stage'.[53]

London Pride's look and feel echoed popular photo-weeklies such as *Life*, published in the United States since 1936 and *Picture Post*, published in

Britain since 1938. During the Second World War *Picture Post* had become an extension of government communications, with special issues subsidized by the MOI.[54] Despite restrictions on paper, the upbeat tone and visual appeal of the magazine stimulated its circulation during these years. *Picture Post* fused the English tradition of social comment and reportage with developments in layout, typography and photography that had flowered on the Continent in commercial, political and avant-garde circles in the interwar years.[55] *London Pride* deployed *Picture Post*'s innovative fusion of typography with photography, laid out in sequence but with an additional spatial element, encompassing the spectator and creating onward momentum, to propel visitors through an unfolding narrative and along a prescribed route. It also had ideological qualities in common with the wartime *Picture Post*, with its upbeat and encouraging tone, its commitment to social democratic values and its evocation of a nation pulling together.

In this context, exhibitions were imagined as mass media, equipped to speak to a mass audience. Its viewers were schooled in seeing such content through their familiarity with such weeklies.[56] The exhibition shared *Picture Post*'s intimacy, with its focus on ordinary acts like the private, domestic task of doing washing; from sparsely populated photographs and from the descriptive accounts and personal testimonies that accompanied them. These allowed viewers to connect and identify with the exhibition's subjects, to create a 'structure of feeling', to use Raymond Williams' phrase: a structure to think with and to feel through while in an ongoing state of uncertainty, appealing to them as personal, rather than merely held at a distance.[57] Parallel 'mass' cultural projects that may have influenced those creating *London Pride* included popular radio programmes like the BBC's *Brains Trust* and popular book series such as the Penguin paperbacks, which had been sold cheaply in Britain since the mid-1930s. However, the tone of MOI exhibitions – as with these other projects – regularly missed the mark, coming across as patronizing, patrician and giving misplaced advice.

Photographs, as an immediate, easily reproducible and highly expressive medium, were central to the MOI's display strategy, considered the best way of evoking feeling in *London Pride*. They could show a collective response to a common enemy and indicate the appropriateness of mass mobilization in the face of a common threat. Explaining what photographs could achieve as propaganda, MOI civil servant Francis Bird wrote just after the war that 'Photographs were one of the most potent instruments of war-time information. . . . The really superb picture [. . .] could have the same effect upon public opinion abroad as a great victory', noting that their special quality was in bringing subjects closer.[58] While hearing of a remote victory in a news bulletin might resonate, showing people's responses in photographs brought the war 'closer', Bird thought. While photographs were expected to speak generically to this wartime context, they could also resonate powerfully and personally with their viewers. In *London Pride* photographs were both the material from which the exhibition was made but then the exhibition, in itself being 'photogenic', created further photo opportunities.

One such opportunity was the series of photographs of visitors to *London Pride* taken by the MOI's home front photography team, including several of a man in flat-cap and overcoat with a child in cap and tie (Figure 5.3). Being themselves London 'types', this performed a kind of double-mediation: inviting viewers to identify with these exhibition-goers who were, themselves, in the process of looking and identifying with the exhibition's subjects, viewers and viewed seen in the same sort of mode of brave and cheery endurance.[59] Photographs of people interacting with the exhibition were included in the home picture library, available as an element in the ministry's wider propaganda effort, to be reproduced in government publications or sold to the illustrated press.

Picking up on its literary form, with its combination of photographs 'of heroic size' and lively captions, trade magazine *Shelf Appeal* described *London Pride* as the MOI Exhibition Division's 'first essay', enthusing that 'no picture

Figure 5.3 Visitors to *London Pride*. © Imperial War Museum (D 1756).

was used which was not in itself interesting'.[60] Given the exhibition's modest site and scale, it had garnered a huge amount of praise, with much of this focusing on the exhibition's hybrid qualities as visual and literary propaganda. The success of London Pride was built on the propaganda power of photography, realized as viewers moved around the site, viewing the exhibition's storyboards sequentially.[61]

The critical response was positive. Mass-Observation reported a steady stream of visitors to London Pride, which 'seemed to be received as well, or indeed better than most exhibitions at . . . Charing Cross'.[62] Mass-Observation charted the MOI's activities across all its areas of production including exhibitions, spending time in twenty-two exhibitions at Worcester, Bolton, Portsmouth, Port Sunlight and Stockport. They reported that exhibitions had been more successful in arousing people's interest and secured better results than many other better-known methods, but often drew very small audiences.[63] Detailed accounts of the impact of MOI exhibitions on individuals are hard to find.

Architectural Review magazine reported that despite its small scale, London Pride made an impressive visual impact and remarked on its being a 'semi-portable exhibition', which could be transferred to other sites.[64] Modern Publicity in War, a survey of 1941 publicity showing the best of wartime display techniques, reproduced images of London Pride.[65] Trade magazine Display was also fulsome in its praise, describing the exhibition as 'one of the most attractive propaganda displays we have seen', 'the best presentation of British spirit that we have seen' and 'the best piece of propaganda display yet seen since the war started'.[66] In the next issue of the magazine, Display again praised London Pride for its 'simple dignity', but 'with sufficient unusual angles to arouse . . . interest'. The exhibition appealed first and foremost to visitors' feelings, 'Never has a display or exhibition made so big an appeal to the emotions or held so much topical and local interest. London Pride is outstanding.'[67] The magazine's admiration was closely related to its support for the profession of display design, with such exhibitions keeping their readers admirably well occupied, with work that was close to that of their civilian lives. After its closure, London Pride toured a dozen London department stores including Selfridges, Whiteleys and Kennards, while a more modest version created as four sets toured the United States.

Shortly after the war, exhibition designer Misha Black reflected on the British government's use of exhibitions as wartime propaganda. After years languishing 'at the tail of the class', Black wrote, Britain had come to the 'front row', because of their development through MOI of 'informative and story-telling' exhibitions, a form in which Britain now led the world.[68] The programme that had started with *London Pride* had developed through dozens of subsequent exhibitions and displays across village halls, bombsites and evacuated department stores. The use of this scripted form of exhibition was closely related to its perceived utility for sharing clear and specific ideas and instructions. However, the text-heavy character of exhibitions was also to become their downfall. Immediately after the war the government continued to use them to communicate with home audiences, as a means of demonstrating early plans for post-war reconstruction, explaining the structures of the embryonic welfare state or presenting Britain's status as a social democracy in the early Cold War. By the end of the 1940s, however, such 'long-winded' and verbose exhibitions were increasingly failing to deliver visually, causing critics to doubt the ongoing validity of this 'storytelling' form.[69]

Notes

1 Research for this article was carried out during the AHRC Leadership Fellowship 'The Materialisation of Persuasion', Project Reference: AH/S001883/1. Every reasonable effort has been made to seek copyright permissions for use of the visual material reproduced in this chapter.
2 For a more detailed elaboration of this subject see Harriet Atkinson, *Showing Resistance: Propaganda and Modernist Exhibitions in Britain, 1933–53* (Manchester: Manchester University Press, 2024).
3 G. S. Kallmann, 'The Wartime Exhibition', *Architectural Review*, October 1943, 95–106.
4 This material is drawn from my book *Showing Resistance* with kind permission of Manchester University Press.
5 The National Archives, Kew (hereafter TNA), INF 1/132, 'Home Planning Committee: Programme for Exhibitions', part 1 (addendum).
6 A particular image-text relationship discussed by Roland Barthes in *Image-Music-Text*, ed. and trans. Stephen Heath (New York, NY: Noonday Press, 1977).
7 Richard Harman, editor of *Display*, in a lecture to Design and Industries Association, reported in *Display* 22. no. 1 (April 1940), 28 and repeated in *Display* 22. no. 3 (June 1940), 74. For sources on British wartime propaganda on the home front see James Chapman, *The British at War: Cinema, State and Propaganda, 1939–45* (London: I.B. Tauris, 2011); Jo Fox, *Film Propaganda in Britain and Nazi Germany: World War II Cinema* (Oxford: Berg, 2007); Henry Irving, 'The Ministry of Information on the British Home Front', in *Allied Communication to the Public During the Second World War*, ed. Simon Eliot and Marc Wiggam (London: Bloomsbury Academic, 2019), 24; Ian McLaine, *Ministry of Morale: Home Front*

Morale and the Ministry of Information in World War II (London: Routledge, 2021); David Welch, *Persuading the People: British Propaganda in World War II* (London: British Library, 2016).

8   Trevor Fenwick reported in *Display* 22, no. 4 (July 1940), 115.
9   Michael H. C. Baker, *London Transport in the 1930s* (Hersham: Ian Allan, 2007), 10.
10 This is the subject of Scott Anthony's *Public Relations and the Making of Modern Britain* (Manchester: Manchester University Press, 2012), in which Anthony discusses how Stephen Tallents developed exhibitions within the short-lived Empire Marketing Board and other organizations.
11 TNA, INF 1/132, A.G. Highet, 'A Note on Exhibition Technique', 3 (undated).
12 Ibid.
13 After Munich (where it was displayed from 19 July to 30 November 1937), *Degenerate Art* toured to Berlin from February to May 1938, to Leipzig from May to June 1938 and to Düsseldorf from June to August 1938.
14 This is an important focus of my book *Showing Resistance*.
15 Avril Blake, *Milner Gray* (London: Design Council, 1986).
16 Gray also appointed graphic designer Norbert Dutton to assist on organization and design, as is clear from internal memos from December 1940 (TNA, INF 1/132). The fact that Black was Russian and had not yet become naturalized as a British citizen meant he could only be employed on a fee basis.
17 Misha Black, 'Propaganda in Three Dimensions', in *The Black Papers on Design: Selected Writings of the Late Sir Misha Black*, ed. A. Blake (Oxford: Pergamon Press, 1983), 119–29; see also Misha Black, *Exhibition Design* (London: Architectural Press, 1950) and Harriet Atkinson, '"Lines of Becoming" Misha Black and Entanglements through Exhibition Design', *Journal of Design History* 34, no. 1 (March 2021): 37–53.
18 TNA, INF 1/132, 'Home Planning Committee: Programme for Exhibitions', part 1 (addendum).
19 Adrian Thomas, 'Exhibition Scripts', in *Exhibition Design*, ed. Misha Black (London: Architectural Press, 1950), 118.
20 Ibid., 119.
21 Ibid., 120.
22 TNA, INF 1/132, 'Home Planning Committee: Programme for Exhibitions', 3.
23 Imperial War Museum (hereafter IWM), Ministry of Information Second World War Official Collection, Home Front photograph series, D1753.
24 'London Pride' became the name of a popular song by Noel Coward of the same year, which opened 'London Pride has been handed down to us; London Pride is a flower that's free'.

25 'Courage of London in War-Time', *The Times*, 18 December 1940, 6. The Blitz began in earnest in London in September 1940, lasting eight months, and in November 1940 the Blitzkrieg had started to attack other large, provincial cities in Britain, continuing until May 1941.

26 The MOI had taken over exclusive use of the station site, by then an established exhibitions venue, for a year (TNA, INF 1/132, memo from Milner Gray to Aynsley, 15 October 1941). Gray wrote that with Treasury approval of the ATS Large Touring exhibitions, the USSR Large Touring Exhibition and the use of the Charing Cross site for the period of a year, the volume of sanctioned work for which the Branch was responsible had so increased that further additions to staff had become necessary.

27 TNA, INF 1/ 132, 'Home Planning Committee: Programme for Exhibitions', 4.

28 MOI's Photograph Library, which collected and organized photographs was based at Senate House. For further information about MOI's Photograph Library see 'Photographs, Motorbikes and the Ministry of Information: An interview with Anne Olivier Bell', MOI Digital (https://moidigital.ac.uk/blog/photographs-motorbikes-and-ministry-information-interview-anne-olivier-bell/) [accessed 14 November 2023]. For discussion of the Photograph Library see also *Display* 22, no. 12 (March 1941), 273.

29 Discussed by Jeremy Aynsley in 'Pressa Cologne, 1928. Exhibitions and Publication Design in the Weimar Period', reprinted in *Public Photographic Spaces: Exhibitions of Propaganda, from Pressa to The Family of Man, 1928–55,* ed. Jorge Ribalta (Barcelona: Museu d'Art Contemporani de Barcelona, 2008), 99–100.

30 See *Public Photographic Spaces*, ed. Ribalta.

31 Herbert Bayer published his 'Diagram of Field of Vision' within the catalogue of the German Werkbund section of *Exposition de la Société des Artistes Décorateurs*, Paris, 1930, as 'Fundamentals of Exhibition Design', *Production Manager* 6, no. 2 (1937): 17–25.

32 Olivier Lugon, 'Dynamic Paths of Thought: Exhibition Design, Photography and Circulation in the Work of Herbert Bayer', in *Cinema Beyond Film: Media Epistemology in the Modern Era*, ed. François Albéra and Maria Tortajada (Amsterdam: Amsterdam University Press, 2010), 145–70.

33 In *Von Material zu Architektur* (1928), published in English as *The New Vision* (1932) Moholy-Nagy explained his experiments with kinetics, light and space and shared information about Bauhaus methods, in particular the merging of theory and practice in design.

34 As Valeria Carullo shows in *Moholy-Nagy in Britain, 1935–7* (London: Lund Humphries, 2019), Moholy-Nagy's displays for Simpson's and other shops made it into the pages of contemporary trade magazines. See also *Albers and Moholy-Nagy: From the Bauhaus to the New World*, ed. Achim Borchardt-Hume et al.

(New Haven, CT: Yale University Press, and London: Tate, 2006) and Kerry Meakin, 'The Bauhaus and the Business of Window Display – Moholy-Nagy's Endeavours at Window Display in London', *Journal of Design History* 35, no. 3 (September 2022): 265–80.

35 As F. H. K. Henrion recalled in his 1986 interview with Richard Hollis ('Henrion, Frederic Henri Kay (Oral history)', IWM, 9592 (http://www.iwm.org.uk/collections/item/object/80009378 [accessed 20 November 2023]).
36 *Display* 22, no. 12 (March 1941), 272–3.
37 In his 1940 'Theses on the Philosophy of History' Walter Benjamin wrote that 'For every image of the past that is not recognized by the present as one of its own concerns threatens to disappear irretrievably' (Walter Benjamin, 'Theses on the Philosophy of History', in *Illuminations*, ed. Hannah Arendt (New York, NY: Schocken Books, 1968), 253). Benjamin's belief in the importance of the quality of contemporaneity (*Aktualität*) was central to his writings.
38 The 'Keep Calm and Carry On' poster created by the British government on the eve of the Second World War has become well known in recent years but was little known at the time, so the overlap of language is most likely coincidental.
39 *Display* 22, no. 12 (March 1941), 273.
40 Discussing Henrion's poster work, typography historian Robin Kinross describes the use of photographic elements to communicate urgency as 'unEnglish', since this was characteristic of modern European graphic design beyond Britain before the 1940s. (Kinross, 'Design in Central-European London', in *Modern Typography in Britain: Graphic Design, Politics, and Society (Typography papers 8)*, ed. Paul Stiff (London: Hyphen, 2009), 107).
41 'Synecdochic' is a phrase drawn from Benjamin H. D. Buchloh, 'From Faktura to Factography', *October* 30 (Autumn 1984): 111. Stuart Hall observed that *Picture Post* showed the tendency of 'the democratization of the subject in photography' (Stuart Hall, 'The Social Eye of Picture Post', *Modern Typography in Britain: Graphic Design, Politics, and Society (Typography Papers 8)*, 82).
42 *Display* 22, no. 12 (March 1941), 273.
43 'Courage of London in War-Time', *The Times*, 18 December 1940, 6.
44 *Display* 22, no. 11 (February 1941), 266–7.
45 Hall identifies a 'quality of usualness' in *Picture Post* photography (Hall, 'The Social Eye of Picture Post', 82).
46 Hall writes that the 'Standard Voice' of the early BBC licensed to broadcast news in 1923, with its 'received' pronunciation, accent and tonal pitch, set out to forge a unified voice 'not of the state, the government, or even "the people", so much as the nation, controlling and subordinating regional and class difference' (Stuart Hall, 'Popular Culture and the State', in *Popular Culture and Social Relations*, ed. Tony Bennett, Colin Mercer, and Janet Woollacott (Milton Keynes and Philadelphia, PA: Open University Press, 1986), 43–4).

47 'Courage of London in War-Time', *The Times*, 18 December 1940, 6.
48 John Berger in *Understanding a Photograph* (London: Penguin, 2013), 20–1 asserts that reading a photograph is only possible through knowing what is beyond the frame. Walter Benjamin criticized the new style of photographic documentary flourishing in Germany in the 1920s, writing 'It has even succeeded in making misery itself an object of pleasure, by treating it stylishly and with technical perfection' (Benjamin, 'The Author as Producer', reproduced in *New Left Review* 62 (July/August 1970), 83).
49 'Courage of London in War-Time', *The Times*, 18 December 1940, 6.
50 TNA, INF 1/132, 'Home Planning Committee – Programme for Exhibition'; *London Can Take It!* (1940) (see https://www.youtube.com/watch?v=bLgfSDtHFt8 [accessed 20 November 2023]).
51 Kallmann, 'The Wartime Exhibition', 106.
52 *Display* 23, no. 4 (August 1941), 81.
53 Also mentioned in 'These Exhibitions of Ideas are Planned', *Shelf Appeal: Merchandising, Design, Packaging and Display*, July/August 1941, n.p.
54 An important precursor to these magazines was the Parisian illustrated magazine *VU* (founded in 1928) which assembled photographs in essay form, as Tim Satterthwaite describes in *Modernist Magazines and the Social Ideal* (London: Bloomsbury, 2020). *Picture Post* was launched in 1938 by Hungarian refugee Stefan Lorant. Other less successful picture magazines included *Weekly Illustrated* and socialist *Clarion*.
55 As discussed by Hall in 'The Social Eye of *Picture Post*', 70.
56 Allan Sekula argues for the need to learn photographic literacy – that photographs are not intrinsically legible or significant – in 'On the Invention of Photographic Meaning', *Artforum* (January 1975) (see https://www.artforum.com/print/197501/on-the-invention-of-photographic-meaning-37302 [accessed 14 November 2023]).
57 Raymond Williams uses this term in *Marxism and Literature* (Oxford: Oxford University Press, 1977), 128.
58 Francis Bird, *Press, Parliament and People* (London: William Heinemann, 1946), 126.
59 IWM Ministry of Information Second World War Official Collection, Home Front photograph series, D1750-1766.
60 *Shelf Appeal*, July/August, 1941, n.p.
61 *Display* 22, no. 11 (February 1940), 454–8, 465.
62 Mass-Observation Online, File report 531, 'Exhibition at Charing Cross Underground Station, December 1940' (https://www.massobservation.amdigital.co.uk/Documents/Details/EXHIBITION-AT-CHARING-CROSS-UNDERGROUND-STATION/FileReport-531 [accessed 27 July 2023]).
63 Mass-Observation's response was noted in 'Britain Shall Not Burn' (*Shelf Appeal*, November 1941, n.p.) and probably referred to Mass Observation 'File Report

869' (September 1941), based on exhibitions observed in August 1941. See 'XIII Exhibitions and Demonstrations', n.p. (https://www.massobservation.amdigital.co.uk/Documents/Details/SALVAGING-HISTORY/FileReport-869 [accessed 27 July 23]). I have found limited evidence of further Mass-Observation reports or diaries.
64 G. S. Kallmann, *Architectural Review*, October 1943, 97.
65 *Modern Publicity in War*, ed. F. A. Mercer and Grace Lovat Fraser (London and New York: Studio Publications, 1941), 50.
66 *Display* 22, no. 11 (February 1941), 266–7.
67 *Display* criticized MOI for not taking the opportunity to tour *London Pride* to 'all parts of this country and the neutral countries of the world'. If exhibited 'in New York, Buenos Ayres [sic], Montreal or Melbourne' the exhibition 'would be the rage of the town', the magazine suggested in its March 1941 issue (*Display* 22, no. 12 (March 1941), 272–3).
68 Black, 'Propaganda in Three Dimensions'; Black, *Exhibition Design*.
69 See, for example, design bureaucrat Paul Reilly's criticism of the over-use of text in government exhibitions in *Printed Advertising* 3 (April 1948), 54, describing the display's 'long-winded' text, smothering its 'worthy message with too many words'.

6

Propaganda as elegy in the Ministry of Information's *Britain in Pictures* series

Megan Faragher

Introduction: 'PRIDE IN THE BRITISH ACHIEVEMENT'

During the Second World War, British print propaganda used increasingly complex registers of emotional appeal to make its case. This chapter examines the Ministry of Information's (MOI's) innovative book series *Britain in Pictures* (1941–8), which deployed strategies of nostalgia and mourning to sustain morale at home and foster support for the British cause abroad. These illustrated books, which also acted as *objets d'art* and educational repositories, adapted discussions of cultural minutiae to garner support for a Britain in peril. Endorsements printed on the dust jackets of the series suggested a highly reverential attitude towards Englishness, but this was infused with sadness that Englishness had been so poorly promoted to date. One such remorseful endorsement reads: 'The English have never been good at describing themselves or their ways, either for their own benefit or for the benefit of others [. . .] At this time, when it has become essential for citizens throughout the Empire to take stock of themselves and their ideas and to express them to others, it is desirable to fill this gap.'[1] To this end, the series was commonly understood at the time as an example of what Jacques Ellul calls 'open and aboveboard' propaganda, intent on influencing a particular audience.[2] With high-quality production values, illustrated in both colour and black and white at a time of severe wartime restrictions on paper and printing, the books were nevertheless available at a low cost (3s 6d) to a wide readership, thereby serving as a form of adult art education and a source of visual appeal.

By 1941, when the first of the series was published, MOI propaganda efforts reflected the 'growing realization of the need to create and diffuse a positive image of Britain abroad through "indirect propaganda"'.[3] A fuller appreciation of 'Britishness' aligned with such a project.[4] *Britain in Pictures* (*BIP*) was widely understood as propaganda by reviewers, advertisers and readers at the time; its volumes also aimed to fill a market niche in the increasingly crowded propaganda field by doubling as beautiful books of art. One hundred and thirty-two editions were published on a wide range of topics related to British history, culture or daily life such as ports, farming, sport, birds, horses, gardening, philosophy and fiction. The series was so totalizing in scope that one 1947 reviewer argued it had 'now absorbed so much material that must at first sight have seemed unpromising that there seems no reason why it should ever stop'.[5] The series deployed a unique psychological stratagem of Second World War propaganda, identified and defined by Paul Saint-Amour as the 'weaponization' of 'anticipation'.[6] As threats of aerial bombardment left the British home front particularly vulnerable, books which weaponized the 'future-conditional' loss of English cultural artefacts and practices were uniquely positioned to reach audiences at home.[7] Saint-Amour argues in *Tense Future* (2015) that '[w]eaponizing anticipation mak[es] the future seem a predetermined site of catastrophic violence and therefore capable of inflicting damage in the present'.[8] In elucidating the threat to such a wide range of cultural forms and activities – from fishing to novel-writing – the authors of *BIP* weaponized anticipated cultural losses as a propaganda strategy abroad as well as at home. It was rumoured that a similar series of illustrated books addressing a wide array of topics had been produced in Germany, so *BIP* can also be understood as an attempt to match Germany's propaganda efforts.[9]

The series was conceived of by Hilda Matheson, one-time BBC Talks Director and director of the Joint Broadcasting Committee (JBC), a group eventually responsible for wartime radio propaganda targeted abroad.[10] The series co-editor W. J. Turner was a poet and music critic for the *New Statesman* before his appointment as Literary Editor of the *Spectator* in 1941.[11] Like Matheson, Turner was frustrated by the formulaic nature of institutionalized propaganda efforts in the early stages of the war; according to his biographer Wayne McKenna, Turner lamented the 'sterility of most propaganda'.[12] An impressive list of author-contributors were recruited and paid £50 for their work, which was significant given their length (books were generally between 12,000 and 14,000 words). These included Elizabeth Bowen, Rose Macaulay, Kate O'Brien, George Orwell, Vita Sackville-West and Rex Warner, some of whom were also involved in other propaganda efforts.[13] However, most *BIP* authors were not famous authors, but rather content experts like zoologist Charles Maurice Yonge, ecologist F. Fraser Darling and Arabian horse expert Lady Wentworth. The books' beauty and totalizing scope were accompanied by chest-puffing nationalism. Headlined as 'PRIDE IN THE BRITISH ACHIEVEMENT', a March 1941 *Times* story introducing the series claimed that its aim was 'to encourage the British reader, at home and in the Empire, to take pride in the achievements of his race, and to give the foreign reader some idea of the British heritage'.[14] This was partly accomplished by promoting the books as aesthetic objects, with Collins advertisements for the series highlighting their 'Splendid Colour Plates'.[15] They were pleasing on the outside as well, with an iconic common design employing single bright colours with white text to attract collectors (see Figure 6.1 and Figure 6.2). Reviews noted these aesthetic qualities: one claimed that '[a] series the beauty, variety and extent of which seem inexhaustible, [has] come to hand'.[16] Another promoted it as '[a] series of books of interest to all readers', stressing the 'splendid colour plates' scattered throughout each book.[17] While contributing to the MOI's 'indirect methods of persuasion', the series was also popular: in the first nine months of sales no volume sold fewer than 5,000 copies, and over the first 10 years over 3 million copies of the 132 books were sold, a particularly striking success given 1940s rationing.[18]

Figure 6.1 Cover of Peter F. Anson's *British Sea-Fishermen*. Reprinted by permission of HarperCollins Publishers Ltd © 1943 Peter F. Anson.

Figure 6.2 Cover of Geoffrey Grigson's *Wild Flowers in Britain*. Reprinted by permission of HarperCollins Publishers Ltd © 1944 Geoffrey Grigson.

If the topics of books were diverse, the sense of mourning they evoked was more unified. While individual books gave the appearance of covering only the minutiae of wildflowers or fishermen, the books' subjects were tied to larger questions of cultural progress and even to the preservation of democracy itself. To that extent, *BIP* authors engage what Jed Esty has described as the 'the metaphor of lost totality' in relation to their subjects, each topic becoming symbolic of larger losses. Significantly, Esty recognizes the use of this metaphor as not only 'one of the central deep structures' of modernism, but also of imperialism.[19] To that end, as *BIP* authors contemplate anticipated losses, they inevitably do so towards the defence of a colonial past. The series used banal, everyday subjects to assiduously defend so-called 'British' values to readers at home and abroad – namely, democratic norms and their institutionalization in everyday life. The threat to these traditions demanded both resistance to fascism and reckoning with Britain's pervasive anxiety around its inevitable loss of colonial power. Despite this complex mission, when examined as a multi-authored textual corpus, *BIP* exhibits demonstrable cohesion in addressing the British everyday through a lens of anticipatory nostalgia for a threatened nation. Further close and distant readings of the series demonstrate that these similarities are not merely incidental and suggest that editorial preferences influenced the rhetorical choices of many *BIP* authors. In their elegiac defence of Britishness, these books demonstrate that editorial input and influence can produce a body of propaganda that maintains formal and rhetorical coherence as a corpus despite being multi-authored and covering diverse topics.

The elegiac defence: The aims of *Britain in Pictures*

To the extent that the English needed to become better at 'describing themselves or their ways' to others, it is worth previewing how that led to a very particular rhetorical pattern in the books, which I am calling the 'elegiac defence'. This pose accomplishes two rhetorical aims. Topics such as British wildflowers or English table manners functioned as metonyms for a liberal, democratic social order, meaning that seemingly inconsequential subjects were inscribed onto larger debates over the future of democracy itself. By further recognizing the impact of the war on these British cultural sectors, the authors engage in an elegiac defence of national accomplishments – conveniently sidestepping critiques of empire and colonial exploitation. Cricket, or any other supposedly British practice, stands in for the larger democratic Western traditions that the series intends to defend. So, the elegiac defence is both an effort to come to terms with Britain's waning global dominance and an appeal to protect it.

The series took an alternative approach to propaganda to meet the unique challenge of countering the appeal of fascism. As Valerie Holman argues, the MOI had the difficult mission of having to 'be more effective than its Axis equivalent while appearing the antithesis of totalitarian'.[20] This was most evident in the increasing concern over perceptions of Britain in colonies and Allied nations, as radio guaranteed that German propaganda infiltrated into the global consciousness. It was within this media landscape that Matheson conceived of a multi-book project expanding upon the heavily illustrated single volume *The Story of the British People in Pictures* (1937), written by Harley V. Usill and published by Odhams.[21] The series was launched at the Mayfair Hotel in London in 1941; tragically, this launch took place without Matheson, who had passed away following a thyroid operation in 1940. Turner, who became sole editor after her death and the departure of the third editor, Dorothy Wellesley, saw

BIP's expansiveness as a cure for British cultural restraint and conservatism.[22] The nation continues to be a focus of *BIP* however, and it is this nuance – the alignment of nationalist propaganda with a totalizing vision – that characterizes the series' unique approach. The contributions of Matheson and others cannot be underestimated, but Turner's role in establishing the style and format of the written elements of *BIP* was vital. A poet in his own right, he valued the propagandistic aims of the project, calling it 'the most solid and worthwhile propaganda effort of the war', and contributed two entries in the series, on *English Music* (1941; #3) and *English Ballet* (1944; #80), both of which employed the sense of anticipatory mourning characteristic of the series.[23]

As a critic who loathed dogmatism and was prone to writing harsh criticism of orthodoxy, particularly an 'antipathy to [. . .] the characteristic restraint of the English when confronted by the most original new work', Turner was perhaps an unexpected figure to be recruited to an overtly propagandistic project.[24] He shared this antipathy with Matheson, whose departure from the BBC was at least in part due to her frustration at institutional resistance to broadcasting reviews of modernist writers like James Joyce and D. H. Lawrence.[25] For Warner, Turner's propensity to embrace the 'extraordinary depth and complexity of life' aligned him with literary modernists and against what he called the 'realists' and more clumsy 'propagandists'; he also railed against a propaganda of 'simple catchwords'.[26] Turner viewed the inclusion of colour illustrations as a means of pursuing an aesthetic as well as a polemic approach to propaganda. A 1939 diary entry envisages the series as a project that would avoid the 'sterility of most propaganda' and would instead 'show the value of British cultural heritage'.[27] The number of full-colour illustrations and Turner's careful attention to design displays a conviction that the aesthetic experience was capable of catalysing political transformation.[28]

In the third volume of the series, *English Music*, Turner not only discusses the continuation of the English musical tradition, but purposefully pivots to a discussion of a renewal of civilization itself, lending the text an eschatological tone:

> The future of English music now depends on the social conditions existing after the present war. The same is certainly true of music in other European countries. In fact, in the present writer's opinion, the chief hope of music lies in a renewal of the general unity in civilization which once prevailed throughout the western world.[29]

Turner's conclusion becomes an ur-example of the elegiac defence. If English music is to continue – if the beautifully illustrated story just read is to go on – pre-war social conditions must be preserved, as they must be everywhere. The scope of the threat expands as Turner moves from English to European music, and then to music in general; by the end of the passage, he is suggesting that the war must be won if only to defend music, and that if music is to survive, we must *return* to the social stability once enjoyed. The 'unity in civilization' which emerges from art's transformational potential can restore a version of Western democracy that was directly challenged by the rise of fascism across Europe. But Turner's claims here also unveil a contradiction that persists through many books in the series; if the books' innovative design and form are unorthodox, they necessarily succumb to a nostalgic vision of empire as they seek to defend and promote democratic ideals.

Turner's tone is prevalent across the series. One further example illustrates this: F. S. Smythe's *British Mountaineers* (1942; #22), which depicts mountaineering as a proxy for Anglo-German tensions. This is no surprise, given that the politicization of the pursuit itself in the lead up to the war was widely recognized in wartime literature such as W. H. Auden's *The Ascent of F6* (1937), which likewise staged mountaineering as a proxy for ideological struggle. Smythe argues that the 'past twenty years' have subjected the sport to the 'taint of nationalism'.[30] He berates the 'cheap and sensational' press coverage of the Everest expeditions (Smythe had taken part in one of these in 1938) and bemoaned the spread of 'Hitlerism' to mountaineering. Smythe's tone then turns morose instead of angry, suggesting that rejecting mountaineering's symbolic allegiance to fascism is the only hope for the sport's future: 'It is to be hoped that from now on the sportsmen of the world will realize that it is the sport alone that counts and that future international contests will help to promote the best, not bring out the worst in men, for it is only thus that the sportsman can truthfully say, "it was worth while [*sic*]."'[31] So, for mountaineering to progress, the fascist tide must be reversed, just as for the future of music we must restore civilization from its sundered state.

A corpus analysis of *Britain in Pictures*: Methods and preliminary findings

Turner's *English Music* and Smythe's *British Mountaineers* demonstrate the emergence of the 'elegiac defence' – a desire for returning to pre-war norms combined with mournful hints of a dystopian future if such a goal was to fail. Quantitative analysis shows that this tone pervades the whole wartime corpus, however. The methods for analysing tone are complex, and it may (rightly) seem counter-intuitive that anything so subjective can be understood via quantitative methods. The process began by digitizing a selection of the books. The line of inquiry was based on the series' value as propaganda during wartime, so the study's scope was limited to editions published between 1941, when the series began, and 1945, when the war ended.[32] These parameters resulted in a limited survey of eighty-two distinct books published from 1941 to 1945.[33] The eighty-two-book digitized corpus was entered into the online platform Voyant, which enables the quantitative examination of digital texts. Voyant examines a text or corpus along several vectors. The programme not only conducts frequency analysis – counting instances of individual words across a corpus – but provides other insights such as collocation – mapping words used adjacently to other key words. This study used both tools as starting points for examining the *BIP* corpus, though these quantitative insights were necessarily supplemented with close reading and contextual analysis to identify the overriding thematic similarities in the books.

It is fitting that the first findings of note were related to the word 'war', which features in Turner's version of the 'elegiac defence' in *English Music*. 'War' was among the top twenty words used in this corpus, featuring in more than half of the books. This is not particularly surprising; a history of any subject is likely impacted by war, even subjects as seemingly detached as Women's Institutes or dogs. A systematic reading of the sections that mention the outbreak of the present war revealed that these moments often featured in the final paragraphs of the books, in tones eerily reminiscent of Turner's earlier contribution, tying the possible imminent loss of everyday cultural practices to a larger and more sustained threat against democracy itself. Further analysis suggested this rhetorical tactic was prevalent throughout the oeuvre. Out of the eighty-two books in the corpus, fifty-one (62 per cent) featured a reference – mostly at the end of the book – to current war-time conditions and their impact on their topic's future repair after the war, as shown in Table 6.1. Each embraced a particular zeitgeist – a mixture of hope, dread and desperation – to defend Britishness to the world.

There is also textual evidence that the elegiac defensive tone was not solely a case of authors aligning unceremoniously with a given structure of feeling.[34] Of course, authors knew the project was propagandistic. Orwell described his contribution as 'a piece of propaganda' while Woolf, who refused to contribute, characterized the series as 'money patriotism, literature & some organising [?] arranging [?] motive, all embracing & intertwining'.[35] Beyond this awareness, the style and tone of the series is self-perpetuating, with new contributors following those of previous books. In fact, an extant letter from Collins to Rose Macaulay soliciting a contribution on Turner's behest included with it a copy of a published

Table 6.1 *Britain in Pictures* Books under Analysis (Author's Own Table)

Book Series Number*	Year	Title	Author	Book Series Number*	Year	Title	Author
1	1941	The English Poets	Lord David Cecil	50	1944	British Soldiers	S. H. F. Johnston
2	1942	English Sport	Eric Parker	51	1944	The English at Table	John Hampson
3	1941	English Music	W. J. Turner	52	1943	Wild Life of Britain	F. Fraser Darling
4	1941	The Government of Britain	G. M. Young	53	1943	British Polar Explorers	Admiral Sir Edward Evans
5	1941	Australia*	Arnold Haskell	55	1943	English Diaries and Journals	Kate O'Brien
6	1941	East Africa*	Elspeth Huxley	57	1944	Horses of Britain	Lady Wentworth
9	1941	Canada*	Lady Tweedsmuir	58	1943	British Seamen	David Mathew
10	1941	India*	Sir Firozkhan Noon	59	1944	English Gardens	Harry Roberts
11	1941	English Villages	Edmund Blunden	60	1943	British Philosophers	Kenneth Matthews
12	1941	British Medicine	R. McNair Wilson	61	1943	Women's Institutes	Cicely McCall
13	1941	British Statesmen	Sir Ernest Barker	62	1943	The Story of Wales	Rhys Davies
14	1941	British Scientists	Sir Richard Gregory	63	1943	British Clubs	Bernard Darwin
15	1941	English Country Houses	V. Sackville-West	64	1944	The Londoner	Dorothy Nicholson
16	1941	English Farming	Sir John Russell	65	1944	Wild Flowers in Britain	Geoffrey Grigson
17	1941	English Education	Kenneth Lindsay	66	1943	The English Bible	Sir Herbert Grierson
18	1942	South Africa*	Sarah Gertrude Millin	67	1943	English Inns	Thomas Burke
21	1942	The Story of Scotland	F. Fraser Darling	68	1944	Britain in the Air	Nigel Tangye
22	1942	Britain Mountaineers	F. S. Smythe	69	1943	British Sea Fishermen	Peter F. Anson
23	1942	English Novelists	Elizabeth Bowen	70	1944	British Marine Life	C. M. Yonge
24	1941	English Social Services	Sir George Newman	71	1944	British Photographers	Cecil Beaton

(*Continued*)

Table 6.1 (Continued)

Book Series Number*	Year	Title	Author	Book Series Number*	Year	Title	Author
25	1942	British Cartoonists Caricaturists and Comic Artists	David Low	73	1944	British Maps and Map-Makers	Edward Lynam
26	1942	New Zealand*	Ngaio Marsh & R. M. Burden	74	1944	The British Red Cross	Dermot Morrah
27	1942	British Merchant Adventurers	Maurice Collis	75	1944	Boy Scouts	E. E. Reynolds
28	1942	The English Church	The Bishop of Chichester	76	1944	British Portrait Painters	John Russell
29	1942	English Women	Edith Sitwell	78	1944	Battlefields in Britain	C. V. Wedgwood
30	1942	English Children	Sylvia Lynd	79	1944	British Botanists	John Gilmour
31	1942	Life Among the English	Rose Macaulay	80	1944	The English Ballet	W. J. Turner
32	1942	British Dramatists	Graham Greene	81	1945	English Letter Writers	C. E. Vulliamy
33	1942	British Rebels and Reformers	Harry Roberts	82	1945	The Guilds of the City of London	Sir Ernest Pooley
34	1942	British Romantic Artists	John Piper	83	1945	British Railways	Arthur Elton
35	1942	British Ports and Harbours	Leo Walmsley	84	1945	English Rivers and Canals	Frank Eyre and Charles Hadfield
36	1942	The Birds of Britain	James Fisher	85	1945	Islands Round Britain	R. M. Lockley
37	1943	British Orientalists	A. J. Arberry	86	1945	British Journalists and Newspapers	Derek Hudson

38	1943	British Craftsmen	Thomas Hennell	87	1945	Sporting Pictures of England	Guy Paget
39	1943	The Story of Ireland	Sean O'Faolain	88	1945	English Watercolour Painters	H. J. Paris
40	1943	The British Colonial Empire*	Noel Sabine	89	1945	British Furniture Makers	John Gloag
45	1942	British Trade Unions	Sir Walter Citrine	90	1945	English Public Schools	Rex Warner
46	1942	Fairs, Circuses and Music Halls	M. Willson Disher	92	1945	Early Britain	Jacquetta Hawkes
47	1942	British Engineers	Metius Chappell	93	1945	English Cricket	Neville Cardus
48	1943	English Cities and Small Towns	John Betjeman	94	1945	Insect Life in Britain	Geoffrey Taylor
49	1943	British Historians	E. L. Woodward	96	1945	British Dogs	A. Croxton Smith

Books highlighted include a passage about the current war with 'elegiac defense'.

*Britain Commonwealth in Pictures Books.
Source: Book list adapted with dates and numbers from Michael Carney, *Britain in Pictures: A History and Bibliography* (Werner Shaw, 1995).

Britain in Pictures book, suggesting that authors may have been plied with models for their work by Turner.[36] The style of Turner's book thus represents the ur-example of the elegiac defensive posture of *BIP*; the formal decisions of the editor set the course for what would follow.

On insects and editorial influence

The conclusion of Rose Macaulay's *Life Among the English* (1942, #31) captures Turner's tone in cautiously hoping ('we cannot know yet', she writes) that the English will 'grope a way through wreckage and smouldering ashes' of war to strengthen democracy, but a further example explicitly supports the theory that writers in the series were inspired by the formal decisions of other writers and editors.[37] *Insect Life in Britain* (1945, #94) by Geoffrey Taylor begins by hailing the '[t]en thousand forms! ten thousand tribes!' of British insects, phrases which he borrows from naturalist James Thomson and the ecstatic tones of which are in keeping with the triumphalist sentiments of others in the series.[38] Understanding that insects provide suboptimal avenues through which to appeal to feelings of national solidarity, Taylor quickly concedes that while the list of British insects would fill a book and more, 'there is nothing distinctive about any particular English insect'.[39] Taylor then claims a level of generic discomfort, recognizing that unlike other topics, the global nature of his subject cannot easily be assimilated into a nationalistic propagandistic genre and explicitly outlines his uneasiness with the template of elegiac defence: 'My problem, therefore, is different from W. J. Turner's on *English Music*, or John Betjeman's on *English Small Towns*.'[40] The overt, specific reference to Turner's and Betjeman's books is of particular interest, indicating an authorial apprehension that each book should fit within the *BIP* series and further suggesting that this impulse derives from editorial motivations behind the corpus. Having introduced this quandary, Taylor wrangles with the inconsistency in making insects metonymic of the British aristocratic tradition: 'English insects are members of our oldest families, tracing a descent from the period of our most ancient fossil-bearing rocks.' Making a further effort to synthesize nature and nationalism, he asks: '[W]hat *is* an insect – of any age or nationality?'[41] Although he avoids mentioning the war, Taylor acknowledges the anomalous nature of his book within the *BIP* series.

Despite his discomfort, Taylor ends his book by gesturing towards the value of British culture to others, citing British poetry about insects including

Tennyson's 'The Two Voices' and John Clare's 'Clock-a-Clay'. The final lines then seek, unexpectedly, to promote entomology-centric literary achievement in nationalist and xenophobic tones: 'Professor Lafcadio Hearn, that odd Japanese-Irish-Greek, complained that the English did not write about insects. He was wrong. There they are – Coleoptera, Odonata, Diptera, Lepidoptera – and with more space, English insects of other natural orders that might have been added to these, for many Englishmen have written curiously and lovingly of their native Hexapoda.'[42] Taylor closes with a strikingly defensive assertion, affronted at the mere suggestion that the English neglected their duties in properly bestowing literary attention to the common housefly ('diptera'). So, even *despite* Taylor's recognition that insects are not the proper subject of propagandistic rhetoric, he still finds a way – via the citation of literature – to make insects and the academics who study them a political and national concern, just like Turner before him.

Elegiac defence in practice: Pride and its complications

The direct reference to Turner's mode in Smythe's *British Mountaineers* and Taylor's *Insect Life in Britain* are just two examples of the elegiac defence that permeates the series. Lord David Cecil's survey *The English Poets* (1941; #1) – the first book in the *BIP* series – ends with a brief homage to the 'imaginative and philosophical poetry' of co-editors W. J. Turner and Dorothy Wellesley, before noting that 'war is sweeping the country. How far it will affect literature and in what direction, it is too early to say.'[43] This ominous tone is more explicit in other books. In *English Education* (1941; #17), Kenneth Lindsay concludes by claiming education as an essential part of national service and the maintenance of civic democracy: 'If England is to be a champion of an alternative new order and the victory is to be not only over Germany, but over a false set of values, then the schools and the whole spirit and apparatus of education must begin to express it here and now.'[44] English education thus becomes a way to defend democracy. Lindsay continues to imagine teachers, parents – and, presumably, students – on the front lines of the conflict, defending themselves by embracing an educational system steeped in freedom: 'to-day the armies of freedom are engaged in an international civil war. In every country education is on trial; it is for teachers and parents alike to awaken to the challenge.'[45] Other books in the series stage the war as a threat to British natural environs. In the final paragraph of *English Gardens* (1944; #59), Harry Roberts notes that 'the future history of the English garden is doubtful', but then references a 'recent Mass-observation enquiry' which found that most working people continue to envision a garden as part of their ideal home. The book concludes, 'Should this bit of democracy materialize, the English cottage garden will have come into its own.'[46] Somehow, it would seem even the maintenance of the garden necessitates the defence of democratic principles in the present.

Notwithstanding the seeming innocuousness of topics like gardens and classrooms, the defence of 'Britishness' in the context of war against Germany was not without obvious complications; this point reveals itself in the series' ambiguity over national and cultural identity. Individual titles in the series were just as likely to feature 'England' or 'English' in titles as 'Britain' or 'British'. In fact, there seems to be little pattern in whether a particular field was best captured by the more expansive 'British' or the more exclusive 'English' title. Topics like historians, photographers, romantic artists and engineers were paired with 'British' in their titles, while ballet, water colour painters, cricket and inns were all paired with 'English' in theirs. But the agnostic stance of the series regarding the distinction between British and English is upended when considering a sub-section of the series – *British Commonwealth in Pictures* – which featured seven books. Of the first twenty books published between 1941 and 1942, five were from the Commonwealth series, suggesting its importance to the series' aims. These early Commonwealth books included *Australia* (1941; #5), *East Africa* (1941, #6) *Canada* (1941; #9), *India* (1941; #10) and *South Africa* (1941; #18).[47] The prioritization of Commonwealth topics suggests that the propaganda aims of *BIP* were directly designed to counter German propaganda abroad by appealing to collective self-interest by means of an opaquely defined 'British' culture. The extent to which German propaganda, particularly radio propaganda, exploited colonial frustrations over empire in its messaging abroad is well known and Matheson knew this better than most. In her 1934 essay 'Politics and Broadcasting', Matheson had already identified that '[i]n Germany, as most British listeners know almost too well, wireless is ceaselessly used to inspire, admonish, encourage and instruct National Socialists, *outside* as well as inside the Reich'.[48] The *Britain Commonwealth in Pictures* sub-series acknowledges the problem with its defensive nature; in presenting a universal appeal to democracy, writers also necessarily balanced the obvious hypocrisy that colonialism posed to the scheme to 'defend Britishness'. Perhaps unsurprisingly, then, each of the five Commonwealth books listed above integrate some version of Turner's original tactic of the elegiac defence.

Mourning empire in *Britain in Pictures*

The Commonwealth books dealt with colonial tensions either by praising productive allegiance with the allies or by suggesting the potential of new, more 'enlightened' relationships between Britain and the colonies, all while minimizing the negative impacts of empire. In *Australia*, Arnold Haskell argues that the 'unhesitating' response of Australians in signing up for the war reveals an implicit, even 'unbreakable' bond between the British and Australian causes:

> I marvel at the unhesitating response of the Australian to take part in the Second World War. Others, nearer home, have hesitated [. . .] Once again they have answered the call, once again the enemy expected them to fail. None but a free man can understand that mysterious link, in peace seemingly so slender, unbreakable in trouble.[49]

These bonds are not often comforting, as we find in several of the books that necessarily address the complexity of the colonial situation.

In the Commonwealth sub-series, the elegiac defence is more nuanced. The defensive posture outlined in many other *BIP* books continues, but is specifically applied to empire, the horrors of which are minimized and negated. In his introduction to *The British Colonial Empire* (1943; #40), Dominion and Colonial Office Publicity Officer Noel Sabine categorizes 'the British Empire' or 'British Commonwealth of Nations' as 'a living political association in full working order', despite its lack of 'deliberate planning'.[50] Anticipating resistance to any praise for imperial policy, Sabine suggests in the conclusion that Britain has simply failed to appropriately 'dramatise or romanticise' empire. He goes further in defending empire to the international audience:

> The traditional background of our Empire story has been characterized, as we have seen, by a general lack of perception of its significance, amounting at times to a dangerous apathy, accompanied by sharp cleavages of opinion and strong, often bitter criticisms of public policy and private activities in the Empire. The criticisms and questionings alike are healthy symptoms of a political order which has always attached high importance to freedom of opinion and speech.[51]

By recognizing that criticisms of empire exist, Sabine amplifies the democratic qualities of free speech that would be lost under a Nazi occupation.

Like other books in the series, *The British Colonial Empire* concludes with a more traditional version of the elegiac defence. Sabine cites, to the credit of the British Empire, 'the famines, pestilences and wars we have prevented' and the 'material developments, the spiritual contribution of fair play and honest dealing', all of which have sadly been 'forgotten' because Britain failed to market its victories properly, a claim acting as a subtle counter to German propaganda's emphasis on the harms of British colonization.[52] Sabine's book concludes with a suggestion that the current war is solidifying these beneficial bonds of empire, and that the defeat of fascism depends on a united support for empire's past: 'The war, so far from driving the peoples of the Empire apart, is drawing them closer together. The future, I firmly believe, depends largely on whether understanding and sympathy can be maintained not only between the governments, but between the peoples of the Commonwealth. The colonies must be fitted and enabled to take their place in the post-war world.'[53] In Sabine's argument, colonies may develop only by maintaining proximity to imperial power.

In *East Africa* (1941; #6), Elspeth Huxley cannot avoid mentioning the violence of colonial rule on the continent. Like Sabine, Huxley alludes to, but minimizes, the struggles facing the region, asking 'whether the African can successfully blend his inheritance and traditions with the new western ideas that have poured in on him so quickly and so roughly'.[54] The suggestion of 'rough' treatment is egregious evasion which enables her to further defend the 'western ideas' with which Africans had been assaulted. In contrast to other books in the sub-series, Huxley does acknowledge the loss of traditions and old ways. For Huxley, abandoning tradition *for* western ways is ideal, and traditional practices might be assimilated only insomuch as they do not upset western values or norms. This argument is a problematic but inevitable outcome of a propaganda mission that defends 'western' ideology as a bastion of progress. Huxley's concerns do not stop at assimilation; Africa's main problem will be 'how to preserve for the use of future generations the only real resource that Africa possesses, its good earth'.[55] It can hardly be coincidental that Huxley connects East Africa's future to its richness of resources, since her family held a 500-acre plantation in Kenya. Maintaining an interest in farming, she studied agriculture at Cornell, and later took up a position as a 'press officer' at the Empire Marketing Board.[56] To return to Huxley's discussion of 'how to preserve' the 'good earth' of Africa, the elegiac defence – the proposal of the earth's fragility and of its preservation – is matched with a defence of her own position as one who can provide 'solutions' to the problems facing Africa. The solution, for Huxley, is as follows: 'the tribal bonds that Europeans have broken can be replaced by a new discipline of the African's own making before a state of spiritual anarchy intervenes.'[57] In her reading, the loss of East African traditions and bonds should not be mourned but celebrated as opportunities for productive assimilation with the colonizer. These uncomfortable allusions to the empire were also evident in Sarah Millin's *South Africa* (1942; #18), where the author defends nineteenth-century colonist Cecil Rhodes, stating that although 'Rhodes had the legal right [. . .] to take a savage land', his 'moral right' was compromised: 'His moral right [. . .] depended on whether in taking the black man's land he was also prepared to regard the black man's soul'.[58] At times, the implied *mea culpas* in these texts are overshadowed by ominous threats about the fascist alternative. Millin reminds readers that '[t]he whip-chain-forced labour system prevailed in all the German colonies. And should the Nazis ever return to Africa it will (as they themselves declare) do so again'.[59] Such passages fabricate a counterfactual history of empire whereby the British colonizer is reimagined as a paragon of democracy. There is a sense of anticipatory mourning over the loss of empire in books like these, slyly admitting the prospective losses of traditional colonial relationships, while mourning the war's threat to shared senses of identity in advance and using these as motivation to join the cause of anti-fascism.

Conclusion: The propaganda of anticipatory mourning

In the Commonwealth sub-series, *BIP* authors deployed anticipatory mourning to assuage and persuade audiences in colonial and neutral territories, as anticipatory trauma was deployed to persuade readers to come to Britain's aid despite the legacy of empire. That books on everyday cultural pursuits and artforms in the wider series were bound to this colonial project attests to the important and unique relationship between the Second World War and the everyday. As Thomas Davis reminds us in his book on literature of this period, *The Extinct Scene* (2015), 'encounters with everyday life [are] not primarily aesthetic or ethical' but are 'simultaneously aesthetic *and* political'.[60] And as the Commonwealth books demonstrate, the editorial focus on mundane histories enables the *BIP* authors to deploy the rhetoric of elegy to reach political registers beyond the immediate war.

While not all images across the *BIP* series weaponized the anticipation of loss as astutely as E. D. Hewland's painting of Hawker-Hurricane assembly work in *Britain in the Air* (1944; #68), the painting is uniquely demonstrative of the mission of series editors, as demonstrated by both corpus-based and close textual analysis (see Table 6.1).[61] As reflections on the history of

ASSEMBLING A HAWKER-HURRICANE
Oil painting by E. D. Hewland

Figure 6.3 'Assembling a Hawker-Hurricane', by E. D. Hewland. Reprinted with permission of Bridgeman Images.

everyday objects, hobbies or practices, the *BIP* books mourn the wartime destruction that threatens everyday customs, tying these customs to a universal fight to protect democratic norms and values from fascism. And while the books present themselves as tomes of self-aggrandizing cultural historiography, their rhetorical play exhibits a more sophisticated brand of propaganda. Following the vision of the series editors of a propaganda that embraced beauty while eschewed dogmatism, authors' luminous prose mourned swathes not just of British, but of human, experience, promising a nearly universal scope to its emotional reach. The expansionist logic of the series attempts what Jet Esty calls a 'synthesizing universalism', a feature Esty associates not only with modernism (like that of editors Matheson or Turner) but also with imperialism. If, as Esty argues, imperial modernist culture always registers an 'absent totality' at its centre, *Britain in Picture*'s books stage anticipatory trauma as a new venue for registering this central absence, making it an important series in understanding the nuances of Second World War propaganda.[62]

Notes

1. Original dust jacket cited in Michael Carney, *Stoker: Life of Hilda Matheson OBE* (Llangynog, Wales: Michael Carney, 1999), 129.
2. Ellul refers to this as 'white' propaganda. While Ellul's distinction between various types of propaganda and its opacity is vital, the continued use of the black/white/grey distinction seems problematic in its refusal to acknowledge the racial connotations of the phrase. See Jacques Ellul, *Propaganda: The Formation of Men's Attitudes*, trans. by Konrad Kellen and Jean Lerner (New York, NY: Vintage Books, 1965), 15.
3. Valerie Holman, 'Carefully Concealed Connections: The Ministry of Information and British Publishing, 1939–1946', *Book History* 8 (2005): 199.
4. The series uses 'British' and 'English' almost interchangeably in the titles of the series, a point I discuss later.
5. 'Books of the Day: Britain in Pictures', *The Scotsman*, 6 November 1947, 7.
6. Paul Saint-Amour, *Tense Future: Modernism, Total War, Encyclopedic Form* (New York, NY: Oxford University Press, 2015), 8.
7. Ibid., 7.
8. Ibid., 8.
9. Carney, *Stoker*, 127.
10. While the JBC had primarily targeted Germans, it began to target 'friendly and neutral' countries to 'reinforce the links with Britain' while Matheson was employed there. See Carney, *Stoker*, 119.
11. Wayne McKenna, *W. J. Turner: Poet and Music Critic* (Gerrards Cross: Colin Smythe, 1990), 54–5.
12. Ibid., 56.
13. This would be about £12,000 today. Rose Macaulay had worked in the British Department of Propaganda during the First World War, but others would have influence in the Second World War. Bowen wrote reports about morale in neutral Ireland for the MOI; although O'Brien probably did not work with the MOI as she often claimed, *Farewell Spain* was a direct rejection of Franco's fascism (see Eibhear Walshe, *Kate O'Brien: A Literary Life* (Dublin: Irish Academic Press, 2006)). Orwell's political writings of the war against Hitler were widely publicized and highly acerbic, though his work for the BBC was in part unsatisfying for its connection to a more direct form of propaganda Orwell disliked, and whose propaganda networks *Nineteen Eighty-Four* satirizes (see Melissa Dinsman, 'Propaganda, Literature, and New Networks', chapter four of *Modernism at the Microphone: Radio, Propaganda, and Literary Aesthetics During World War II* (London: Bloomsbury Academic, 2015), 97–120).

14 'Pride in the British Achievement: Books by Authoritative Writers', *The Times*, 12 March 1941, 7.
15 The description reads 'Every volume in the series is fully illustrated with specially chosen pictures reproduced in colour, as well as with at least 20 black and white pictures', Collins Advertisement, 'Britain in Pictures', *The Times*, 31 October 1941, 9.
16 Advertisement, 'Britain in Pictures', *The Times*, 31 October 1941, 9.
17 'Pride in the British Achievement', *The Times*, 12 March 1941, 7.
18 McKenna, *W. J. Turner*, 57; David Finkelstein and Alistair McCleery, 'Publishing', in *The Cambridge History of the Book in Britain: Volume 7, The Twentieth Century and Beyond,* ed. Andrew Nash, Claire Squires, and I. R. Willison (Cambridge: Cambridge University Press, 2019), 167; Carney, *Britain in Pictures*, 36.
19 Jed Esty, *A Shrinking Island: Modernism and National Culture in England* (Princeton, NJ: Princeton University Press, 2004), 7.
20 Holman, 'Carefully Concealed', 200.
21 Carney, *Britain in Pictures*, 28.
22 McKenna, *W. J. Turner*, xiv.
23 Ibid., 56.
24 Ibid., xiv.
25 Matheson pushed for a generous and positive broadcast review of Lawrence and Joyce by Harold Nicholson (Carney, *Stoker*, 73).
26 McKenna, *W. J. Turner*, 23, 56.
27 Ibid., 56.
28 McKenna claims that Turner aligned with Yeats against what he called the 'Ezra, Eliot, Auden school' (McKenna, *W. J. Turner*, 44).
29 W. J. Turner, *English Music* (London: William Collins, 1941), 48.
30 F. S. Smythe, *British Mountaineers* (London: William Collins, 1942), 46.
31 Ibid., 48.
32 This rubric may exclude books written during the war and published afterwards. One example of the former is Orwell's *The English People* (1947; #100), commissioned in 1943 (George Orwell, *I Have Tried to Tell the Truth*, ed. Peter Davison (London: Secker & Warburg, 1998), 199).
33 Carney, *Stoker*, 128. The survey also excluded the books *Shelley* (1941; #7), *Byron* (1941; #8), *Tennyson* (1942; #19), *Keats* (1942; #20), *Coleridge* (1942; #43) and *Wordsworth* (1942; #44), on the grounds that these books were part of a different sub-section of the series – *English Poets in Pictures* – all written and edited by Dorothy Wellesley. They were unique in that they did not provide larger histories of fields within British society, but instead consisted solely of elongated close readings of the poets' oeuvres. Additionally, some books in the numbered series as recorded by Michael Carney (1995) were never published, leaving gaps in the common numbering of the series. The unpublished books include such promising titles as

British Biographies (#56) by Rebecca West and *English Conversation* by Lord David Cecil and Lettice Fowler (#54).

34 Raymond Williams describes structures of feeling as concepts or ideas that appear holistically and are 'emergent or pre-emergent, they do not have to await definition, classification, or rationalization before they exert palpable pressures and set effective limits on experience and on action' (Raymond Williams, *Marxism and Literature* (Oxford: Oxford University Press, 1977), 132).

35 Orwell, *I Have Tried to Tell the Truth*, 199; Virginia Woolf, *The Diary of Virginia Woolf: Volume Five 1936–1941,* ed. Anne Oliver Bell (New York, NY: Harcourt, 1984), 302.

36 A letter from the office of William Collins included a copy of Cecil's *The English Poets* and cites Turner as being responsible for soliciting manuscripts (1941, #1). Collins to Rose Macaulay, 2 April 1941 (243/1/11/5: Authors' Correspondence 1937–1943. Records of William Collins, Sons and Co Ltd, publishers, University of Glasgow Archives, Glasgow). Thanks to the archivists at the University of Glasgow for their assistance in finding these records, many of which were destroyed in the war.

37 Rose Macaulay, *Life Among the English* (London: William Collins, 1942), 48.

38 Geoffrey Taylor, *Insect Life in Britain* (London: William Collins, 1945), 7.

39 Ibid.

40 Ibid., 8.

41 Ibid.

42 Ibid., 46–7.

43 Lord David Cecil, *The English Poets* (London: Britain in Pictures Ltd, 1941), 48.

44 Kenneth Lindsay, *English Education* (London: William Collins, 1941), 46–7.

45 Ibid., 48.

46 Harry Roberts, *English Gardens* (London: William Collins, 1947), 48.

47 Notably, Seán Ó Faoláin's *The Story of Ireland* (1943; #39) was included as part of *Britain in Pictures* but separate from the Commonwealth series.

48 Hilda Matheson, 'Politics and Broadcasting', *The Political Quarterly* 5, no. 2 (1934): 182 (emphasis added).

49 Arnold Haskell, *Australia* (Britain in Pictures Limited, 1941), 48.

50 Noel Sabine, *The British Colonial Empire* (London: William Collins, 1943), 7.

51 Ibid., 47.

52 Ibid.

53 Ibid.

54 Elspeth Huxley, *East Africa* (London: Britain in Pictures Ltd, 1941), 48.

55 Ibid.

56 Sarah Lyall, 'Elspeth Huxley, 89, Chronicler of Colonial Kenya, Dies', *New York Times,* 18 January 1997, 13.

57 Huxley, *East Africa*, 48.

58 Sarah Gertrude Millin, *South Africa* (London: William Collins, 1941), 33.
59 Ibid., 36.
60 Thomas Davis, *The Extinct Scene: Late Modernism and Everyday Life* (New York, NY: Columbia University Press, 2015), 6.
61 Saint-Amour, *Tense Future*, 8.
62 Esty, *Shrinking Isle*, 7.

Part III

7

Colonial insurgency, propaganda and the British 'soldier-aesthete'

Maurice Cardiff, Lawrence Durrell, Patrick Leigh Fermor and Freya Stark in the Cyprus Revolt

Maria Hadjiathanasiou

Introduction

'I have wondered if British influence would so survive the loss of Britain herself?' wrote Freya Stark after the fall of France in 1940.[1] Almost half a century later, in his *New York Times* article on the occasion of Patrick Leigh Fermor's death, Robert D. Kaplan claimed that '[t]he British Empire lasted as long as it did partly because it produced soldier-aesthetes like Fermor'.[2] The intriguing concept of the 'soldier-aesthete' becomes particularly relevant when describing British individuals of the arts and letters who engaged in overt and/or clandestine propaganda activities on behalf of the British government in lands away from their own. This chapter examines contacts between such individuals and different arms of the British propaganda effort such as the British Council, the Ministry of Information (MOI), the Political Warfare Executive (PWE), the Special Operations Executive (SOE), embassy press offices and others during the Second World War. Taking late colonial Cyprus as a case study, I then explore how these figures came to find themselves in the Mediterranean colony after the end of the war, arguably continuing to serve Britain's national interest as cultural diplomats and propagandists. The chapter focuses on the period from the 1950s until Cyprus gained its independence in 1960, following the four-year anti-colonial armed Revolt (1955–9) mounted by EOKA (*Ethniki Organosis Kyprion Agoniston*),[3] the Greek Cypriot guerrilla organization demanding liberation from British rule and *enosis* (political union) with Greece. The chapter reveals a network of individuals who shared a faith and loyalty to Britain, and who fought using their wits to win hearts and minds at the end of empire: in this period, the aim was to foster and maintain intangible connections between colonial populations soon to gain independence and their former imperial ruler. The chapter also traces the social and personal connections which bound this network together: the individuals in question shared long-standing friendships and offered practical support to each other in diverse ways, ranging from arranging accommodation or providing contacts to literary agents.

Since the beginning of the British occupation in 1878, the Church of Cyprus, representing the majority population of the Greek Orthodox people of the island, extended verbal and written appeals requesting a political union with Greece. These requests were ignored by Britain until the Government House in Nicosia was consumed in flames in October 1931 in the first local rebellion against the British occupation. This event was followed by ten years of illiberal colonial rule championed by the hastily imported hardline Governor Richmond Palmer.[4] Measures were relaxed only when Britain needed support in its war against the Axis powers, and the people of Cyprus were called to fight in the name of the Crown and Greece.[5] With the end of the Second World War, organized attempts to end British colonial rule and unite with Greece led to the Greek Cypriot Revolt.[6] By the 1950s, the *enosis* movement was supported by the vast majority of the Greek Cypriot community of the island, owing a large part of its strength and inspiration to the Greek Orthodox Church of Cyprus and specifically to its leader Archbishop Makarios III, elected to this position in 1950. An armed resistance campaign against British rule ended only with the establishment of the independent state of the Republic of Cyprus in 1960 under his presidency.

The British Council opened its first institute in Cyprus in 1940, the same year it opened institutes in Aden, Iraq, Palestine and Turkey; others had been established in Egypt in 1938 and Greece in 1939.[7] These were designed to counter so-called 'alien cultural influences' which threatened British economic, strategic and political interests in the Eastern Mediterranean and the wider region.[8] The establishment of the British Council in Cyprus brought a number of British individuals of the arts and letters to the island, usually to give lectures on their areas of expertise at the Council's institutes.[9] Most of these figures were acquainted before arriving in Cyprus, some of them having worked together in the past or having enjoyed long-standing friendships. Although their accommodation was generally organized by the Council, the visitors were free to act independently and unsupervised, and were therefore largely able to escape the growingly distrustful local gaze.

This chapter focuses on four such individuals active in Cyprus at the end of empire: the writer, and Representative of the British Council in Cyprus from 1953–5, Maurice Cardiff, the writer and special forces veteran Patrick Leigh Fermor, the internationally acclaimed novelist, poet and travel writer Lawrence Durrell, and the travel writer and adventurer Freya Stark. Published writings by these authors and their biographers typically include only brief references to their stay in Cyprus, usually short notes about a summer vacation in the island, a professional visit, a work stint or a brief stop on their way to a different destination. Consequently, apart from Durrell (for whom the literature is more extensive due to his international fame), the rest remain largely unknown in the modern literary and cultural history of Cyprus. However, I argue that these writers acted as the type of 'soldier-aesthetes' identified by Kaplan. All four had forged close connections with various aspects of the British propaganda apparatus during the Second World War and all four visited Cyprus during the Revolt to produce cultural propaganda on the British government's payroll and/or for private or professional reasons. Their wartime skillset was effectively harnessed specifically for propaganda purposes before and during the EOKA insurgency and the British counter-insurgency campaigns (1955–9).

In what follows, I detail these figures' wartime activities before exploring their role in the Revolt, identifying ways in which their wartime experiences appear to have overlapped with the colonial counter-insurgency campaign. Drawing on unpublished documents including colonial files and private correspondence, as well as memoirs and novels, I argue that these cosmopolitan intellectuals sought to further British official interests, not just through conventional propaganda activities but also by mingling with local populations, gathering and disseminating information and contributing to the formation of Cypriot, Greek, Turkish, British and international public opinion, with the ultimate aim of maintaining Britain's geostrategic influence in the region. The most evident example of this enduring presence is the Sovereign Base Areas of Akrotiri and Dhekelia which, in the Treaty Concerning the Establishment of the Republic of Cyprus (1960), were retained as British sovereign territory.

British writers in Cyprus

The activities of the writers under study varied from information gathering and information dissemination to incitement. Their targets included influential Cypriot leaders and opinion shapers as well as segments of the wider society. The writers in question served the Empire in Cyprus for the most part in unofficial capacities, and it is important to acknowledge that none of them were explicitly linked to propaganda and intelligence work in Cyprus during the Revolt except for Lawrence Durrell, whose role was increasingly disputed by his contemporary counterparts and has also been questioned by current research on the subject, as will be discussed later in the chapter. Cardiff's, Stark's and Leigh Fermor's roles in Cyprus at this time are largely absent from the literature, partly due to the inaccessibility and scarcity of published material, but also simply because their activities and contacts were not supposed to be common knowledge.

According to Panagiotis Dimitrakis, during the Second World War, '[t]he small Cypriot cities and the villages with their dusty roads were the epicentres of propaganda, political espionage, anti-colonial agitation, intrigue and crime'.[10] At the time, the island had its fair share of agents and informers, including SOE operatives, coordinating along with the colonial government the propaganda strategy to support the British war effort. One British wartime document advised that 'to be really successful here [in Cyprus], propaganda must not be recognizable as such, nor its source recognizable as officially British'.[11] The 'peculiar value of oral dissemination, which appears more spontaneous, more independent, at a time when printing is controlled and publishing licensed' appears to have been recognized by the ex-wartime propagandists examined in this chapter.[12] Oral propaganda was believed to be the only way to maintain anonymity and secrecy, which were obligatory in order to protect the central and/or colonial government from being exposed as its source. Surveillance and rumour-mongering were the key methods employed by agents during the war, but also by the soldier-aesthetes after the end of it.[13] Oral propaganda was thought to have been 'very successful in a country in which there are many minorities and much political dissatisfaction'.[14] After the end of the war, even though the 'political problems' – as they were called – in Cyprus were many, maintaining a covert propaganda organization there was considered both 'uneconomical and unnecessary', 'unless S.O.E. receives a general post-war charter'.[15]

Available secondary literature gives only limited information about these writers' clandestine activities during the Second World War, but nevertheless offers a useful starting point for exploring their wartime and post-war activities in Cyprus. Cardiff worked for the British Council from the mid-1940s to 1973, during which time he was posted to no fewer than seven stations, including in Greece, Italy and Cyprus.[16] He joined the British Council in a full-time capacity in 1945, taking up the management of the Council in Athens due to his knowledge of Greek. In 1943, before his recruitment by the SOE, Cardiff was attached to the PWE in Cairo and worked with resistance organizations in the Aegean Islands. Later, in Athens, 'as a pseudo civilian [he] began daily stints at the office' in civilian clothing.[17] Cardiff served as Acting Representative before Steven Runciman took over as Representative (1945–7), and at a time when the Council appears to have been extremely influential in the Greek capital: a former Greek Minister for Culture observed that 'the intellectual life of Athens after the [Civil] war was formed by the British Council'.[18] The years before the start of the Greek Cypriot anti-colonial Revolt have also been described as 'the high point of the British Council's presence in Greece'.[19] However, the 1950s Cyprus crisis brought about a 'splitting of sympathy' between these foreign writers and intellectuals (such as Steven Runciman, Lawrence Durrell, Henry Miller, Rex Warner, Osbert Lancaster, Leigh Fermor, Philip Sherrard) and the Greek intelligentsia.[20] The rupture was genuine, and since then numerous Greek and Greek Cypriot authors have conveyed it through literature and poetry. Patrick Leigh Fermor, who worked with Cardiff as Deputy Director for the Council in Athens, had joined the Irish Guards on the outbreak of war. He was quickly transferred to the Intelligence Corps, serving as a liaison officer with Greek resistance forces in Albania and then in Crete, where he took part in the unsuccessful attempt to hold the island against the German invasion. Having been evacuated, he was recruited by the SOE, and sent back to Crete where, dressed as a Cretan shepherd and using his knowledge of the Greek language, he helped organize local partisan sabotage operations.[21] Of Leigh Fermor's recruitment to the SOE, Penelope Tremayne writes: 'Whatever may be the army's talent for cramming round pegs into square holes, all should be forgiven them for fitting him into the only just formed SOE for which he was ideally suited.'[22] As I argue here, the soldier-aesthetes' wartime skills were then employed in post-war theatres of operations. Their previous experiences may have assisted their work in the field of cultural diplomacy, but the lifestyle was often very different, especially for Leigh Fermor, who had played a significant role in the resistance as an SOE agent in Crete and led the legendary operation to abduct German General Heinrich Kreipe.[23] In post-war Athens, for example, Leigh Fermor 'was clearly not suited to the disciplines of army life in peacetime, and still less to teaching or office routines': he was employed by the British Institute (the 'teaching branch' of the Council) mainly for lecturing.[24] As Leigh Fermor recalled, '[i]t was a fascinating time to be in Athens. The war was over and the later troubles had not yet really begun. [. . .] When it was thought that I might be more useful outside the capital, I was sent to lecture all over the mainland and the islands. This involved six months in the remotest places I could find'.[25] Cardiff recalled that Rex Warner, the director of the British Institute, was indulgent of the younger members of staff: 'Quick to spot the comedy in our not infrequently misplaced endeavours, the merest amateurs that we were, to live up to the high ideals in cultural diplomacy [Warner] tempered our dismay at the worst of our failures by his deep and reassuring chuckle.'[26] Nevertheless, Leigh Fermor was arguably a very successful cultural diplomat, forming friendly, long-lasting relationships with several Greek intellectuals and opinion-formers of the time such as the writer George Katsimbalis (portrayed by Henry Miller as 'The Colossus of Maroussi') and his circle, the Greek Nobel-winning poet and diplomat George Seferis, and the author and diplomat Rodis Roufos, even though he fell out with some of these individuals during the period of the Revolt.[27] During the troubled 1950s, the British Council was soon branded by both Greeks and Greek Cypriots as a propaganda instrument, tarnishing the good name of many of its British employees and contributors.[28]

Durrell's official roles as government propagandist in Greece, and then in Cyprus, made him 'a fair game for the assassin's bullet' during the Revolt.[29] Durrell had also worked for the British Council in Greece, teaching English in the early years of the war in Kalamata. Previously, he had worked as a press attaché at the British Embassy in Athens due to his fluency in Greek (he had lived in Greece from 1935 until 1941) and continued this career at the British embassies in Cairo and Alexandria from 1941 to 1944. It has been speculated that Durrell's frequent moves were due to the secondary posts he was assigned by the Foreign Office.[30] After the war, Durrell became press officer for the Dodecanese islands and was based on Rhodes, before moving to Argentina for two years and then to Yugoslavia, before arriving in Cyprus in early 1953 where he continued his information and propaganda work.[31]

Freya Stark, the well-known British travel writer and adventurer, is perhaps the most established propagandist of the individuals studied in this chapter. Stark joined the MOI on the outbreak of war in 1939 as an expert on southern Arabia, 'earning prominence and honours for enhancing British influence and countering Axis propaganda in Aden, Yemen, Egypt, Iraq and India'.[32] The Brotherhood of Freedom, the organization she founded to build support for democracy and bring together pro-British sympathizers in Baghdad while at the same time deterring the spread of communist ideas, has been described by James Vaughan as taking 'the concept of oral propaganda to new levels of effectiveness'.[33] Despite identifying with the struggles of people she met on her travels, Stark remained a believer in the necessity of empire and was hostile to nationalist movements;[34] as Guy Woodward observes, her wartime career is representative of a contradiction central to any study of British deployment of covert propaganda, between the 'professed and often-proclaimed faith in idealistic and nebulous concepts such as British values or Western democracy [...] and the shady and deceptive means used to promote these abstractions'.[35] The Brotherhood reportedly succeeded because its propaganda was 'not only spread but conceived by the people of the country in which it was to act', and Stark's activities suggest that propaganda is at its most successful when the propagandist *assists* the audience in understanding on their own their needs and wants – needs and wants that in this case also happened to serve Britain's interests.[36] In order to achieve this, the propagandist has to form a relationship of trust through close interactions with influential figures in local society (such as religious and political representatives), an approach which all the writers examined in this chapter adopted in Cyprus.

Personal relations played a significant role in these propaganda campaigns, both in terms of relationships between British propagandists and local communities, and those between propagandists themselves. The 'soldier-aesthetes' shared long-standing friendships, mutually beneficial social and intellectual relations and national interests. These figures often stayed at each other's local places of residence, offered their expertise at their friend's place of work (giving lectures at British Institutes or contributing articles to magazines published by relevant departments) and shared stories that fuelled their literary imaginations. Lawrence Durrell was a friend of Stark and wrote many letters to her during his stay in Cyprus. He also wrote the foreword to *The Journey's Echo* (1963), her selected travel writings, where he extolled the 'singular qualities of heart and mind which informed' these, thus making an oblique allusion to the wartime business of winning hearts and minds.[37] In her own letters, Stark also alluded to her wartime propaganda activities, illuminating methods in persuasion and propaganda that could arguably be applied in contexts such as Cyprus. She wrote that 'propaganda in districts where the other side is powerful should be as intangible as possible, so as to offer no target. [... A] tour of private talks with influential people would probably be more useful in results. One could send a series of people at intervals, and have small drawing room meetings – but with the Press strictly excluded'.[38] When Stark was in Cyprus in 1942, staying at Prodromos village, where a cottage had been provided by the British Council, she 'was already involved in clandestine operations',[39] interacting with British administrators and local people alike, collecting and disseminating information, as she had done successfully in the Middle East and elsewhere.

Apart from a few sentences in Stark's and Durrell's published letters, we lack detailed information about Stark's activities in Cyprus, with little available to retrieve from archival sources. However, we do know that she was often invited to give lectures at the British Council's premises on the island. The limited information on her stays means the purpose of her trips to Cyprus in 1952 and then in 1956 during the Revolt are not known, but the fact that all her publications had 'to be approved by the Foreign Office' suggests official interest in her work at this time and the sensitivity of what she was recording.[40] In 1952, she stayed in Kyrenia, where she was 'plunged into Cyprus society', meeting with 'the widows', going 'to see the church built' and 'pass[ing] through the hospital'.[41] Letters reveal that she went on excursions with a Greek poet and Archbishop Makarios's secretary. In 1956, during the EOKA armed revolt, she was in the village of Lapithos, a 'dangerous village but seems very peaceful – simply owing to the fact that Austen [Harrison, a British architect living in Cyprus] has always been friendly with the mayor and people around'.[42] This reference reinforces the argument – popular among colonial administrators – that in Cyprus 'all depends upon personal relations'.[43] Lapithos, a village with increased EOKA activity, obtained a semblance of peace due to the fact that a British intellectual living there had a good relationship with the locals.

Given her role as a successful propagandist during the 1940s, it seems likely that in this late colonial context Stark continued to pursue Britain's interests in Cyprus, using her connections with Cyprus society to gain intelligence and feed information to influential local people in both the Greek Cypriot and the Turkish Cypriot communities.[44] Her Turkish lessons with a local teacher are suggestive of these activities.[45] Teachers in 1950s Cyprus were highly respected, especially among the peasantry, as they were literate and educated, and were therefore used by EOKA as conduits for propaganda intended to influence the young. Staying in Cyprus unofficially and therefore, unlike Durrell, unburdened by a colonial public servant's identity, Stark was an unsuspected source of intangible propaganda for the local population. It is clear that she had strong views on both the political situation and what were the most effective diplomatic strategies to address this, writing that: 'if I were a Cypriot Turk I would not waste my time protesting here, but would see to it that Ankara made it quite clear, preferably in private, that she will not stand a purely Greek Cyprus – and of the two, one may be sure that modern Turkey is not the country that will be treated with disregard.'[46] Given her reading of the situation and Stark's extensive propaganda work in the past, it is therefore likely that Stark's interactions with influential local figures were designed to shape public opinion on behalf of Britain.

Stark's methods and observations were not always approved by her counterparts in the colonial administration. In a letter to her publisher and friend John Grey Murray (also publisher of Durrell's and Leigh Fermor's work), she was critical of how the government had failed to identify the Church of Cyprus as the key actor that had to be approached in order to exert influence over the Greek Cypriot population, writing 'we must either be working with this Church or, eventually, fail [. . .] [N]ow I suppose it is too late . . . One can certainly not win out on the track we are going on now, with the spiritual force all on the other side. How silly governments are!'[47] Displaying more honesty and foresight than colonial administrators at this time, Stark intuited that a political union of Cyprus with Greece would not be decided on Cyprus' merits but on relations between Britain, Turkey and Greece, commenting that 'one may be sure that Britain will not seriously offend either of these – intentionally (but I didn't say that)'.[48]

Stark's substantial photographic collection also provides a useful insight into her time in Cyprus, revealing that in addition to documented visits in 1942 and 1956, she also visited the island in 1943, 1952 and 1954.[49] The vast majority of the eighty-two photographs in the collection were taken in 1954, less than a year before EOKA's campaign began. These show extensive interactions with members of both Greek and Turkish Cypriot communities on an informal and personal level, as a tourist being shown around by locals. There are also several photographs of priests, reinforcing the sense that she understood that building a personal connection with the Church was of particular importance.

Propaganda operatives in the Cyprus Revolt

Propaganda, for John M. MacKenzie, can be defined as the 'transmission of ideas and values from one person, or groups of persons, to another, with the specific intention of influencing the recipients' attitudes in such a way that the interests of its authors will be enhanced'.[50] The boundaries between propaganda and other types of information sharing are often blurred: according to Simon J. Potter, information and education 'often blend into one another', and 'it is often in the interests of the propagandist consciously to blur the boundaries that separate them'.[51] Furthermore, the production of propaganda depends on intelligence, and the two functions overlap and inform each other.

During the Cyprus Revolt, systems of this type can be observed in action. 'Grapevine telegraph', or word of mouth, was a significant, useful and effective propaganda method, used by both the Greek Cypriot and British sides.[52] Rumours travelled through the coffee shops, churches and village squares. Collators of gossip, whisperers and informers infiltrated (sometimes successfully, sometimes not) the Greek Cypriot, Turkish Cypriot and other communities in the island. These informers could be Greek Cypriots, mainland Greeks, Turkish Cypriots, British colonial public servants or individuals with clandestine connections visiting Cyprus for this purpose. Field Marshal John Harding, who served as the Governor of Cyprus from 1955 to 1957, said that during the 'Emergency'[53] the colonial police had depended to some extent on what he called 'gossip sources', in the same way as the police had originally done in Malaya during the Emergency there.[54] This, he explained, was due to the lack of intelligence and the lack of an effective intelligence organization in Cyprus. Nevertheless, Harding recalled that these 'gossip sources' were inadequate, as there was no clear or credible information about EOKA, its strengths and its armed men and tactics. Such an absence of reliable information gathering compromised the colonial government's counter-insurgency efforts.

General Georgios Grivas, the military leader of EOKA, accused Harding of misinformation and deception for propaganda purposes, but after the end of the Revolt admitted that during the campaign there were times when he had also used misinformation. According to Grivas, and unlike Greek Cypriots, the 'gentlemen of the Press' were 'easily deluded', a fact that he made use of himself 'when it became necessary. [. . .] At once extraordinary rumours would begin [. . .]. It was a trick that worked however many times it was used'.[55] Grivas used misinformation and rumours not only to influence impressionable foreign press representatives and boost the morale of the Greek Cypriot public, but also to divert British attention. For example, when Grivas feared being caught during a manhunt for his head, he used Deacon Anthimos 'to put out a strong rumour' that he was hiding in the Troodos mountains to divert attention.[56] At the same time, British colonial forces also deployed secret propagandists who infiltrated the local communities in order to influence their representatives and, by extension, the wider community.[57] Stark's relationship with her Turkish Cypriot teacher, and Durrell's, Cardiff's and Leigh Fermor's various friendships with members of the intellectual and artistic elites in Greece and Cyprus can all be viewed in this context.

Both Cardiff and Durrell found themselves in Cyprus during the critical years of the 1950s. Cardiff was the British Council's Representative from 1953 to 1955 and collaborated closely with Durrell, even though the latter was not directly employed by the Council. In Cyprus, the Council offered a safe base from which expatriate writers and cosmopolitans could interact unobtrusively with local society, maintaining a cover if their work crossed into propaganda activities. Both Cardiff and Durrell acted as hosts of several British artists and intellectuals, who could have acted as 'soldier-aesthetes', and who stayed at their houses in Kyrenia and Nicosia, thus facilitating their stay and allowing them to focus on their literary and other endeavours.[58] At this time, Cardiff and Durrell often met at informal and friendly gatherings, at the same time maintaining a professional relationship and working together as part of the activities of their respective organizations (such as social gatherings, film screenings, lectures and art exhibitions).

Leigh Fermor, who was a friend of both, visited Cyprus more than once during the 1950s, either as a writer seeking inspiration for his own literary endeavours, as a British Council lecturer and journalist and sometimes along with his wife Joan Leigh Fermor. Durrell and Leigh Fermor had met back in 1942 in Cairo, the latter being at the time a SOE operative.[59] Leigh Fermor visited Durrell in Cyprus in May 1955 during the inaugural year of the Revolt, merely a month after EOKA's official commencement. During his visit, which was briefly covered in the local Cypriot press, he gave two lectures, one at the British Institute in Nicosia (on 4 May, addressing 'The difficulties of being a travel writer')[60] and one at the Limassol branch (on 'The difficulties and the art of travel writing').[61] One press clipping mentions that Leigh Fermor had previously faced accusations in the Athenian press that he had informed British authorities in Cyprus about the movements of the Greek oil tanker *Agios Georgios*,[62] 'an explosive-laden ship'[63] which had arrived in the village of Chloraka on 25 January 1955, and the contents of which were intended for use by EOKA. Leigh Fermor refuted the accusation and addressed it in a letter published in the Athenian newspaper *Kathimerini*, where he also conveyed his support for the Greek people of Cyprus in their pursuit of self-determination. During his stay, and with Durrell, he even attended the trial for conspiracy of the men captured following the tanker incident in Paphos. Some months later Leigh Fermor published two extensive articles in the *Spectator* in which he publicly voiced his support for the self-determination of Cyprus, ending the second with the following lines: 'It is within our grasp to solve it [the Cyprus crisis] with a courageous and unorthodox decision not only to admit the principle, but to discuss the practice of self-determination and plan the details in concert with the Greeks'.[64] While his published articles overtly express support for the Greek Cypriot cause, there are doubts about the genuineness of this in private correspondence with Greek friends. For example, in a letter Fermor received from George Katsimbalis, Katsimbalis reproaches him for '[his] infinite admiration for Mr Macmillan and Mr Eden, and [his] blind faith in English diplomacy'. Katsimbalis accused the Foreign Office of inciting Turkey against Greece and of kidnapping Archbishop Makarios, exiling him to the Seychelles in 1956 after negotiations over self-determination broke down. Although Katsimbalis acknowledged Leigh Fermor's affection for Greece, he was enraged by Leigh Fermor's inability to see British politics, in the case of Cyprus, for what they were, which he viewed as nothing less than criminal.[65]

In a recent article, Leigh Fermor's philhellenic sentiments are disputed by one researcher who goes so far as to accuse him of being 'basically a classical agent who faithfully served the interests of England and, as a cultured gentleman, wrote good travelogues'.[66] In 1956, Fermor was at least once again in Cyprus as pages from his personal diary confirm,[67] and private correspondence shows that he was in contact with his friend Durrell. Apart from an invited lecture to the British Institutes, Leigh Fermor had also contributed to *The Cyprus Review*, a local British illustrated monthly magazine edited by Durrell.[68] Leigh Fermor's role in the Cyprus Revolt warrants further exploration, but the limited yet significant information we have retrieved so far allows us to begin understanding his contribution.

Official government propaganda

Compared to Patrick Leigh Fermor's enigmatic role, Lawrence Durrell conducted propaganda operations in Cyprus during his stay from 1953 to 1956 officially and openly via press, radio and other cultural diplomatic outlets, while on the British government's payroll. He also developed friendships with many Greek and Cypriot intellectuals and artists such as George Seferis, the Greek Cypriot author Evangelos Louizos and the Greek Cypriot painter and teacher Adamantios Diamantis. Durrell's activities in Cyprus are much better documented than those of any of the other writers examined in this chapter.

Durrell suggested that he came to Cyprus in the hope of finding a peaceful and inexpensive place to write his novel *Justine* (1957). In need of money, his friend Cardiff introduced him to Konstantinos Spyridakis, the headmaster of the Pancyprian Gymnasium in Nicosia, described by Cardiff as 'a known hotbed of anti-British propaganda'.[69] Durrell subsequently managed to secure a job as a teacher of English. In 1955, and again via Cardiff's intercession, Durrell became Director of Information at the Cyprus Public Information Office (later 'Press and Information Office'), much to the disappointment and 'considerable suspicion' of the Greek Cypriots.[70] From 1954 to 1956, he was editor of the *Cyprus Review* (1946–56), after which he left the island.

Under his leadership, the *Cyprus Review* followed the policy of 'communalism', publishing articles and visual material by Greek Cypriot, Turkish Cypriot and

British artists and writers, thus promoting a 'mix-and-match' Cypriot identity.[71] Durrell was tasked with reviving the publication and using it as a medium to gain the Cypriots' support and thus to promote British interests in the island.[72] In a letter to his friend – and contributor to the magazine – Freya Stark, Durrell suggested that the changes he was about to effect in the magazine were intended to make it an instrument of more effective propaganda for the Government: 'I am grappling with the moribund Information Services of the island, trying to make our case against the united howls of Enotists, British Pressmen and fact-finding M.P.s'.[73] Less than a year later, in another letter to Stark, Durrell boasted that although the administration considered it a frivolous publication, the Governor was very pleased with the magazine and it was popular with tourists. He aimed to make the *Review* 'something to stand the government in good stead – something worth owning'.[74] Durrell therefore took a primary role in shaping a cultural identity for Cyprus, promoting this on and outside the island. Indeed, the *Review* was designed for consumption not only by the local population, but also and perhaps more importantly by tourists, journalists and other opinion shapers who visited and then left to narrate Cyprus abroad. Durrell was also responsible for the Cyprus Broadcasting Service, a British radio station based on the island. He aimed to surpass the reach of Athens Radio, which was fervently supportive of the Greek Cypriots' cause during the preparatory years of the Revolt and during the Revolt itself. Durrell considered the radio to be the 'new metal God' of the times.[75]

Durrell was identified by EOKA as a threat to the cause to the extent that, whenever his doorbell rang, he opened his door 'armed with a 12-bore double barrelled shotgun pointed at close range at one's chest' and, in daytime, carried 'a minute pearl-handled pistol stuffed into his breast pocket'.[76] In August 1956, just before he fled Cyprus for France, Durrell wrote that 'after this long spell of Balkan service – nearly seven years flat I feel I need Debarbarizing and re-gilding', and openly expressed his distaste for 'certainly the most obstinate of Mediterranean problems'.[77] Durrell's philhellenic politics may still seem convincing to some, but he did not believe that the Greek Cypriot population of the island was Greek, even though the two shared an identity through their common language, religion and customs. Some Cypriot and Greek intellectuals were fast to pick up his false tone in *Bitter Lemons* (1957) and almost immediately replied to his propaganda through their writings, in Greek and in English. Costas Montis's *Closed Doors: An Answer to Bitter Lemons by Lawrence Durrell* (1964) is perhaps the most prominent example of these texts. In his poem 'Salamis in Cyprus' (1954), Seferis questioned the role of the British in the development of events in late colonial Cyprus. Roufos's novel *The Bronze Age* (1960), set during the events of the Revolt in Cyprus, meanwhile offered an account that provided an implicit contrast to Durrell's. And, increasingly, other novelists and researchers continue to revisit and contest this vision of the era in their writing.[78] Recent research has also critically examined Durrell's role in Cyprus, usually through readings of his literary texts.[79] Detecting 'colonialist nostalgia' in *Bitter Lemons*, Jim Bowman questions Durrell's 'supposed affection for the locals', and suggests that 'Durrell ultimately views Cypriots – Greek and Turkish – as unfit to rule themselves and in need of British steering to usher the poor islanders to modernity's doorstep'.[80]

Conclusion

'[S]ometimes [it] seemed like almost every figure from the literary and scholarly worlds gathered around the Mediterranean after the Second World War.'[81] Cyprus, part of this 'tough neighbourhood',[82] and 'certainly the most obstinate of Mediterranean problems',[83] as Durrell later suggested, was visited in this period by a number of British 'soldier-aesthetes', whose activities in the island remain largely under-researched. In this initial exploration of the figure of the 'soldier-aesthete' in 1950s Cyprus, I have thrown new light on four British authors that during their lifetime, in Cyprus and other territories, served the Crown as propagandists. For Lawrence Durrell and Maurice Cardiff, this claim gains validity primarily via their official roles at the British Council and the Information Services of the colonial government. Freya Stark's and Patrick Leigh Fermor's roles in the Cyprus Revolt remain enigmatic and warrant further research. Nevertheless, their presence in Cyprus at the time suggests that Stark and Fermor may have contributed to the British propaganda effort during the Cyprus Revolt that primarily aimed to safeguard British national interest on the island even after 'the end of Empire'. If these 'irregular warriors' are remembered today, it is primarily because of their literary work, but this chapter has sought to demonstrate that the 'soldier' existed alongside the 'aesthete', by beginning to trace the propaganda roles played by members of the British intelligentsia during their visits to Cyprus.

Notes

1 Freya Stark, *The Journey's Echo: Selections from Freya Stark* (London: John Murray, 1963), 128.

2 Robert D. Kaplan, 'The Humanist in the Foxhole', *New York Times*, 11 June 2011 (http://www.nytimes.com/2011/06/15/opinion/15Kaplan.html?_r=0 [accessed 22 November 2023]).
3 In English the National Organization of Greek Cypriot Fighters.
4 See Alexis Rappas, *Cyprus in the 1930s: British Colonial Rule and the Roots of the Cyprus Conflict* (London: I.B. Tauris, 2014).
5 See Anastasia Yiangou, *Cyprus in World War II: Politics and Conflict in the Eastern Mediterranean* (London: I.B. Tauris, 2012); Marios Siammas, *Cyprus and its Regiment in the Second World War* (London: Palgrave Macmillan, 2023).
6 Indicative bibliography on the Cyprus Revolt includes David M. Anderson, 'Policing and Communal Conflict: The Cyprus Emergency, 1954–60', *Journal of Imperial and Commonwealth History* 21, no. 3 (1993): 177–207; Robert Holland, *Britain and the Revolt in Cyprus, 1954–1959* (Oxford: Oxford University Press, 1998); Andrew R. Novo, *On All Fronts: EOKA and the Cyprus Insurgency, 1955–1959* (PhD thesis, University of Oxford, 2010); David French, *Fighting EOKA: The British Counter-insurgency Campaign on Cyprus, 1955–1959* (Oxford: Oxford University Press, 2015).
7 Frances Donaldson, *The British Council: The First Fifty Years* (London: Jonathan Cape, 1984), 373–6.
8 Undated draft speech by Lord Tyrrell, quoted in Philip M. Taylor, 'Cultural Diplomacy and the British Council: 1934–1939', *British Journal of International Studies* 4, no. 3 (October 1978): 260.
9 For more detail on the activities of the British Council in Cyprus, see Maria Hadjiathanasiou, 'Colonial Rule, Cultural Relations and the British Council in Cyprus, 1935–55', *Journal of Imperial and Commonwealth History* 46, no. 6 (2018): 1096–124.
10 Panagiotis Dimitrakis, 'The Special Operations Executive and Cyprus in the Second World War', *Middle Eastern Studies* 45, no. 2 (March 2009): 321.
11 The National Archives, Kew (hereafter TNA), HS 3/ 120, Captain R.A. Dray to DSO(A), Special Propaganda – Cyprus, Most Secret, 10 March 1944, quoted in Dimitrakis, 'The Special Operations Executive and Cyprus in the Second World War', 321.
12 Ibid.
13 Ibid, 324.
14 TNA, HS 7/85.
15 Ibid.
16 Artemis Cooper, 'Maurice Cardiff: Writer and Cultural Attaché', *The Independent*, 20 May 2006 (https://www.independent.co.uk/news/obituaries/maurice-cardiff-548950.html [accessed 22 November 2023]). Cardiff's service in the SOE (and for the PWE) is also mentioned in a second obituary by Geoffrey Wheatcroft (Wheatcroft, 'Maurice Cardiff: British Council Officer Who Wrote Incognito', *The Guardian*, 20 June 2006 (https://www.theguardian.com/news/2006/jun/20/guardianobituaries

.booksobituaries [accessed 22 November 2023]). Cardiff describes his wartime career in *Achilles and the Tortoise: An Eastern Aegean Exploit* (London: Heinemann, 1958). See also *One Man's Mexico: A Record of Travels and Encounters* (London: The Bodley Head, 1967). Both were published under the pseudonym 'John Lincoln'. *Friends Abroad: Memories of Lawrence Durrell, Freya Stark, Patrick Leigh Fermor, Peggy Guggenheim and others* (London and New York, NY: The Radcliffe Press, 1997) was published under his true name several years later.

17 Maurice Cardiff, *Friends Abroad*, 3.
18 Quoted in Donaldson, *The British Council*, 47. The Greek Civil War took place from 1946 to 1949, between communist opposition and government forces backed by Britain and the United States.
19 Jim Potts, 'Truth Will Triumph: The British Council and Cultural Relations in Greece', in *Greece and Britain Since 1945*, ed. David Wills (Newcastle-upon-Tyne: Cambridge Scholars Publishing, 2010), 115.
20 John Akritas, 'Seferis, Leigh Fermor and the Cyprus Crisis', *Hellenic Antidote*, 4 February 2012 (https://hellenicantidote.blogspot.com/2012/02/seferis-leigh-fermor-and-cyprus-crisis.html [accessed 22 November 2023]).
21 John Ure, 'Fermor, Sir Patrick Michael [Paddy] Leigh', *Oxford Dictionary of National Biography* (http://www.oxforddnb.com/view/article/103763 [accessed 22 November 2023]); see also Artemis Cooper, *Patrick Leigh Fermor: An Adventure* (London: John Murray, 2012), 120–43.
22 Penelope Tremayne, 'Falling for Paddy': Review of Artemis Cooper, *Patrick Leigh Fermor: An Adventure*, *The Salisbury Review* 31, no. 2 (Winter 2012): 38.
23 Patrick Leigh Fermor, *Abducting a General: The Kreipe Operation and SOE in Crete* (London: John Murray, 2014).
24 Cardiff, *Friends Abroad*, 11; Tremayne, 'Falling for Paddy', 38; Katerina Krikos-Davis, 'Sir Steven Runciman and "The Nicest Greek" He Knew: The Chronicle of His Friendship with George Seferis', in *'His Words Were Nourishment and His Counsel Food': A Festschrift for David W. Holton*, ed. Efrosini Camatsos, Tassos A. Kaplanis, and Jocelyn Pye (Newcastle-upon-Tyne: Cambridge Scholars Publishing, 2014), 218.
25 Patrick Leigh Fermor, 'Remembering Steven Runciman', *The Spectator* Archive, 13 January 2001 (http://archive.spectator.co.uk/article/13th-january-2001/43/remembering-steven-runciman [accessed 22 November 2023]).
26 Cardiff, *Friends Abroad*, 11.
27 The inventory of the Sir Patrick Leigh Fermor Archive at the National Library of Scotland suggests that Leigh Fermor corresponded with Durrell and Stark in the period under study here; the archive also features two letters from Cardiff dating from 1988 and 1997. See https://digital.nls.uk/catalogues/guide-to-manuscript-collections/inventories/acc13338.pdf [accessed 22 November 2023].
28 Hadjiathanasiou, 'Colonial Rule, Cultural Relations and the British Council in Cyprus', 1102.

29 Cardiff, *Friends Abroad*, 32.
30 «Κάθε αλλαγή κατοικίας του την περίοδο 1939–54 οφειλόταν σε δευτερεύοντα πόστα απευθείας ή πλαγίως εξαρτημένα από το Φόρειν Όφφις.». G. P. Savvides, 'The "cynical and philhellene" Lawrence Durrell' («Ο 'κυνικός και φιλέλλην' Λορέντζος Δαρέλλης»), *To Vima tis Kyrakis*, 11 November 1990.
31 Durrell's biographer writes that Durrell landed in Limassol on 26 January 1953 (Ian MacNiven, *Lawrence Durrell: A Biography* (London: Faber and Faber, 1998), 386).
32 Peter B. Flint, 'Dame Freya Stark, Travel Writer, is Dead at 100', *New York Times*, 11 May 1993 (https://www.nytimes.com/1993/05/11/obituaries/dame-freya-stark-travel-writer-is-dead-at-100.html [accessed 22 November 2023]).
33 James R. Vaughan, '"A Certain Idea of Britain": British Cultural Diplomacy in the Middle East, 1945–57', *Contemporary British History* 19, no. 2 (2005): 161.
34 Writing in June 1939 Gladwyn Jebb, private secretary to Sir Alexander Cadogan, the Permanent Under-Secretary of State for Foreign Affairs, suggested that 'If war broke out, we might very well have to make some use of Miss Stark's special knowledge and experience'. At this point the Colonial Office and the Ministry of Labour were both keen on securing her services, and Jebb wrote further 'Miss Stark might be of considerable use to some friends of mine in the event of war and I should be very grateful if the Ministry of Labour would allow us to have first claim of her services' (Gladwyn Jebb to H. M. Phillips, 21 June 1939, TNA, CO 732/85/7). During the war Jebb was to serve as chief executive of the SOE.
35 Guy Woodward, '"The Celestial City is as Real as Any Swamp": Freya Stark in the Middle East', 27 February 2019 (https://writersandpropaganda.webspace.durham.ac.uk/2019/02/27/the-celestial-city-is-as-real-as-any-swamp-freya-stark-in-the-middle-east/ [accessed 22 November 2023]).
36 Vaughan, 'A Certain Idea of Britain', 160.
37 Lawrence Durrell, 'Foreword' to Freya Stark, *The Journey's Echo: Selections From Freya Stark* (London: John Murray, 1963), xi.
38 Stark to Harold Bowen, Prodromos, 19 September 1942, in Freya Stark, *Letters. Vol. 4: Bridge of the Levant*, ed. Caroline Moorehead (Salisbury: Michael Russell, 1977), 246.
39 'Nigel Clive', *Daily Telegraph*, 18 May 2001 (https://www.telegraph.co.uk/news/obituaries/1330618/Nigel-Clive.html [accessed 22 November 2023]). Clive, who shared a house in Prodromos with Stark, had served as an MI6 intelligence officer.
40 Stark to Flora Stark, Latakia, 18 August 1942, in Stark, *Letters. Vol. 4*, 238.
41 Stark to John Grey Murray, Kyrenia, 15 December 1952, in Freya Stark, *Letters. Vol. 7: Some Talk of Alexander*, ed. Caroline Moorehead (Salisbury: Michael Russell, 1982), 39.
42 Stark to Grey Murray, Lapithos, 7 April 1956, in Stark, *Letters. Vol. 7*, 152; Jane Fletcher Geniesse, *Freya Stark: Passionate Nomad* (London: Chatto & Windus, 1999), 301, 354.

43 TNA, BW 26/1, British Cultural Propaganda extract from Report by Sir Angus Gillan on a Tour in the Middle East, February–April 1946.
44 Stark to Grey Murray, Kyrenia, 15 December 1952, in Stark, *Letters Vol. 7*, 39.
45 Stark to Grey Murray, Kyrenia, 2 March 1952, in Stark, *Letters Vol. 7*, 66–7.
46 Ibid.
47 Stark to Grey Murray, Kyrenia, 2 February 1952, in Stark, *Letters Vol. 7*, 64–5.
48 Stark to Grey Murray, Kyrenia, 2 March 1952, in Stark, *Letters Vol. 7*, 66–7.
49 The archive is held in the Middle East Centre Archive at St. Antony's College, Oxford, and contains many photographic albums from her travels in Asia, the Middle East, South and South-Eastern Europe.
50 John M. MacKenzie, *Propaganda and Empire: The Manipulation of British Public Opinion 1880–1960* (Manchester: Manchester University Press, 1984), 3.
51 Simon J. Potter, 'Propaganda and Empire', in *The Encyclopedia of Empire*, ed. John M. MacKenzie (Hoboken, NJ: John Wiley & Sons, Ltd., 2016), online.
52 The term 'grapevine telegraph' is used by Penelope Tremayne in her book *Below the Tide* (Boston, MA: Houghton Mifflin; Cambridge: Riverside Press, 1959), 24.
53 Emergency regulations were imposed on 26 November 1955, shortly after Field Marshal Harding took up the island's governorship, and ended in early 1959 with the end of the Revolt.
54 John Harding, Imperial War Museum Interview (Oral History), Reel 41/50, 24:55, https://www.iwm.org.uk/collections/item/object/80008532 [accessed 22 November 2023].
55 Georgios Grivas, *The Memoirs of General Grivas*, ed. Charles Foley (New York, NY: Praeger, 1964), 83.
56 Ibid., 16.
57 See Susan Carruthers, *Winning Hearts and Minds: British Governments, the Media and Colonial Counter-insurgency 1944–1960* (London and New York, NY: Leicester University Press, 1995); David French, *The British Way in Counter-insurgency, 1945–1967* (Oxford: Oxford University Press, 2011); Erik Linstrum, *Ruling Minds: Psychology in the British Empire* (Cambridge, MA and London: Harvard University Press, 2016); Andrew Mumford, *The Counter-insurgency Myth: The British Experience of Irregular Warfare* (Abingdon: Routledge, 2012).
58 Lawrence Durrell to Freya Stark, 1 June 1954, Bellapaix, Cyprus, in Durrell, *Spirit of Place: Letters and Essays on Travel*, ed. Alan G. Thomas (London: Faber and Faber Ltd., 1969), 124; Durrell to Alan G. Thomas, 14 March 1954, Bellapaix Abbey, Cyprus, in Durrell, *Spirit of Place*, 124; Durrell to Thomas, 1953, Bellapaix, Cyprus, in Durrell, *Spirit of Place*, 120.
59 MacNiven, *Lawrence Durrell: A Biography*, 241.
60 Press clipping, *Eleftheria* newspaper, 30 April 1955 (in Greek).
61 Press clipping, *Ethnos* newspaper, 4 May 1955 (in Greek).
62 'Mr Patrick Fermor Arrived in Cyprus', *Ethnos* newspaper, 3 May 1955 (in Greek).

63 Carruthers, *Winning Hearts and Minds*, 196.
64 Patrick Leigh Fermor, 'Friends Wide Apart', 16 December 1955, *The Spectator* Archive (http://archive.spectator.co.uk/issue/16th-december-1955 [accessed 22 November 2023]).
65 Sir Patrick Leigh Fermor Archive, National Library of Scotland, George Katsimbalis, letter to Patrick Leigh Fermor, Athens, 20 March 1956, (original in Greek, translated by M. Hadjiathanasiou). Hereafter 'NLS'.
66 Antonis Sanoudakis, 'Leigh Fermor was a Typical Agent', 5 August 2011 (https://archive.patris.gr/articles/204664 [accessed 22 November 2023 (original in Greek)]).
67 NLS, Journal of Patrick Leigh Fermor: 'England, Greece, Cyprus, March 1956'.
68 NLS, Lawrence Durrell to Patrick Leigh Fermor, 4 July 1955.
69 Cardiff, *Friends Abroad*, 25.
70 Ibid., 28–9.
71 Rita Severis, *'Although to Sight Lost, to Memory Dear': Representations of Cyprus by Foreign Travellers/Artists 1700–1955* (PhD thesis, University of Bristol, 1999), 233.
72 On Durrell, the *Cyprus Review* and the concept of 'Cypriotism' see Maria Hadjiathanasiou, *Propaganda and the Cyprus Revolt: Rebellion, Counter-Insurgency and the Media, 1955–59* (London: Bloomsbury Academic, 2020), 51–9.
73 Durrell to Stark, 1954, Press and Information Office Nicosia (hereafter PIO Nicosia), Cyprus, in Durrell, *Spirit of Place*, 126.
74 Durrell to Stark, 31 March 1955, PIO Nicosia, Cyprus, in Durrell, *Spirit of Place*, 127–8.
75 Vangelis Calotychos, *Modern Greece: A Cultural Poetics* (Oxford and New York, NY: Berg, 2003), 264.
76 Cardiff, *Friends Abroad*, 32.
77 Durrell to Thomas, 1956, PIO. Nicosia, Cyprus, in Durrell, *Spirit of Place,* 129; Durrell, 'This Magnetic, Bedevilled Island that Tugs at My Heart', *Daily Mail*, 22 August 1974, 6.
78 Evripidis Kleopas, '"Cynical and Philhellene": The Political Role of the British Author Lawrence Durrell in Cyprus', *Nea Estia* 1865 (March 2015, in Greek); Ninos Fenek Mikelides, 'Lawrence Durrell: Philhellene or Agent? An Unknown Aspect of the Activity of the Famous British Writer', 25 May 2007 (in Greek), uploaded on *Ta Skonakia Blogspot* on 18 February 2014, see https://ta-skonakia.blogspot.com/2014/02/blog-post.html [accessed 22 November 2023].
79 See José Ruiz Mas, 'Lawrence Durrell in Cyprus: A Philhellene Against *Enosis*,' *EPOS* XIX (2003): 229–43; Calotychos, *Modern Greece: A Cultural Poetics*; Anna Lillios, *Lawrence Durrell and the Greek World* (Cranbury, NJ: Susquehanna University Press, 2004); Hadjiathanasiou, *Propaganda and the Cyprus Revolt*.
80 Jim Bowman, *Narratives of Cyprus: Modern Travel Writing and Cultural Encounters Since Lawrence Durrell* (London and New York, NY: I.B. Tauris, 2014), 40, 53.
81 'Joan Leigh Fermor', *Daily Telegraph*, 5 July 2003 (https://www.telegraph.co.uk/news/obituaries/1434893/Joan-Leigh-Fermor.html [accessed 22 November 2023]).

82 Christopher Hitchens, 'The Last of the Scholar Warriors', *Slate*, 13 June 2011 (https://slate.com/news-and-politics/2011/06/patrick-leigh-fermor-1915-2011-scholar-writer-hero.html [accessed 22 November 2023]).

83 Durrell, 'This Magnetic, Bedevilled Island that Tugs at My Heart', 6.

8

John Bankole Jones, *London Line* and the Central Office of Information in the era of cultural propaganda

Scott Anthony

Created in 1964 and running until 1978, *London Line* became one of the Central Office of Information's (COI's) longest running 'telezines'.[1] From taxi cabs and buses to motorways, electric typewriters and a VC10 jet, the opening titles of *London Line* distilled a self-confident vision of modern Britain into an attractive shorthand, which was then broadcast to audiences across the globe. While the choice of images used by the show may have become familiar, the verve and humour of *London Line's* opening animated sequence cuts against contemporary stereotypes about the COI's output.[2] The film critic David Thomson famously characterized work at the COI, set up in the aftermath of the war as a non-ministerial department, as 'about as an unrewarding experience as it is possible to imagine'.[3] Thomson's judgement remains the dominant view of the COI, which during its sixty-five years of existence served as producer, commissioner and consultant for the UK government's media communications. Yet on television, at mobile film shows and in a variety of civic venues, screenings of series like *London Line* proved that the COI was capable of producing programmes that achieved extraordinary popularity with overseas audiences. The cultural afterimage of the COI may be dour, but during the mid-century, it produced several film series which showed that it was capable of extremely effective work that was fresh, optimistic and confident in its handling of popular culture.[4]

The COI produced four versions of *London Line*: one aimed at 'the Old Commonwealth' (the Dominions of Canada, Australia and New Zealand), one at 'the New Commonwealth' (the newly independent nations in Africa and Asia), one at Latin America and an Arabic edition entitled *Adwa Wa Aswat*.[5] While the edition aimed at the 'Old Commonwealth' swiftly fell out of policy fashion and was rapidly driven to extinction by economic pressures and technological change, 'the New Commonwealth' and Arabic versions of *London Line* retained their popularity and influence with overseas audiences into the mid-1970s.

This chapter focuses on the West African and Caribbean 'New Commonwealth' versions of *London Line*, exploring the genesis of the programme against the backdrop of technological, institutional and policy developments that reshaped British filmic propaganda in the post-war period. It examines shifts in policy and implementation, but also tracks the professional and biographical history of John Bankole Jones and other presenters of *London Line*. The argument here is that in addition to the propaganda value of its content, *London Line* played an even more significant role in linking together a series of professional and personal relationships. Indeed, the formation of these new social networks preceded and enabled the development of new forms of propaganda developed by the COI and other organs of the British state. The rise of the televisual was particularly important to this evolution – whether conscious or not – of the COI's approach.[6] The abrupt shifts of tone, focus and subject visible in *London Line*, alongside the unrelenting pace of televisual production cycles, had the effect of constantly establishing and re-establishing a range of social and professional connections, affinities and assumptions. This was also a form of propaganda that was particularly well suited to the political and social moment. In the post-war era, as attentive commentators such as Jacques Ellul noted, propaganda was no longer about advancing specific political aims but sating the emotional anxieties, needs and desires of an emerging post-industrial middle class.[7] The post-war boom, the demographic shift towards 'youth' and the fracture of old social and political structures created a generational opening for programmes like *London Line* that figures such as Bankole Jones and his peers were able to capitalize on. However, while large media organizations could establish an image of rapid individual and collective ascent, the actual social position of these new media figures remained politically, psychologically and socially precarious. As the post-colonial period progressed, Bankole Jones's fortunes declined precipitously. Ultimately, the argument underpinning this essay is that the content of propaganda was less important to its 'success' than the support it offered to new social and professional patterns. Counter-intuitively, the dissemination of a particular message, or set of messages, was secondary to its role in knitting together new intellectual, cultural and political coalitions.

The post-war resurgence of the British propaganda film

In histories of British cinema, state filmmaking is often still said to end with the dissolution of the Crown Film Unit in 1952. The decision of the Conservative government to scrap the Crown Film Unit has often been characterized as short-sighted, if not nakedly spiteful.[8] Although thinly justified by austerity and the geopolitics of the Cold War, many commentators at the time saw it as an attempt to clip the wings of an activist state. According to this view, it was here that Britain closed off the option to create a high-status national film industry (what we might call 'the French model') and instead accepted specialized roles at the margins of a global film industry dominated by America. Increasingly, the British state's interventions in the film industry would happen at arms-length. In place of the direct government intervention of the Second World War, when an unprecedented wave of cinematic propaganda was produced by the British state, visual media was now posited as a softer tool of cultural relations. State intervention in the film industry would be conducted through tax breaks, seed funding and international partnerships. As far as it existed, state funding for film would be justified on economic grounds as a way to help sell British holidays, goods and services.[9] Instead of the propaganda of political mobilization, there was an attempt to encourage greater consumption.

Aside from the fact that advertising might be considered a particularly insidious form of propaganda, this perspective on the British state's approach to film is deeply simplistic.[10] Unsurprisingly, having developed a taste for intervention, the political impulse to shape the content produced by the nation's media industries did not simply evaporate. Instead, the British propaganda film was reconstituted. One of the legacies of the Second World War was a shared popular understanding of what a propaganda film looked like. The films of directors such as Leni Riefenstahl were codified by critics and educators as impressive, if terrifying, examples of totalitarian cinematic mass manipulation. Accordingly, the mode of propaganda film that developed in post-war Britain avoided aesthetic virtuosity, obvious exaggerations and appeals to transcendence. Instead, the British propaganda film would be muted, mundane and televisual. It would self-consciously engineer reasonableness. By purporting to be apolitical, it would be deeply political.

Central to the post-war resurgence of the propaganda film would be Garrett Ponsonby Moore (1910–89), better known as the Earl of Drogheda. Hailed in his obituaries as the consummate networker who had reinvigorated the Royal Opera House and made the arts pages of the *Financial Times* 'the best in the world', Drogheda was also the protégé of Brendan Bracken, who had served as Minister of Information during the War.[11] The lessons Drogheda drew from his mentor became essential not just to furthering the success of his twin professional passions – opera and the *FT* – but to the lesser-known story that is the reconstitution of the mid-century British propaganda film. Drogheda was an impresario whose professional and financial standing enabled him to create appealing cultural environments where financiers could mingle comfortably with artistic talents such as Georg Solti, as well as intellectuals like Lord Annan and Sir Isaiah Berlin. Drogheda gathered an eclectic mixture of representatives from the world of art, politics and business to try and build a new consensus to promote Britain's overseas information services. His personal networks would provide the initial social and cultural basis for the Conservative government's expansive approach to overseas propaganda.

Throughout the 1950s, Drogheda's name became attached to a range of articles and reports that gave voice to the cultural preferences of both his cultural and economic circles, as well as the elements of the British state – including, apparently, the Secret Intelligence Services – who regretted the Conservative retreat from the state production of information.[12] While his reports initially made little political headway, having kept the flame of government information alive, the ideas and human infrastructure that Drogheda had laid out in advance were perfectly positioned to take advantage of the surge in government spending on overseas propaganda which was the legacy of the Suez Crisis of 1956.[13] Between 1954 and 1962, the budget of the COI's film and TV division increased from £170,000 to over £1.5 million.[14] Importantly, the growing global demand for televisual content saw the COI move away from film into the field of telemagazine programmes that could be edited and reconfigured to suit local needs. Programmes like *London Line* therefore emerged as a preferred format for navigating this new technological and political climate. It could be screened at embassies and special events, included in the programme of touring mobile film shows, as well as used by independent national and local television stations. Even *London Line*'s striking credits had been designed to work on their own, so that, in the words of Linda Kaye, they 'effectively functioned in a similar way to an advertisement, distilling Britain into a single package lasting around twenty seconds'.[15] It was a format of production and distribution that arguably worked against high culture. Instead of the artistic or intellectual avant-garde, the focus became the everyday concerns of 'the informed citizen'. Unlike the stately prestige of the propaganda film, televisual propaganda was both culturally innocuous and relatively cheap.

John Hall, who worked as Director of the COI's Films Division in the 1980s, remembered a British ambassador to the United States once complaining that he was not interested in talking to 'little people', but the Foreign Office increasingly realized that winning over wider public opinion had become a prerequisite for securing a sympathetic hearing with political leaders.[16] Or, as Drogheda put it, 'the government must concern itself with public opinion abroad and be properly equipped to deal with it.'[17] Existing practices of diplomacy were reordered and reemphasized as they were translated into the formats of new media technology. In the immediate post-war period, this concern with popular opinion tended to entail a focus on cultural attainment. In the context of the Cultural Cold War, this sensitive approach was also thought to contrast favourably with the ideological nature of communist propaganda.[18] To this end, COI programmes championed the increasing accessibility of 'high' British political values and culture. For example, the working-class soprano Rita Hunter became a staple of COI film programmes for overseas audiences in the early 1960s. However, as the decade progressed, the subjects of veneration began to shift from idiosyncratic characters like Hunter towards 'pacemakers', a new generation of professionals 'shaking up' the established conventions of British society. In the British propaganda film, middle-class radicals began to nudge aside working-class aspirants as campaigning lawyers, social workers and educators moved to the centre. Rather than celebrating working-class advancement through old social scales, COI films began to advance an image of a burgeoning new middle class in formation.

We can plot the rapid emergence of this trend in the shifting editorial emphasis visible in *London Line*. Many of the people interviewed by the programme were well on their way to becoming figureheads of this new Britishness. Figures such as the journalist and agony aunt Marjorie Proops became part of a familiar conveyor belt of British experts and talking heads used by the COI to tackle a broad range of political debates and social issues. Engineers, educators and doctors were pushed to the foreground of the new British propaganda film, as well as popular crazes, sport and the emergence of a new generation of celebrities that had begun to take advantage of the platform offered by new media technologies. Alongside the celebration of new literary works, *London Line* featured items celebrating prefabricated buildings, affordable fashions and new media trends. Although the programmes are infused with a sense of propriety – overseas viewers often expressed the need for the presenters to speak English 'properly'[19] – the programme also played on a widespread desire to comprehend the new forces shaping the world. By the mid-century, the COI was producing a wide range of biography-led cinemagazines for foreign audiences including *British Sporting Personalities* (1959–62), *Moslems in Britain* (1961–4), *Commonwealth Review* (1964–5), *The Enthusiasts* (1967) and *The Pacemakers* (1969–71). Instead of high politics, the films of the COI shaped an era that I have elsewhere characterized as being dominated by the cultural propaganda film.[20] '*London Line* reflected the optimism and confidence which had invaded almost every aspect of British life', remembered Hannah Neale (then Bright-Taylor), one of the shows' presenters, 'youth power had taken over; innovation, creativity, dynamism in fashion, music, art and culture all had new and exciting forms of expression. The skirts of the female presenters got shorter, and the men had brighter shirts.'[21]

Perhaps predictably, *London Line* was especially attracted to political debates and social issues that effected new professions in the cultural industries. There is an argument that *London Line* existed to reflect, and was mainly 'about', contemporary media discourse. Indeed, other than relatively high rates of pay, one of the appeals of the show for freelancers was the opportunities it provided for introductions to industry moguls such as Lord Thomson of Fleet who, through his control of newspapers, television companies and publishing concerns, was already shaping a future that would be defined by supranational cross-media ownership. Here, it is instructive to compare Drogheda's vision for overseas audiences against more programmatically anti-communist activities aimed at domestic audiences. Christopher Mayhew, the Labour MP responsible for creating the Information Research Department, wrote instead of the importance of harnessing working-class suspicion of surveillance, officiousness and the idea of state informers.[22] While domestically anti-communism was often negatively defined as a threat to hard won freedoms, for overseas audiences, greater weight was placed on stories which stressed the expansiveness, relatability and attractiveness of Western trends. Presenters like John Bankole Jones bemoaned the amount of 'lifestyle' pieces *London Line* produced, seemingly without recognizing that this output was to some extent calculated to both flatter and excite the tastes of an emerging post-colonial elite. The British propaganda film offered a world defined by relative plasticity, prosperity and individual freedoms.

London Line and the new world of cultural propaganda

'Cultural work was bringing British life and thinking to many parts of the world', wrote the politician Charles Hill; 'for a philistine who would rather go to the

Crazy Gang than to *Godot* this is saying a great deal.'[23] Hill's appointment as coordinator of government information services in 1957 was both essential to systemizing Drogheda's vision and to the purging of 'politics' from the British propaganda film. Working in tandem with Harold Evans, a PR manager Harold MacMillan had recruited from the Colonial Office, Hill attempted to steer the British overseas services away from potential sources of aggravation by avoiding topics liable to cause embarrassment or friction. There was a technological motivation for this – for instance, the increasing availability of both televisions and short-wave radios among local elites encouraged greater attention to private individual desires – as well as an ideological one. Sweeping decolonization against the backdrop of the Cold War necessitated the development of new social and cultural affiliations able to circumnavigate ideological friction.

Across the information services, Hill's direction strengthened the position of the technicians, artists and teachers that would be responsible for maintaining Britain's international reputation. Once the parameters of political acceptability had been safely established, Hill was able to free the practitioners of British cultural propaganda from strict administrative oversight. Where high diplomacy had failed, lines of cultural communication could still operate through the distribution of subsidized textbooks, the organization of cultural tours and the awarding of educational scholarships. Gordon Johnston and Emma Robertson have described how, during the immediate post-war period, the focus of the BBC's Overseas Services shifted away from servicing 'British exiles' towards attracting foreign audiences.[24] This strategic shift had important ramifications for how overseas listeners were imagined. Britain was no longer positioned as 'the mother country', but instead the BBC attempted to adopt a breezy descriptive style that – in its own estimation – would be tourist-compelling. With the reconstitution of the BBC Overseas Services into the BBC World Service in 1965, the task of representing Britain to non-Britons moved further to the fore. The resulting output aimed for a colour-blind African version of affluent Britishness.

To an extent, we can understand the creation of *London Line* against the reconfiguration of the BBC's Overseas Services. In the case of many West African countries, the BBC's output was apparently valued because it gave local populations the opportunity to hear news of relatives and compatriots working or studying in the UK. The deluge of letters, postcards and Christmas cards received by *London Line* demonstrates a similar dynamic was at work in the COI. Indeed, the vast majority of the COI's presenters were recruited from the BBC.[25]

Britain was to be projected overseas through the eyes of local interlocutors. The employment of African presenters in *London Line* both accompanied and followed a shift in approach across the British information services. There was an attempt to create a media environment that was homely for international elites. While news programmes criticized the centralizing impulses of 'imperial' Soviet Russia, the outputs of the COI, the BBC and the British Council began promoting diasporic cultures in Britain back to former colonies while at the same time enthusing about the reception that visiting artists, broadcasters and writers from the Commonwealth received in Britain.

To give a particularly striking example of how the information services were able to link together a diverse range of activity, after the South African musical *King Kong* toured the West End in 1961, a small nucleus of the actors and actresses involved in the production opted to remain in the UK.[26] The presence of this émigré talent encouraged the BBC to commission young African writers to develop radio plays.[27] This patronage helped nurture a range of interesting and increasingly influential cultural figures as, after first airing on the BBC World Service, the work of writers like Obi Egbuna, Ngũgĩ wa Thiong'o and Efua Sutherland subsequently reached British audiences through repeats on the BBC Third Programme. By running interviews with playwrights like Badamassie Mahdi, as well as poets and writers such as John Ruganda, and through a range of writing competitions, *London Line* played an important role in fostering a new strand of post-colonial African culture.

The programme's presenters also made important contributions to this strand. The Nigerian dramatist Wole Soyinka wrote 'The Detainee', about the aftermath of a coup, for the BBC World Service in 1965. The following year, the station broadcast extracts of Soyinka's play *The Lion and the Jewel* as it premiered at the Royal Court Theatre in London. Widely acclaimed on its debut, *The Lion and the Jewel* starred the *London Line* presenters Jumoke Debayo, Hannah Neale and Lionel Ngakane. Debayo and Ngakane both went on to develop impressive careers in theatre, film and television. COI productions such as *London Line* were thus so integrated into the British state's communication apparatus that they were capable of representing, embodying and actively shaping important new cultural strands. In propaganda terms, the value of this output was in creating a 'British' response to an emerging form of affluent modernity. While the Americans sold consumer products, the British sold a different kind of aspirational cultural discernment that could be exported overseas through education, publishing and a variety of popular commercial media. Social and cultural interactions, rather than high politics, were *London Line*'s focus. As much as shaping the politics of a new generation, the propaganda film of the mid-century would sell the mores of an increasingly internationalized middle class.

James Bankole Jones: The biography of an African correspondent

Over the course of its history, *London Line* provided an apprenticeship for many interesting and significant cultural and political figures. Although it was fronted by a rotating team of presenters, James Bankole Jones was something of a figurehead for the programme and was the only presenter to have featured in the opening credits of the 'New Commonwealth' version.[28] The complexity and contradictions of Bankole Jones's professional life exemplified many of the struggles faced by his peers.

When I interviewed former COI producers, they disparaged the idea that the presenters of *London Line* played a significant role in the propaganda value of the programme,[29] their rationale for this being that while they may have been valued for their presentation skills, figures like Bankole Jones were not employed as reporters, and did not write scripts or choose subjects. 'The versions for Nigeria feature a Nigerian artist', as COI guidelines explained, 'similarly, an Indian artist is seen in the Indian version, but the bulk of the shooting is in common to all versions.'[30] Each line of every script was signed off by civil servants. Presenters were given precise instructions on how and when to move around the set. Bankole Jones even described himself as 'an insignificant cog in a vast societal machine'.[31] However, as Tom Rice argued in his study of the Colonial Film Unit (1939–55), the employment of local presenters had long played a central role in determining how propaganda films were received by local audiences.[32] By weaving jokes and stories into screenings, the Colonial Film Unit ensured its work became part of a dynamic social infrastructure where new associations and friendships could be forged. Indeed, this approach to propaganda film was well established. The belief that media activism could only be effective if it collated and amplified existing strands of civic activism had been a cornerstone of Sir Stephen Tallents's work in the 1930s.[33] As the inaugural president of the Institute of Public Relations, Tallents developed ideas and an ethos at organizations like the Empire Marketing Board and the GPO Film Unit during the interwar period that were slowly codified into accepted post-war practices.[34] Not only does *London Line* sit squarely in this tradition, but beyond his role as a sympathetic 'interpreter' for the COI, Bankole Jones's life story provides insights into both the operation and longer-term impacts of British propaganda.

Born out of wedlock to a White English mother and a Black Sierra Leonean father (Sir Samuel Bankole Jones, who from the 1960s served as a Chief Justice and as Acting Governor General), Bankole Jones was fascinated by the nature of personal and political identity. In his autobiography, entitled *A Mother's Dilemma. An English Mother. An African Father. England, 1936* (2018), Bankole Jones recounted his mother's decision to foster him while his father moved back to Africa, married and built a new life: 'She stubbornly resisted societal disapproval and was determined to keep me', he reflected, 'she did not want me around, but she never let me go either'.[35] While Bankole Jones's early years in Britain were relatively modest – he would reminisce about holidays in Weston-super-Mare – he lived a privileged life in Sierra Leone. As a young man, he contrasted the abundance of family life in Freetown with the dirt, decadence and squalor of London. His British family were down-at-heel snobs ('We are descendants of the Duke of Wellington!'),[36] but his family in Sierra Leone sent him to an exclusive public school.

This ambivalence – and lack of centre – appears to have become a running theme of Bankole Jones's life. As an admirer of James Baldwin and Stokely Carmichael, he was thrilled to win a scholarship to study in America during the heyday of the Civil Rights movement. But while in the United States he came to believe that 'today's Africans are no longer part of black American history', as a visiting student at Howard University, the leading African American university, Bankole Jones described the uncomfortable relationship that existed between African and American students. 'Africans two or three generations removed from the slave trade cannot be held responsible for the sale of their brothers into slavery', he wrote, 'we should acknowledge the past, lay it to rest and move on.'[37] Towards the end of his life Bankole Jones reflected that he had been born at a time when there was still a great divide between white and Black. His mother both complained that 'the country (Britain) had gone to the dogs' since the arrival of Black immigrants from Africa and the West Indies, but also that 'you (Bankole Jones) are thoroughly British and don't you forget it.'[38] At the same time, he recounted how Syrian and Lebanese migrants were discriminated against in Sierra Leone and how even uglier ethnic and tribal divisions tore through the post-colonial state. Eventually, Bankole Jones married a Fijian woman of Indian ethnic origin. It seems a reasonable supposition that Bankole Jones's work as a propagandist was partly enabled by his cosmopolitan professional affinities outweighing more rooted forms of personal identity.

By his own admission, the BBC played an important role in socializing Bankole Jones, providing both a professional identity and an institutional anchor for social and political advancement. Examining his BBC files, it is striking how often Bankole Jones interviewed journalists: interviewees included *Sunday Times* editor Harold Evans, Richard West and a young Peter Kellner. When working for the BBC in America, he recounted being so overawed in the presence of Charles Wheeler, the BBC's long-serving foreign correspondent, that he was unable to speak. Insights drawn from Lord Denning's radio lectures pepper his memoir.

Meanwhile, flagship BBC radio programmes such as *From Our Own Correspondent*, *My Word*, and *Letter from America* became important forums for the testing and retesting of his attitudes to Britain. Bankole Jones's work for the BBC also provided the fostered child with 'the one and only occasion that I can recall on which I was ever allowed to introduce her to everyone as my Mother. It was the only way she could take personal credit for what she considered a massive achievement'.[39] With such itinerant personal circumstances, as well as an upbringing lacking emotional intimacy, it is perhaps unsurprising that an institution like the BBC would play an important role in Bankole Jones's life. He later reflected:

> I embraced my broadcasting career with enthusiasm. I thought I was more important than I actually was. I perceived journalism as being not too dissimilar from law. In both professions the journalist and the lawyer stood up for and advocated for justice . . . I liked the idea and was proud to be part of it, although I did precious little to influence or change anything. I knew that the BBC was not as independent as it made itself out to be and was an instrument of British propaganda, especially its overseas services. I did write critical pieces contrary to the established view, but they were heavily edited by my radio producers until they lost their import.[40]

Although he dismissed much of his work on the BBC programme *Calling Sierra Leone* as 'a propaganda tool for all things British', this bias is less evident from the surviving scripts. During his time at the BBC, Bankole Jones made programmes on 'African Universities', 'African Law' and 'The African Intellectual', as well as on cults, missionaries and the prospects for African socialism.[41] He also interviewed figures such as Dr Milton Obote, Ali Al'amin Mazrui and Professor A. A. Kwapong.

Indeed, before the political failures of post-colonial Africa were so obviously manifest (post-colonial Africa, he reflected, had been governed by 'a rollercoaster of corrupt and self-seeking morons'),[42] Bankole Jones often exhibited an ambitious impatience with his colleagues at the BBC and the COI. For example, Bankole Jones sharply and publicly criticized how Cold War politics shaped the forms in which capital, know-how and machinery were offered to newly independent African nations while covering a conference on 'Aid to Africa' at Rhodes Hall, University of Oxford, for *London Line*.

While he may not have been able to set the editorial direction to the degree that he wished, Bankole Jones did manoeuvre himself into a role which would enable him practically to address the economic and social problems raised by his media work. As he admitted himself, the BBC World Service operated as 'a form of social networking'.[43] Bankole Jones both interviewed influential Sierra Leonian figures such as John Akar and later followed them into senior careers in diplomacy and broadcasting in post-colonial Sierra Leone. Indeed, his friends and colleagues from public school in Africa and the BBC became a *Who's Who* of post-independence Sierra Leone. He may have felt 'an insignificant cog in a vast societal machine', but Bankole Jones used his position to help secure his place in post-colonial politics.

In 1970, Bankole Jones became Press and Information Attaché in London for Siaka Stevens, the then Prime Minister of Sierra Leone. Later, Bankole Jones was given responsibility for the creation of the Sierra Leone News Agency and the reorganization of the Ministry of Information. He continued working for the Sierra Leonian government until 1980, when threats to his life led Bankole Jones to flee West Africa, return to London and join the UK's Crown Prosecution Service.

Conclusion

In Britain, the world of secular filmic propaganda grew out of the bureaucratic conviction that if the internal life of the nation could be made visible, it would renew the bonds between 'the masses' and Britain's elites that had been threatened by the rise of communism: intervention in the private psychological sphere could be justified in order to shape the emergence of a newly democratized public sphere. Broadly, by bringing together a large coalition of what Arthur Marwick termed 'middle opinion', victory in the Second World War was seen to have vindicated this strategy.[44] Yet new ideological (Cold War), political (decolonization) and technological (televisual) challenges, along with economic and generational shifts, entailed a gradual but substantive reformulation of the sociological assumptions of the interwar propaganda film. Post-war practices accordingly saw a shift away from collective experiences and towards the brokering of transnational affinities. The national was now more usually communicated through stories of iconic individuals setting new intellectual, cultural and consumer fashions. The eclecticism of *London Line*, in which a single episode could jump wildly from development economics to sport, poetry and medicine, exemplifies this transition. Formats first popularized by newsreels in the interwar years would become dominant in the post-war era.

We can also see the growth of cultural propaganda like *London Line* as part of a larger governmental attempt to usher society away from ideological extremes. Unlike the propaganda films of the early twentieth century, COI telemagazines lent themselves to a mode of visual communication that emphasized disjuncture, critical distance and a recognition of the complex and multifactorial genesis of new ideas. The televisual magazine show was no friend of the revolutionary vanguard. But perhaps this reading is too complacent. In a series of books published in the mid-century, the French scholar Jacques Ellul argued that modern society had been captured by the logic of the machine (which he called 'technique'),[45] setting in chain a kind of technocratic reordering of society that undermined individual human autonomy. In this brave new world, propaganda became a social necessity, functioning as a mechanism to soothe the social, physiological and psychological stress caused by the perpetual reordering of the human environment.[46] Ellul's work also challenged the assumptions of twentieth-century theorists of propaganda, who had tended to focus on the manipulability of 'the masses'. Instead, Ellul argued that because intellectuals, writers and film makers were employed in the psychological, technological and sociological reshaping of the world, they were also the groups most exposed to, and susceptible to, its claims.[47] By contrast, ignorance, indifference and the pressures of everyday life often had the effect of inoculating ordinary people from the excesses of propaganda. Bankole Jones came to agree.

By the end of his career Bankole Jones saw youth, personal ambition and insulation from social and historical reality as prerequisites for a career as a propagandist. He realized that not only had he been shaped by the propaganda he disseminated, but he had ultimately become politically and socially trapped by it. 'I believed that I could have been an agent for curbing the abuses and excesses of power', Bankole Jones admitted, 'I had deceived myself that it was better for me to remain in the system.'[48] Bankole Jones's experience led him towards a more generous acceptance of human fragility and limitation, as well as a recognition of the importance of religious faith. As an old man, Bankole Jones held an overwhelmingly negative view of the mass media, along with the vanity, superficiality and impatience he believed it encouraged. 'As a lawyer and a journalist myself I fervently believed in democracy, the freedom of the press and the rule of law', he reflected, 'it never even occurred to me to question their appropriateness or workability in the developing countries into which they were imported.'[49] The hunger for rapid development he had expressed while working for the COI had been replaced by a much more cautious espousal of the importance of honesty, discernment and incremental improvement. While the development of the propaganda film in the early twentieth century reflected political anxieties provoked by working-class enfranchisement, Drogheda's mid-century reforms had fed into an emerging type of propaganda film that existed to manage the social anxieties of a new middle class.

Notes

1 With thanks to the editors, Alice Byrne, Peter Mandler and Martin Stollery for constructive feedback on an earlier draft.
2 See, for example, David Robertson, 'Spending Cuts Drive Deep and Charley Says It No More', *The Times*, 24 June 2011, 47.
3 David Thomson, 'John Grierson', *A Biographical Dictionary of Film* (London: Deutsch, 1994), 305.
4 For a more balanced post-war history see David Welch, *Protecting the People: The Central Office of Information and the Reshaping of Post-War Britain, 1946–2011* (London: British Library, 2019).
5 A full list of *London Line* episodes can be found at the British Universities Film and Video website: http://bufvc.ac.uk.
6 This was also a process later observed by Roger Silverstone in *Television and Everyday Life* (London: Routledge, 1994).
7 See Jacques Ellul, *The Technological Society*, trans. John Wilkinson (New York, NY: Vintage Books, 1964) and *Propaganda: The Formation of Men's Attitudes*, trans. Konrad Kellen and Jean Lerner (New York, NY: Vintage Books, 1965).
8 See Alan J. Harding, 'The Closure of the Crown Film Unit in 1952: Artistic Decline or Political Machinations?', *Contemporary British History* 18, no. 4 (2004): 24–5.
9 See Andrew Higson, *Film England: Culturally English Filmmaking Since the 1990s* (London: I.B. Tauris, 2011), 40–2.
10 See, for example, Steve McKevitt, *The Persuasion Industries: The Making of Modern Britain* (Oxford: Oxford University Press, 2018).
11 'Lord Drogheda', *Financial Times*, 28 December 1989, 11.
12 *Summary of the Report of the Independent Committee of Enquiry into the Overseas Information Services* (London: HM Stationery Office, 1954).
13 Fife Clark, *The Central Office of Information* (London: George Allen & Unwin, 1970), 40.
14 Linda Kaye, 'Reconciling Policy and Propaganda: The British Overseas Television Service, 1954–1964', in *Projecting Britain: The Guide to British Cinemagazines*, ed. Emily Crosby and Linda Kaye (London: British Universities Film & Video Council, 2008), 75.

15 Ibid., 89.
16 John Hall, personal communication, 7 October 2019.
17 Quoted in Kaye, 'Reconciling Policy and Propaganda', 73.
18 See Frances Stonor Saunders, *Who Paid the Piper? The CIA and the Cultural Cold War* (London: Granta Books, 1999).
19 Private information passed to the author.
20 Scott Anthony, *The Story of Propaganda Film* (London: BFI, forthcoming).
21 Hannah Neale, personal communication, 9 June 2020.
22 See Andrew Defty, *Britain, America, and Anti-Communist Propaganda, 1945–1953: The Information Research Department* (Abingdon: Routledge, 2004); Lashmar and Oliver, *Britain's Secret Propaganda War 1948–1977*; Christopher Mayhew, *Time to Explain* (London: Hutchinson, 1987); Lyn Smith, 'Covert British Propaganda, The Information Research Department: 1947–77', *Millennium: Journal of International Studies* 9, no. 1 (1980): 67–83.
23 Lord Hill of Luton, *Both Sides of the Hill: The Memoirs of Charles Hill* (London: Heinemann, 1964), 190.
24 See Gordon Johnston and Emma Robertson, *BBC World Service: Overseas Broadcasting, 1932–2018* (London: Palgrave Macmillan, 2019), 223–79.
25 Following up on personal interviews, I worked my way through the BBC files of John Bankole Jones, Arnold Gordon and Hannah Neale (née Bright-Taylor).
26 See Shirley Cordeaux, 'The BBC African Service's Involvement in African Theatre', *Research in African Literatures* 1, no. 2 (Autumn 1970): 147–55.
27 John Wyver is doing interesting work on this. See John Wyver, 'Obi Egbuna and the BBC: The Story Continued', *Illuminations* blog, 10 July 2020 (https://www.illuminationsmedia.co.uk/obi-egbuna-and-the-bbc-the-story-continued [accessed 13 November 2023]).
28 For example, Lord Paul Boateng, Britain's first black cabinet minister (and first High Commissioner) worked on the show as a presenter in the 1970s. See Scott Anthony, '"These Were Stars!": How a Forgotten Teleseries Put Swinging London on the Map', BFI Interviews, 2 November 2021 (https://www.bfi.org.uk/features/london-line-paul-boateng [accessed 13 November 2023]).
29 I'm grateful to John Hall for putting me in touch with a number of his former COI colleagues. Hall has also built an excellent online resource detailing the work of the COI Film Division at: https://www.coifilms.co.uk [accessed 13 November 2023].
30 Quoted in Kaye, 'Reconciling Policy and Propaganda', 87.
31 John Edward Bankole Jones, *A Mother's Dilemma. An English Mother. An African Father. England, 1936* (New York, NY: Novum, 2018), 180.
32 See Tom Rice, *Films for the Colonies: Cinema and the Preservation of the British Empire* (Oakland, CA: University of California Press, 2019).
33 Stephen Tallents, *The Projection of England* (London: Faber, 1932), reprinted in Scott Anthony, *Public Relations and the Making of Modern Britain* (Manchester: Manchester University Press, 2012), 234–5.

34 See Anthony, *Public Relations* for a full account of this.
35 Bankole Jones, *A Mother's Dilemma*, 13.
36 Ibid., 168–9.
37 Ibid., 190.
38 Ibid., 167.
39 Ibid., 181.
40 Ibid., 179–80.
41 See BBC Written Archives Centre, Caversham, John Bankole Jones (8 files).
42 Bankole Jones, *A Mother's Dilemma*, 238.
43 Ibid., 132–3.
44 See Arthur Marwick, 'Middle Opinion in the Thirties: Planning, Progress and Political "Agreement"', *The English Historical Review* 79, no. 331 (April 1964): 285–98.
45 See Ellul, *The Technological Society*.
46 See Jacob E. Van Vleet and Jacob Marques Rollinson, eds., *Jacques Ellul: A Companion to His Major Works* (Eugene, OR: Cascade Books, 2020).
47 David Graeber argued that the growth of post-industrial 'bullshit jobs' had the effect of encouraging people to identify with the perspectives and sensibilities of administrators, managers and officials. It may be that this is also an important political consequence of Britain's over-sized public relations industry. See David Graeber, *Bullshit Jobs: A Theory* (London: Allen Lane, 2018).
48 Bankole Jones, *A Mother's Dilemma*, 207.
49 Ibid., 187.

9

The British Council, *Writers and Their Work* and literature as cultural diplomacy

James Smith

This chapter investigates the history of the British Council's work in Cold War cultural diplomacy and specifically examines the role the Council's literary guides played in projecting British cultural prestige in the post-war era. Today, the British Council has a ubiquitous role in the international educational and artistic community. It is run as an 'executive non-departmental public body' which, although allocated a 'government grant in aid', remains 'operationally independent from the UK government'.[1] It has a presence in more than one hundred countries, with its website stating that its mission is to 'support peace and prosperity by building connections, understanding and trust between people in the UK and countries worldwide', and will be particularly familiar to many international students for its role in teaching English as a second language.[2]

Given this contemporary presence and benevolent mission statement, it is easy to overlook the fact that the British Council is one of the world's most enduring and successful organizations conducting 'cultural propaganda' – a term used in 1934 by its founder, Rex Leeper, the senior Foreign Office official who later went on to become a director of the wartime Political Warfare Executive (PWE).[3]

However, while the Council was established to counter the propaganda of other states by 'the projection abroad of British cultural values, attitudes and achievements',[4] its role was never to generate the types of directly government-controlled propaganda created by conflict-focused agencies such as (respectively) the Ministry of Information (MOI), the Information Research Department (IRD) or the PWE. Instead, the British Council had a distinctive mission as a 'peacetime' propaganda agency that worked by building incremental and long-term positive projections of Britain; or, as the 1953 Drogheda Report described, an organization that used the 'long-term investment' of (ostensibly) 'strictly non-political' methods of cultural and educational interaction that nonetheless might result in 'considerable political or commercial benefit [. . . but] only after a period of years'.[5]

Despite its extensive role within the global cultural diplomacy apparatus since the Second World War, the British Council largely remains a missing dimension in current scholarship on Cold War propaganda and the Cultural Cold War.[6] To remedy this lacuna, this chapter will specifically examine the British Council's *Writers and Their Work* (1950–) series of literary study guides, with particular focus on the evolution of the series across its first thirty years of publication. Launched in 1950 as a supplement to the already established *British Book News* magazine, over its initial decades *Writers and Their Work* was published in collaboration with Longmans, Green & Co, the UK's oldest commercial publisher which since 1884 had sought to build its 'educational lists and to develop markets in India and elsewhere'.[7] With monthly issues of what initially were little more than simple pamphlets, the series rapidly became recognized by scholars and students for its concise yet confident introductions to major authors or topics in British literature, with the material specifically commissioned from many of the most prominent scholars and critics of the modern era (early contributors included T. S. Eliot, David Gascoyne, Herbert Read, Stephen Spender and Rex Warner). Having developed across several formats over the decades, the series is now published by Liverpool University Press and continues to occupy a ubiquitous if unassuming presence on the bookshelves of literature students around the world, with its most recent evolution seeing current volumes digitized and available as ebooks.

In its early years, however, *Writers and Their Work* was envisaged by the Council and its contributors as more than an introductory pedagogical tool, and was promoted as a vessel through which positive ideological connections could be forged with a new generation of receptive intellectuals in the wider world. As the poet (and contributor to the series) Edmund Blunden proclaimed in an article in the *Times Literary Supplement* (*TLS*) in 1951, the volumes of *Writers and Their Work* could uniquely serve as 'emissaries' to reach 'the university type of reader in the East', with the 'literary imagination' offering the 'avenue which lies most open and understood between East and West' at a time when other 'political questions' have generated 'suspicion of the West'.[8] In what follows, I therefore pursue this case study across several tracks. First, I contextualize the broader operations of the British Council and the development of its publishing programmes with the aim of promoting British literary studies, before surveying the launch of the *Writers and Their Work* series, its editors and the critical position of its early works. In later sections of the chapter, I consider how the series was received by the academic community and how policy debates within the British Council itself shaped its evolving focus. Overall, this chapter seeks to shed new light on the operations of the British Council itself and, through this, illuminate a key example of the role cultural diplomacy organizations played in the post-war globalization of English literary studies as a discipline.[9]

The British Council and post-war cultural diplomacy

Emerging from what was initially called 'The British Committee for Relations with Other Countries' in 1934 with a modest budget of just £5000, the British Council gained its official name in 1936 and assumed the cultural roles of the Foreign Office News Department (the branch of the Foreign Office tasked with briefing the media and foreign correspondents in London).[10] The Council grew rapidly: by the beginning of the Second World War, its grant was £330,249, and its chairman Lord Lloyd could confidently advocate to the Foreign Secretary, Lord Halifax, that 'I believe more and more [. . .] that it is worth armies battleships & aeroplane and that its effect – unlike those agencies' is both lasting and beneficial'.[11] The Council gained a further degree of independence in 1940 with the granting of its Royal Charter. As Edward Corse has demonstrated, the Council proved a key diplomatic arm for the British government during the war, and Donaldson records that by 1945–6 it commanded a grant-in-aid of £3,500,000.[12] In the post-war period, it addressed the tasks of European reconstruction and was also given an increased presence in the Dominions and Colonies, and from 1948 the Colonial Office delegated to the Council 'activity in the cultural and educational sphere of which the chief purpose is the "projection" of the British way of life and the promotion of closer relations in cultural matters between the people of Great Britain and people of the Colonies'.[13]

Across these political contexts and geographical spheres, the promotion and dissemination of British literature was one of the Council's core activities. The Council's Books and Periodicals Committee (whose members included the Poet Laureate John Masefield and the publisher Stanley Unwin) first met in 1935 to identify 'books [and] periodical' to distribute to 'societies, libraries and institutions' recommended by British embassies.[14] This concern persisted across the twentieth century: later British Council officials described in the 1990s that the organization saw 'the book as an unrivalled vehicle for the transmission of ideas and culture. Books are inexpensive, durable, need no maintenance, travel easily and without complaint and never fall ill or have off days'.[15] To conduct its activity, the Council constructed an impressive international network of operations which included fixed premises, cultural officers and ad hoc events. By 1949 it had established what was claimed to be (at the time) the most geographically extensive library system in the world, and boasted of having 'as far as possible [. . .] a main British Council library in each capital in Europe and the Middle East, and smaller institute libraries in the important provincial towns'.[16] It could also call upon many of the most distinguished figures in modern Anglophone literature and culture to speak at its lecture tours and events, with T. S. Eliot just one of the dozens who travelled abroad at the Council's behest (in Eliot's case, to events in Sweden, Italy and France in the 1940s and early 1950s).[17]

In 1949, the year before the launch of *Writers and Their Work*, the Council suffered the first in a series of major cuts to its budgets and services, with a 42 per cent budget reduction occurring between 1949 and 1954, with cuts falling particularly hard on the Council's European and South American activity.[18] Nonetheless, the promotion of British literature abroad remained a key ambition and was supported by an English Studies Advisory Committee chaired by the academics Ifor Evans (1952–6) and Geoffrey Bullough (1956–63).[19] This committee advised on the Council's Education Department's ongoing activity relating to the teaching of literature abroad, which involved appointing and subsidising literature teachers and academics, arranging for exchange visits and lecture tours, promoting scholarships for the study of literature by visiting students at British universities, organizing summer schools for the study of literature, compiling and disseminating audio recordings of literary texts, advising on the literary syllabi for foreign education systems and promoting literary study guides.[20] This also fed into the activity of the Council's Books and Publishing and Editorial panels, which remained concerned with the material production and dissemination of the Council's selected books.

It was within this context that *Writers and Their Work* emerged and became one of the Council's flagship offerings. The series was initially conceptualized as a supplement to *British Book News*, a book trade magazine run by the National Book Council (a body that aimed to promote books and represent the branches of the publishing trade) that began publication in 1940 to 'acquaint the reader with the best British books on all subjects, including those published in the Commonwealth and Empire', achieved through offering 'bibliographies on specific subjects, and articles of general interest to the bookman'.[21] *Writers and Their Work* would considerably expand this bibliographical remit into pamphlets that offered more sustained forms of critical engagement. As described in a meeting of the Council's Literature Panel, '[t]he original plan of the series [. . .] was to provide an assessment with a select bibliography of all the principal figures in English literature, together with studies of leading contemporaries'.[22] The series was launched under the editorship of T. O. Beachcroft, a short story writer and critic who possessed key connections in the literary world. Part of the *Criterion* circle, he was a friend of T. S. Eliot, who recommended him as 'a man of culture and charm'.[23] Beachcroft had also worked with Mass-Observation, for Unilever's Advertising Service and as Chief Overseas Publicity Officer of the BBC from 1941 to 1961.[24] After Beachcroft, editorship of the series was taken over by Bonamy Dobrée (1954–64) and then Geoffrey Bullough (1964–9). Dobrée also had a strong connection with Eliot, being described as one of 'Eliot's chief lieutenants on the *Criterion* during the 1920s',[25] and had held professorships of English at Cairo (1926–9) and Leeds (1936–55). Bullough, meanwhile, was Professor of English at King's College London (1946–68), with publications ranging across Shakespeare, Greville and Milton through to *The Trend of Modern Poetry* (1934).

The first *Writers and Their Work* to be published was A. C. Ward's *Bernard Shaw*, which appeared in 1950.[26] Ward's study was a simple stapled pamphlet, priced at one shilling, which announced itself on its front cover to be a 'Supplement to British Book News' and 'Published for The British Council and the National Book League by Longmans, Green & Co'. It has been suggested its unremarkable aesthetic reflected the wartime legacies of paper rationing and restrictions on design and typesetting, and certainly there is no sense of an attempt to project cultural prestige through glossy production values (a feature of other mid-century British propaganda campaigns, as illustrated by Megan Faragher's analysis of *Britain in Pictures* in this volume).[27] The format of the coverage was equally concise: of a total of fifty-six pages, thirty-three were given to an 'Introduction' surveying Shaw's major life events, novels, pamphlets, plays and views. This was followed by an index of the first performances of the major plays, a select bibliography and then an index of Shaw's plays and essays – a compact format that allowed a student who might otherwise lack access to a research library to gain a concise snapshot of the career and publications of the author and the current state of the critical field.

If the design and table of contents suggested an uncontroversial work, we can still detect some potentially more pointed critical elements at play. The choice to open the series with a volume on Shaw was notable, for example. As a Nobel Prize-winning dramatist who had achieved fame through plays such as *Pygmalion* (first performed 1913) and *Saint Joan* (first performed 1923), Shaw was both well known to the public and widely studied and performed at schools and universities – as the inner cover attested, Shaw was the 'world's most famous modern dramatist'. His death in November 1950 also rendered the choice of author inadvertently topical. Despite this prominence, Shaw was still in many ways an unusual fit for a series that aimed to project British culture abroad. Although a British subject since his birth in Dublin in 1856, Shaw had become a dual Irish-British citizen in the 1930s, following Irish independence. He was also well known for controversial political and social views, had dabbled with various forms of socialism and praised various dictators (including Stalin, whom he had met during a visit to the Soviet Union in 1931, and who, at the time of the pamphlet's publication, remained in power in Moscow). Ward gives space to some of these tensions, discussing Shaw's Dublin childhood and acknowledging that the dramatist 'consistently proclaimed himself a socialist'.[28] But the compact format also allowed much of this to be elided or repackaged: Shaw quickly becomes 'the outstanding British dramatist of his generation', an 'arch-independent' whose 'socialism' is always secondary 'to his inborn individualism', making him as likely to attract the ire of communists as of fascists.[29] While I highly doubt any direct or deliberate cross-over, it is still interesting to note here that Shaw is positioned as a kind of literary embodiment of the 'Third Force' doctrine – the idea of Britain leading an independent democratic socialist movement in international affairs – that motivated the initial propaganda output of other British agencies such as the IRD in the late 1940s.[30] Disregarding any possible political subtext, initial reviewers praised the volume on other lines as 'exceptionally easy to read', and observing that it 'appears to be a good refresher or introduction to a study of Shaw'.[31] Its print history also suggests that students concurred: revised editions were published in 1951, 1957, 1960, 1963 and 1966, before it was reprinted in 1970 with amendments and additions to the bibliography.

The writers of *Writers and Their Work*

Over the first two years after its launch with Shaw, *Writers and Their Work* rapidly developed its list, with the initial twenty volumes consisting of *Joseph Conrad* by Oliver Warner, *G. K. Chesterton* by Christopher Hollis, *The Brontë Sisters* by Phyllis Bentley, *Henry James* by Michael Swan, *John Keats* by Edmund Blunden, *E. M. Forster* by Rex Warner, *T. S. Eliot* by M. C. Bradbrook and *Arnold Bennett* by Frank Swinnerton (all published 1950); and then in 1951 *Byron* by

Herbert Read, *Tobias Smollett* by Laurence Brander, *William Blake* by Kathleen Raine, *Bertrand Russell* by Alan Dorward, *G. M. Trevelyan* by J. H. Plumb, *George Eliot* by Lettice Cooper, *Osbert Sitwell* by Roger Fulford, *Jane Austen* by Sylvia Townsend Warner, *Sheridan* by W. A. Darlington, *Kipling* by Bonamy Dobrée and *I. Compton-Burnett* by Pamela Hansford Johnson. While hardly an iconoclastic list of titles, it nonetheless shows relatively generous assumptions guiding the Council's projection of British literature at this stage: a volume on Shakespeare was not immediately in sight (he had to wait until volume 58, in 1955), but contemporary authors such as Compton-Burnett were part of the initial run, and contemporary philosophers and historians are also included in what was an expansive definition of the 'literary' – all in all, a rendering of literature that (as will be seen later) irritated F. R. Leavis for its middle-brow tendencies and lack of critical discrimination. The initial twenty volumes also demonstrate the extent to which the British Council was able to marshal a highly credible corps of scholars and critics as authors for the series. A number of those commissioned to write for the series had histories of cultural diplomatic work or other forms of wartime government service. Oliver Warner was Deputy Director of Publications at the British Council, having worked in the Admiralty and on the War Artists Advisory Committee during the war, while Christopher Hollis had served as an RAF intelligence officer before his election as Conservative MP for Devizes in 1945, and was a supporter of the Congress for Cultural Freedom during the 1950s.[32] Meanwhile, Phyllis Bentley had performed 'highly confidential' wartime work in the First World War, also writing articles for the MOI 'urging the importance of munitions to our war effort and describing interesting human incidents in munition factories'.[33] Kathleen Raine had worked for the PWE during the Second World War, and Laurence Brander had served as the BBC's Eastern Intelligence Officer and later as Director of Publications for the British Council. Others came more from outside the government information system, however – Townsend Warner had been a communist in the 1930s (and consequently had been of considerable interest to the security services), while Herbert Read was a prominent proponent of anarchism, suggesting that there were no narrow political preconditions for authors approached to write.

Following its successful launch, the issues of the *Writers and Their Work* series gradually became more sophisticated – from 1953 the pamphlets featured enhanced designs and illustrations – and from 1958 the Council's Editorial Panel, chaired by Charles Snow, took a further role in 'advising on the Council's publishing programme at home and overseas' (which included *Writers and Their Work*).[34] Across the series, it appears that authors, once selected and briefed, were given a loose rein with regards to their choice of approach, although overall editorial control remained the purview of the Council, which held back volumes from publication if they were deemed to be too 'donnish' in tone.[35] The attempts in 1958 to commission J. R. R. Tolkien to write a volume on *Beowulf* for the series offers a useful example of this process, demonstrating the formal requirements of the series and the ambitions of the Council regarding readerships, as well as revealing the informal networks of contacts that the editors called upon in order to select authors to write copy. When contacted by the Council, Tolkien was approaching the peak of both his literary fame and academic gravitas – the three volumes of *Lord of the Rings* had been published between 1954 and 1955, and he was entering his final years as Merton Professor of English Language and Literature at Oxford. The mere fact that he would consider writing an introductory essay for the series indicates the considerable regard with which the Council was held in the academy. Tolkien's recruitment was no doubt helped by Dobrée's personal connections in the academic and literary worlds: in this case, Dobrée sent out a letter addressed to 'My dear Tolkien', which opened with a reminiscence about their last meeting at Oxford. Dobrée proceeded to woo Tolkien with flattery by informing him that it was 'high time' a book was commissioned on *Beowulf*, with Tolkien being the 'only one person' with the skills required to make '*Beowulf* known and appreciated from China to Peru, especially, perhaps, in the Commonwealth'[36] – a pitch which evidently enthused Tolkien, who agreed to write despite various other commitments.

After Dobrée's clubbable initial approach, it then fell to the Council's Director of Publications, at this time Laurence Brander, to follow through with a formal commission, in which he explained exactly the audience this study of *Beowulf* would need to reach:

> The essay is for the educated reader overseas, with an interest in English Literature. He is understood to have a good general knowledge of English reading but I do not think we can suppose that he reads Anglo-Saxon. 'Educated' implies that there must be no writing down, and 'overseas' normally implies that one has to remember the odd island matter that the reader will not understand unless there is a gloss, or some roundabout way of enlightening him. In your case that would be quite different and I can only suggest that you visualise an American or a Hindu or a Japanese whom you wish to interest. Of course, it could be Italian or anyone else you prefer.[37]

Brander's indifference as to the precise nationality of the 'foreign' audience is (at best) somewhat surprising, but also important is his insistence that there should be no 'writing down'. Tolkien was offered a fee of seventy-five guineas for the essay of 9,000 words – a welcome but not lucrative amount, considering a university lecturer in Tolkien's institution at this point might expect to earn up to £1650 per year as a salary (seventy-five guineas converts to just under seventy-nine pounds).[38]

In the following years, the Council sought ways to further broaden the scope of the series: one document from 1971 states that officials were actively considering 'dramatists and writers from the new Commonwealth' (the Nigerian writer Wole Soyinka is suggested as a possible topic), and relatively recent 'Angry Young Men' such as John Osborne were also selected for treatment around this time.[39] But in other ways, the Council's conception of the evolving literary scene failed to always keep pace with contemporary movements. For example, when Iris Murdoch and Doris Lessing were suggested as subjects in the early 1970s, they were initially judged to have 'rather less strong claims' than other (male) authors being considered for treatment at the time,[40] while the conception of the 'literary' also had its limits and could not incorporate every genre: Ian Scott-Kilvert (a successor Director of Publications for the Council who, from 1969, had become editor of the series) admitted that he 'enjoy[ed] Conan Doyle, of course', but warned that a volume on the Sherlock Holmes author risked letting in 'a horde of detective and historical novelists whose presence I do not think we could justify'.[41] Furthermore, it was not until 1997 that Tolkien, distinguished enough as a critic to be approached in the 1950s, was given a volume dedicated to his own work, despite the fact that *Lord of the Rings* had long been one of the most widely read works of Anglophone fiction of the twentieth century.

Reception and reviews

If the motivation behind *Writers and Their Work* was to engage foreign students with a stimulating and positive vision of the key past and present authors in British culture, to what extent did it achieve this goal, or indeed contribute towards the Council's wider mission? Given the long-term and incremental nature of such modes of study-guide cultural diplomacy, the specific impact of the series is hard to gauge, although there is considerable evidence attesting to the reputation of specific volumes and of the series as a whole. Within the British Council itself, there was evidently considerable pride at the uptake and status of the series. This is conveyed by Brander's report to the Literature Panel in 1957, in which he enthused that 'the plan' for the series to cover all the principal figures of past literature as well as leading contemporaries 'is being fulfilled, and the booklets are now familiar in every part of the world'.[42] This report also assesses the relative strengths and weaknesses of the series and the levels of sales and circulation. It noted that the 'most popular work in the series has always been Miss M. C. Bradbrook's study of T. S. Eliot', and that 'other titles with steady sales above average' were those on Austen, the Brontë sisters, Conrad, Keats, Milton, Shakespeare, Shaw, Woolf and Wordsworth. There were 'obvious gaps' in the coverage of the '18th and 19th centuries' that the series was trying to fill, and while the series was 'planned with care', the fact that 'authors write at different speeds' meant that 'the series, keeping obstinately to monthly publication, may well seem to lack adequate design'.[43] In general, the 'Romantics sell well; and the eighteenth century creeps along behind. This reflects the shape of Eng. Lit. courses throughout the world and especially in oriental countries where sales are strongest'.[44] Overall, in 1957, the series had annual sales in the world of around 80,000, with the largest number of sales in Japan – itself perhaps a surprising uptake given the Council had only appointed a representative to Japan in 1952 'with insufficient financial backing for him to do very much'.[45] As the series continued into the 1970s, it appears that the standard print run was 8,000 for each volume, with these being periodically revised and reprinted, and distribution split between the British Council and Longmans.[46]

Outside the Council, the series also attracted praise in prominent venues. The *TLS* in particular often noted new volumes and, on occasion, published longer dedicated reviews which lauded the series with missionary-like zeal for its role in projecting British culture to the non-Anglophone world. Writing for the journal in 1951, the poet Edmund Blunden praised the series in notably Orientalist terms, enthusing that '[n]o recent project [. . .] in the sphere of printed books has been more justifiable and more admirable' than *Writers and Their Work*, due to the 'extent and quality of the attention given to our national literature in the Eastern world', where 'in India, in China, in Japan and other counties a number of the great writers of England have become [. . .] part of their vision and their illumination in the process of common life'. Amid the broader need to allay 'suspicion' in the East, 'works of the literary imagination' offer the 'avenue which lies most open and understood between East and West', and the series therefore provided the required 'emissaries' to go forth with 'applause'.[47] Three years later, the Shakespeare scholar A. H. R. Fairchild elevated the series in similar terms while reviewing C. J. Sisson's *Shakespeare* (1955). Fairchild enthused to readers of *Shakespeare Quarterly* that *Writers and Their Work* demonstrated the 'special genius' possessed by 'England [. . .] that is beneficent for all' – the ability to deploy the country's 'top specialists [. . .] to summarize for publication in booklet form facts and truth in their respective fields'; as a result, he suggested, the British Council 'makes friends and influences people intellectually, morally, educationally'.[48]

Not all critics welcomed the series so warmly, however, and some feared the broader encroachment of the Council on matters of literary criticism.[49] One of the most trenchant assessments was provided by the critic F. R. Leavis in his essay dedicated to 'Mr. Pryce-Jones, The British Council and British Culture', published in the Winter 1951–2 number of Leavis's own journal *Scrutiny*.[50] Alan Pryce-Jones was the editor of the *TLS* from 1948 to 1959, and Leavis's 'vociferous criticism' here flows from broader grievances Leavis felt surrounding the treatment of *Scrutiny* by the *TLS* journal and the British Council, probably sparked, as Asha Rogers has suggested, by the failure of the Council to 'keep *Scrutiny* afloat as he [Leavis] wished' through subsidies.[51] Describing *Writers and Their Work* as 'that growing series of essays on authors past and present which is commissioned by, and published for, the British Council', Leavis folded the series into a broader attack on a 'contemporary literary world [which] is controlled by a system of personal and institutional relations'.[52] Complaining that Council publications have 'the august and authoritative impersonality of an institution', while remaining a system that is 'inimical to the real thing, the new and living', Leavis questioned '[h]ow, and by whom, we ask, are its [the Council's] literary policy determined and its literary jobs distributed?'[53] Leavis's absence from the roll call of authors who produced volumes for the *Writers and Their Work* series is of course notable, and there is also evidence that his grievance was not entirely misplaced, as the Council's archive suggests he had attracted personal enmity from influential figures involved in the organization.[54] But, even if the Council had not commissioned Leavis directly as a critic, as Christopher Hilliard has noted, it was still one of the major institutional supporters of *Scrutiny*, at some points buying around 10 per cent of its print run. In addition, many of Leavis's pupils later took up employment with the Council as education officers and language teachers,[55] and Leavis himself participated in the Literature Panel's Foreign University Interchange scheme, holding a fellowship in Nijmegen in the Netherlands in March of 1959.[56]

Conclusion

After changes in publisher and editors, and an 'abeyance' in the late 1980s,[57] *Writers and Their Work* was relaunched in 1994 by the British Council in collaboration with Northcote House Publishers, before passing to Liverpool University Press in its latest incarnation. The revived series retained the original ambitions of providing 'brief but rigorous critical examinations', but contemporary volumes are now more systematic, substantive and professionalized, employing 'the best of modern literary theory and criticism' in place of the sometimes-eclectic approaches of the shorter early volumes.[58] Still, the endurance of this format testifies to the vision of the initial series, whose editors originally identified the opportunity for such sponsored literary guides to become a fixture in the international teaching of British literature and, through this, to engage generations of international students with a long-term interest in British culture at a time when Britain was rapidly reorientating its position in a post-war, post-Imperial world. More broadly, this case study suggests that while the burgeoning public and scholarly interest in the Cultural Cold War has rightfully concentrated on the clandestine elements of this conflict and the role of actors such as the United States' CIA and the British IRD in subsidizing and organizing aspects of the cultural sphere, this has come at the cost of neglecting other organizations and initiatives that, while lacking the allure of covert operations, nonetheless achieved a far greater reach and impact in influencing the international intelligentsia and creating favourable projections of the British national culture.

Notes

1 These descriptions are taken from the British Council website: 'About Us' (https://www.britishcouncil.org/about-us [accessed 14 November 2023]); 'How We Work' (https://www.britishcouncil.org/about-us/how-we-work [accessed 14 November 2023]).

2 British Council, 'About Us'.

3 For Leeper's advocacy of cultural propaganda see Philip M. Taylor, *The Projection of Britain: British Overseas Publicity and Propaganda, 1919–1939* (Cambridge: Cambridge University Press, 1981), 144. More broadly, the fourth chapter of Taylor's book provides detailed context about the emergence and early years of the Council amid wider British policy debates concerning cultural diplomacy and propaganda.

4 Douglas Coombs, *Spreading the Word: The Library Work of the British Council* (London: Mansell, 1988), 1.

5 Drogheda Report cited in Frances Donaldson, *The British Council: The First Fifty Years* (London: Cape, 1984), 182. Officially titled the 'Report of Independent Committee of Inquiry into Overseas Information Services', the Drogheda Committee Report of 1953 was a wide-ranging review of British information services which shaped much of this activity in the subsequent Cold War. The 'peacetime' lineage of the Council is pointed out by Richard J. Aldrich, 'Putting Culture into the Cold War: The Cultural Relations Department (CRD) and British

Covert Informational Warfare', in *The Cultural Cold War in Western Europe, 1945–60*, ed. Hans Krabbendam and Giles Scott-Smith (London: Frank Cass, 2003), 110. The emphasis on the 'incremental' nature of the British Council's activity is made by Edward Corse at various points across *A Battle for Neutral Europe: British Cultural Propaganda During the Second World War* (London: Bloomsbury, 2013).

6 There is a small but important body of scholarship specifically devoted to the role of the Council in propagating British literature. Most substantive is Asha Rogers's *State Sponsored Literature: Britain and Cultural Diversity After 1945* (Oxford: Oxford University Press, 2020), where chapter 1 is devoted to the Council's role in sponsoring literary activity in the 1930s and 1940s. Further work has been done on the Council's role in supporting the rise of Commonwealth literature as an academic field in the UK by Gail Low in 'Professing the Common Wealth of Literature, Leeds 1957–1969', *The Journal of Commonwealth Literature* 50, no. 3 (2015): 267–81. Most recently, on 8 July 2022 at the English: Shared Futures conference (Manchester, UK) a workshop was held on *Writers and Their Work*, involving papers by three recent contributors to the series. See https://englishsharedfutures.uk/workshops/writers-and-their-work-a-snapshot-of-a-book-series/ [accessed 14 November 2023]. Caroline Ritter, *Imperial Encore* (Oakland, CA: University of California Press, 2021) also gives significant attention to the Council's cultural work in Africa.

7 A history of the publisher is given to accompany the Longman Group Archive at the University of Reading: see https://collections.reading.ac.uk/special-collections/collections/longman-group-archive/ [accessed 14 November 2023].

8 Edmund Charles Blunden, 'A British Council Series', *Times Literary Supplement*, 30 March 1951, 197.

9 See, for example, the argument in Peter Kalliney, *Commonwealth of Letters: British Literary Culture and the Emergence of Postcolonial Aesthetics* (New York, NY: Oxford University Press, 2013). Kalliney explores the post-war growth of what is termed the 'latent cultural neo-imperialism' of 'an empire of English speakers and readers' (183), with regions such as sub-Saharan Africa seeing English become 'one of the dominant disciplines for the ruling classes: it was one of the choice degrees for aspiring bureaucrats, intellectuals, and politicians alike', even in the aftermath of independence (193).

10 Coombs, *Spreading the Word*, 4.

11 Donaldson, *The British Council*, 62.

12 See Corse, *A Battle for Neutral Europe*; and Donaldson, *The British Council*, 140.

13 Brigid O'Connor and Stephan Roman, 'Building Bridges with Books: The British Council's Sixty-Year Record', *Logos* 5, no. 3 (1994): 135.

14 Coombs, *Spreading the Word*, 4. This committee, as tracked by Donaldson, *The British Council*, mutated across several forms and names in subsequent decades (see Appendix 4, 377–81).

15 O'Connor and Roman, 'Building Bridges with Books', 137.

16 Coombs, *Spreading the Word*, 38.

17 See 'Cultural Warfare: Eliot's Work with the British Council' for overview of Eliot's activity, online at: https://tseliot.com/foundation/cultural-warfare-eliots-work-with-the-british-council/ [accessed 14 November 2023].
18 O'Connor and Roman, 'Building Bridges with Books', 135; see also Donaldson, *The British Council*, chapter 11.
19 The terms of reference for this committee initially involved both the teaching of English language and literature. These, however, were soon regarded as distinct activities, with the committee splitting into sub-panels along 'Linguistics' and 'Literary' activity. This is explained in an 8 January 1957 note in The National Archives, Kew (hereafter TNA), BW 138/1. Thanks to the British Council for permission to quote from this material, and Jess Prestidge for initial research assistance.
20 The minutes of the committee across TNA, BW 138/1 – 138/4 capture the activity across these fields.
21 This summary is offered on the inside back cover of the first issue of *Writers and Their Work*.
22 Report on *Writers and Their Work* for 12 March 1957 meeting of the British Council's Literature Panel, TNA, BW 138/1.
23 This was a testimonial on Beachcroft offered by Eliot to the BBC in 1941. For this testimonial and some other details on their relationship, see *The Letters of T. S. Eliot Volume 3: 1926–7*, ed. Valerie Eliot and John Haffenden (London: Faber, 2012), 118 n. 1.
24 These details can be found in a biographical note in *The Letters of T. S. Eliot Volume 6: 1932–1933*, ed. Valerie Eliot and John Haffenden (London: Faber, 2016), 408 n. 2.
25 See Jason Harding, *The Criterion: Cultural Politics and Periodical Networks in Inter-War Britain* (Oxford: Oxford University Press, 2002), 5.
26 This volume was republished in multiple revised editions over subsequent years. A first 1950 edition is available to consult at https://archive.org/details/bernardshaw0000ward_s7d4/ [accessed 14 November 2023], its title page containing a blue stamp that suggests something of how it reached international circulation, stating: 'Review Copy: United Kingdom Information Office: Ottawa'.
27 Michael Lister, 'Writers and Their Work', *Textualities* (no date), online at: http://textualities.net/michael-lister/writers-and-their-work [accessed 14 November 2023]. This useful account is one of the few to give critical attention to *Writers and Their Work*.
28 A. C. Ward, *Bernard Shaw* (London: Longmans, Green, and Co., 1950), 20.
29 Ibid., 9, 20.
30 The rise and abandonment of the concept of the 'Third Force' in British propaganda is covered at length across Hugh Wilford, *The CIA, the British Left and the Cold War: Calling the Tune?* (London: Frank Cass, 2003).
31 This was a brief review in the 'Nonfiction' section of *The English Journal* 41, no. 5 (1952): 285.
32 See Giles Scott-Smith, 'The Congress for Cultural Freedom, the End of Ideology and the 1955 Milan Conference: "Defining the Parameters of Discourse"', *Journal*

of Contemporary History 37, no. 3 (2002), who notes that Hollis was one of the only British politicians who attended the Congress's Berlin conference (449).
33 Phyllis Bentley, *Noble in Reason* (Bath: Cedric Chivers, 1955), 124–5.
34 See Lister, 'Writers and Their Work' regarding design; the Editorial Panel is covered in TNA, BW 2/551.
35 This is conveyed in TNA, BW 2/747.
36 Dobrée to Tolkien, 5 November 1958, TNA, BW 2/650. Tolkien eventually pulled out from this venture, citing an accident suffered by his wife.
37 Brander to Tolkien, 18 November 1958, TNA, BW 2/650.
38 The salary figure is taken from C. Cradden, '"Old" University Academic Staff Salary Movement since 1949', *Higher Education Quarterly* 52 (1998): 396, table 1.
39 The nomination of Soyinka was by John Muir, 16 February 1971, TNA, BW 2/747, and various other letters and minutes in this file from the preceding years record the debate about new authors the series might cover.
40 Ian Scott-Kilvert, 20 January 1971, TNA, BW 2/747.
41 Ian Scott-Kilvert, 16 February 1971, TNA, BW 2/747. The prejudice within the Council against genre fiction seemed to linger for many decades: according to one account, a book on Terry Pratchett by the writer and critic David Langford was considered in the 1990s and then dropped, with the suggestion being that officials from within the British Council had declined the proposal despite support from the academic editors and publishers. See David Langford, *The Sex Column and Other Misprints* (Cabin John, MD: Cosmos, 2005), 71–2.
42 Report on *Writers and Their Work* for 12 March 1957 meeting of English Studies Advisory Panel (Literature), TNA, BW 138/1.
43 Ibid.
44 Ibid.
45 Brander, in minutes of a 12 March 1957 meeting of English Studies Advisory Panel (Literature), TNA, BW 138/1. The point about the Council's role in Japan is made by Donaldson, *The British Council*, 159.
46 This is taken from a 24 February 1972 distribution plan for Bernard Blackstone's *Byron III*, found in TNA, BW 2/685.
47 Blunden, 'A British Council Series'.
48 Review by A. H. R. Fairchild, *Shakespeare Quarterly* 6, no. 4 (1955): 463.
49 More broadly, Donaldson in *The British Council* demonstrates the running antagonism the Council has had from the tabloid press, with the enmity of the Beaverbrook publications casting a particularly long shadow over the Council for much of its history.
50 F. R. Leavis, 'Mr Pryce-Jones, The British Council, And British Culture', *Scrutiny* 18, no. 3 (1951): 224–8.
51 Rogers, *State Sponsored Literature*, 44.
52 Leavis, 'Mr Pryce-Jones', 225–6.
53 Ibid.

54 TNA, BW 2/685 suggests that Ronald Bottrall, the poet who had been the British Council's Directory of Education in the 1950s, had developed a personal grievance with Leavis that, at least in one instance, spilled into the works chosen for listing in the *Writers and Their Work* bibliographies.
55 Christopher Hilliard, *English as a Vocation: The 'Scrutiny' Movement* (Oxford: Oxford University Press, 2012), 95–6.
56 The list of exchange appointments is in TNA, BW 138/1.
57 Lister, 'Writers and Their Work'.
58 This description is in the front matter of recent volumes in the series.

Part IV

Lynette Roberts's *Gods with Stainless Ears* and the poetics of propaganda

Adam Piette

The Second World War was as much a war of hearts and minds as it was a destructive conflict, bringing to a head the lethal struggle against totalitarianism fought through propaganda drives towards mass persuasion alongside the military and police operations of the war. Poetry responded to the lure of propaganda which sought to occupy, like some mad titan cuckoo, the spaces of language normally reserved to the epic and lyric poets, co-opting the history of the nation as well as the intimate desires and obligations of the citizen imagination in the name of state security and war aims. This chapter draws together wartime integration propaganda theory as developed in 1940 by the Ministry of Information (MOI) psychologist F. C. Bartlett and the analysis of propagandized war culture as experienced in Wales by the experimental poet Lynette Roberts. Written during the war but published in 1951, Roberts's long poem *Gods with Stainless Ears* dramatizes both the complex propaganda manoeuvres of the totalitarian states and British democracy as analysed by Bartlett at the same time as it explores the erotic and apocalyptic possibilities of a counter-propaganda poetics.

Bartlett and political propaganda: Soviet, German, Italian, British

Integration propaganda, as defined by propaganda theorist Jacques Ellul, is aimed at the home population during wartime and is designed to sustain morale, increase productivity and encourage commitment and nationalist identifications, working by fostering conformity and cohesion through shared 'stereotypes, beliefs, and reactions of the group' and aiming at the 'total molding of the person in depth'.[1] The widely acknowledged expert in integration propaganda in the 1940s was F. C. Bartlett, Professor of Experimental Psychology and Director of the Psychological Laboratory, Cambridge, whose 1940 book *Political Propaganda*, commissioned by the MOI, proved to be very influential on its strategies and campaigns during the War. Bartlett studies the propaganda styles of the Italian, German and Soviet war machines and suggests a way forward for the British propaganda war effort. For Bartlett, British propaganda should avoid totalitarian propaganda's drive towards 'exaltation of the primitive and the unconscious' and should instead favour propaganda as 'a means of centralising and making concrete affections, loyalties and constructive impulses which are open for everybody to know and which have their basis largely in contemporary events'.[2] From his investigations of the uses of propaganda by totalitarian regimes Bartlett understood the critical significance of radio: 'To-day propaganda is in the air and on it.'[3] British 'democratic propaganda' needed to understand but not mimic Soviet and fascist state propaganda with its infantilization of the populace, its 'uniformity of opinion and of action' and artificially heightened emotions ('in a totalitarian State constant public excitement is needed to help prevent diversity of views').[4] Soviet propaganda specialized in exalting the proletariat and rural worker through highly controlled education of the masses in 'houses of social culture' backed up by extremely severe censorship ('drawing the maps, shaping the plays, directing all the entertainments and amusements').[5] Nazi propaganda worked through highly 'programmised' and 'systematised' manipulations using catchwords and slogans,[6] while Italian propaganda was more creative:

> There is in it all a spirit of daring and audacity, a brilliant inventiveness, both of phrase and manner, a kind of realism in the midst of its most sweeping generalisations, which keep it moving and alive. It has a sort of *ad hoc* character, as if it were not wholly shackled by the chains of a closed and complete system, but can grow and fit itself to the kaleidoscopic change and the opportunities of practical affairs. The machine never seems likely to master the man who has made it.[7]

For Bartlett, the three totalitarian systems shared features such as mass emotion whipped up by manufactured crises, prestige suggestion inculcating ideas of superiority-inferiority and 'symbol and sentiment', all designed 'to paralyse critical analysis and to stimulate all tendencies to thoughtless and slavish acceptance'.[8] Totalitarian propaganda worked by insistence and 'repetition with variations',[9] but each of the three variants had its own style. Soviet propaganda repeated its agitprop language in an analytic manner detached from concrete occasions, with worker heroism as abstract ideal. The Italians emphasized love of display more concretely, a play-acting flair, 'a kind of realism' with characteristic aesthetic emphasis in the control of art production, radio and cinema. The Nazi style leant on 'deliberately constructed symbolism', catchwords and slogans, with 'wireless communication' and statistics key to its disinformation campaigns and prestige suggestion.[10]

To counter these, Bartlett suggests that democratic propaganda should stage a variety of voices (to counter the manufactured 'simple, violent emotions which run swiftly to uniform action')[11] and a reasonable and intelligent style of delivery demonstrating 'control of the intelligence' over emotions,[12] with emphasis on morale and productivity boosting bonhomie: 'the primary aims are the maintenance of a cheerful and high morale and of a willingness to work.'[13] British propaganda should display 'sympathetic understanding' of the masses of people addressed, based on knowledge of 'their common conditions of life, their common interests and their common hopes' and should be characterized by humour and friendliness.[14] Bartlett equates the emotional, crisis-led manipulations of totalitarian propaganda with a machinic consciousness: propaganda works through radio technology, manufactures emotions and is itself a kind of machine aimed to master even 'the man who has made it' – he leans towards the *ad hoc* creativity of the Italian style because it introduces human eccentricity into the machinic uniformity of the Soviet and Nazi styles. Bartlett advises imitation of Italian propaganda, as is made clear at one point when he encourages maintaining '*ad hoc* character' in the British handling of news,[15] deliberately alluding back to the 'sort of *ad hoc* character' he noted as a key feature of Italian creative propaganda.

Lynette Roberts and the propaganda machine of the Second World War

Bartlett's book was so influential on the MOI that we can see it shaping the ways the ministry designed posters, campaigns, public order practices, as well as influencing its interactions with bodies such as the BBC, or with advertising or social research organizations moulding public opinion. Widely reviewed, Bartlett's vision of the fourfold styles of propaganda – German, Italian, Soviet, British – can also be observed infiltrating literary explorations of wartime propaganda. Though there is no direct evidence she read Bartlett, Lynette Roberts's long poem *Gods with Stainless Ears*, a sharply focused meditation on propaganda and the civilian imagination during the Second World War, is strikingly in tune with his analyses of totalitarian and British propaganda styles. *Gods with Stainless Ears* was written in Wales between 1941 and 1943, though only published after the war in 1951. It charts the relationship between a gunner in the British Army and the female poet-avatar as the war hots up, and observes the changes wrought upon Wales by wartime technology, propaganda, industry and culture from the vantage-point of the lovers together, and from a rebellious (and at times Welsh nationalist) counter-hegemonic, counter-propagandist and pacifist-political point of view.

Roberts herself was somewhat of an outsider figure: born of wealthy Welsh-Australian parents in Buenos Aires, she was brought up in London during the First World War, and then had a Catholic convent education in Argentina, before being sent to Bournemouth at fourteen when her mother died of typhus. She trained at the Central School of Arts and Crafts in London and became a familiar figure in 1930s poetry circles. It was in London that she met Welsh poet Keidrych Rhys, a friend of Dylan Thomas and editor of *Wales*, the prominent Anglo-Welsh journal: he is the gunner of Roberts's poem. Roberts and Rhys married in 1939 and spent the war in Llanybri in Wales. Her poetry was admired by fellow poets such as Robert Graves and T. S. Eliot; Faber and Faber published her *Poems* in 1944 and *Gods with Stainless Ears* seven years later. The long poem constitutes not only her identification with Wales, but was also understood within Anglo-Welsh modernism as a major statement of Welsh war culture, as well as a significant modernist long poem.[16] Part of the poem's force lies in its analysis of the mental conflicts generated by wartime cultural propaganda: as a Welsh epic lyric, it is the most significant 1940s exploration of propaganda's psychic and machinic manipulation of the citizen imagination within specific national, cultural, sexual and psychological contexts controlled through psychological warfare and integration propaganda, by London, by the war industrial complex, by the MOI and the institutions of culture. It most importantly maps out a way forward towards a counter-propaganda poetics.[17]

The complexity and subtle layeredness of *Gods with Stainless Ears* takes considerable unpacking. One of the drivers behind its complexity is its blend of targets and aims, its prophylactic satirical bite and its attentiveness to the many lines of force that constitute the hegemonic war culture of the 1940s. These satirical sources to its compositional matrix are accompanied by something quite different, and as important to the poem's structure and substance: its epic and lyric dimensions. The poem fuses its satire with very heartfelt and emotionally baroque writing, seeking to chart an ecstasis of war sexuality and erotic dreamwork as well as serious reflection on Second World War history as an extraordinary next step in the apocalyptic trajectory of twentieth-century culture. These lyric and epic drives to the composition do not clash, however, with the satirical sections: for the satire is principally aimed at war propaganda as it shaped hearts and minds in Wales, defined as a multi-layered set of ideological forces unleashed by the wartime government and military authorities to commandeer and control morale and war production in the subject nations of the United Kingdom.

In the 1949 Preface to the poem, Roberts warns the reader of the strange language they will encounter:

> The use of congested words, images, and certain hard metallic lines are introduced with deliberate emphasis to represent a period of muddled and intense thought which arose out of the first years of conflict, e.g. Factory hands and repetitive lines re-occur with the same movement as with a machine.[18]

The sentence sets up a mimetic relation between war culture as an ideological form of war machine (mechanized according to the forces, design and values of late capitalism and the industrial factory system) and the poem's own metallic finish and automatic processes, the repetition, the machinic movement, while at the same time preserving a space of autonomy in the thinking being generated by the war machine. The 'muddled and intense thought' tracks the psychology and intellectual reflection of the central characters not just as symptom but as analysis and emotional reaction and abreaction.

What is clear, however, is that it is propaganda as the collective voice of machinic war culture that is the principal focus of engagement: the machine being a state apparatus controlling culture through the system of wartime bureaucracy, the collective being the designed image of the people as dreamt up by integration propaganda. Bartlett's study had revealed how propaganda in its American and British forms blends the mind control and public opinion manipulations of official state forms of persuasion and command with commercial advertising techniques encouraging consumption and identity-formation. As such, propaganda aims to record as much as to generate public opinion, and thereby command and control the collective by artificially voicing its desires, duties and needs. The poem mimics this propagandized collective voice as mediatized, as machinic, as internalized, at the same time as seeking modes of resistance with the same compromised means of expression. Roberts had a pronounced faith in the resistance of the ordinary people to the British war propaganda. As she put it in her diary for 21 June 1940: 'The trouble with the modern world is this: THE PEOPLE ARE TOO INTELLIGENT FOR THEIR GOVERNMENT. Both Broadcasting House and the Government are speaking below the standards of the people, consequently most of their statements are jeered at.'[19] On reflecting on her practice in the poem, Roberts broadens the meaning of the machinic collective that is propaganda by including the cinema, the major modernist entertainment technology of mid-century: she draws on the cinema for her sense of the way her poem was composed, and in so doing, hints at wartime propaganda as the key target of its satirical procedures, and the manner in which it might be resisted as a popularly conceived and libidinally charged counter-propaganda:

> when I wrote this poem, the scenes and visions ran before me like a newsreel. The galley sheets on which I wrote the first draft may be partly responsible for this occurrence. But the poem was written for filming, especially Part V, where the soldier and his girl walk in fourth dimension among the clouds and visit the various outer strata of our planet. (Preface, 43)

The machinic is identified with the newsreel, a key emergent mode of wartime propaganda of the conflict.[20] The newsreel shapes not only the form of the poet's composing imagination, the sequentiality holding together the stream of 'scenes and visions', but also the very materiality of the composition. Roberts writes on galley sheets (printed proofs of texts, here possibly of *Poems*), the print analogue to the newsreel machine: the pages fabricated by the printing press. At the same time, another sense of the cinematic is brought into play, the dreamwork of an erotic sublime rising, seemingly, above the newsreel surface, entering an autonomous spacetime continuum above the battle: cinema not as newsreel or manufactured sentiment, the daily sequence of shots detailing history as wartime culture propaganda, but as an art of the collective and erotic unconscious, capturing a loving four-dimensional transcendence of news that stays news.

Braided propaganda styles and Welsh nationalism

As the argument to the poem suggests, Roberts saw a muddled and intense relation between the erotic bond between the gunner and the central consciousness of the poem and the propaganda procedures of the wartime state. She suggests that the important woodpecker figure in the opening section conjoins war technology and Welsh nationality, revealing the way the natural scene of Carmarthen Bay ('bay wild with birds and somewhat secluded from man') is changed by the war:

> War changes its contour. Machine-gun is suggested by the tapping of a woodpecker which gives out the identity of the gunner and provides his nationality, 'a dragon of wings'. Soldiers and armoured corps arrive: military parade and propaganda: factory workers and fatigues.[21]

The invasion of the region by the army and its propaganda equates to the militarization of the natural, provoking an armouring of the bird-life characteristic of the wild natural environment in the form of the lethal aircraft and anti-aircraft gun systems and personnel.[22] Roberts's prose implies another relation too: the alliterative form of Welsh writing is mimicked in her prose (armoured-arrive; parade-propaganda; factory-fatigues), hinting at a militarization of the compositional imagination in Wales, the repetitive sounds (local to specific Welsh trajectories from the *cynghanedd* of the *Black Book of Carmarthen* on) 're-occur with the same movement as with a machine'.

The change to the contour of the region, culturally, is achieved through this totalizing propaganda and its parade of machinic styles. And it is specifically integration propaganda that Roberts is charting. Roberts's poem has a finely tuned ear for the range and variety of integration propaganda styles 'in the air' in Wales as its contours were changed by the war, in particular after the German invasion of the Soviet Union in 1941 that turned the communist state suddenly into a key ally of Britain. Two stanzas from the opening section about the militarization of Wales make this clear:

> Into euclidian cubes grid air is planed.
> Propellors scudding up grit and kerosene, braid
> Hulls waled 5 miles below, spidering each man stark
> On steelweb, hammering in rivets ambuscade
> Interrupted by sirens screaming tirade.
>
> With machine-strength wearing blinkers and mask,
> Will of iron moulding surface to brain chained:
> While below in well shafts soldiers squat and cark,
> Shell and peel pods and spuds: girders craned;
> Into euclidian cubes tempered air is planed. (47)

The rhymes are braided into a web within the cubes of the cinquains to create the 'air' of the poem as manufactured sound-system. This accompanies the vision of the Welsh shipyards, which during the war specialized in refitting merchant ships for war service, alongside docks vital for wartime shipping and logistics, particularly coal and petrol exports.[23] Roberts takes us into the air and spectates on the riveters and welders from on high, then zooms in on their goggles and welding masks before entering the hulls to spy on the men in the ship's canteen. These cinematic shots are machinic insofar as they are screened by the machine of the camera, but also display the mechanical grids of the war machine's geometries of interpretation, planing the airspace into volumes, tracking human and machine targets in its 'steelweb' vectors. This combination of cinema and war machine absorbs the Welsh docks into a military episteme that is designed to display the emergent war culture as a braided exercise in propaganda. Technology assumes space and mind within the war's grids and webs, an informational planification of the war citizen as propagandee. The verse voices propaganda and its consequences in the same lines; for instance, 'Will of iron moulding surface to brain chained' voices both the slogan of the propagandist ('Will of iron') and its effect ('brain chained'). The 'air is planed' insofar as the air of the poem is being shaped by the radiophonic forces of propaganda: we recall Bartlett's 'To-day propaganda is in the air and on it'. The 'moulding' of the war citizen (anticipating Ellul's 'total molding of the person in depth') by the war's ideology is given a visual analogue in the image of the welder's face in blinkers and mask.[24] The two cinquains plot the dominant propaganda styles defined by Bartlett: Nazi propaganda is present in the 'sirens screaming tirade'; Soviet agitprop and worker heroics in the lines 'With machine-strength wearing blinkers and mask, / Will of iron'; Italian style in the aesthetics of the 'euclidian cubes' of poster design; and low-key, comic British democratic propaganda in the soldiers who 'squat and cark, / Shell and peel pods and spuds'.

This braiding of propaganda styles into a 'steelweb' of metallic lines is unsettlingly related to the broader meshing of registers performed by Roberts's long poem. The machinic language is a clear offshoot of modernism's scientism and geometric work, whether it be futurist, constructivist or analytic cubist. The war machine and its propaganda styles offer a wry commentary on the texts and visuals generated by machine modernity, laying bare the industrial and scientific manufacturing of processes and languages, parodied in the poem's own loud scientism: 'bare / Aluminium beak to clinic air' (45). The poem weaves this harsh, bright machinic language into Welsh modernist textures, in particular its Dylan Thomas-esque zesty pastoral surrealism: 'Saline mud / Siltering, wet with marshpinks' (44). Alongside the machinic and pastoral run lines that chart the specific social mores of the Welsh scene, with an eye shaped by Mass Observational codes of class analysis and sociology. Mass-Observation (MO) was a social research organization that developed information-gathering techniques based on the close observation and interviewing of particularly working-class communities, that were later influential in advertising, marketing and public opinion tracking. The MOI often used MO during the war, and MO saw itself as creating a bridge between commercial and official forms of propaganda.[25] Roberts's lines stage MO sociology through its display of democratic surveys of citizens at war, and in its recording of speech and views of the common people: 'Clear as beer sparkle ... "you've had it, mun". / "Where's the 'professor' he should know?"' (49).

This Mass Observational attention is keyed into the nationalism of Wales as a political space, and the poem works hard to chart nationalist culture and visionary Welsh poetry and fiction as deep time background to wartime history: 'Prophets warm in the shade sign black signatures // In the Red Book of Hergest and cross their toes / To confuse the Principality' (48). Lightest of comedy, however, invites suspicion about the nationalism written into the image of the prophets crossing their toes and signing their signatures in the great compilation of Mabinogion stories and Gogynfeirdd poems. The crossing of toes implies silent resistance to the lure of nationalism in wartime, since so clearly recruited by the English for the greater good of the British war effort (just as the Red Book languishes in the library of Jesus College, Oxford). What troubles the nationalism is the force that drives through the green fuse of Wales, the British propaganda drive, which aims to channel nationalist energies according to the grid-like uniformity of integration propaganda. This attention to collective and mass emotion as British propagandized martial uniformity of mind is traceable here: 'He, who comes from Saint Cadoc's Chapter / Giant or Legendary Prince, who loves / One and no other, turns in his mind LEFT – RIGHT / LEFT – RIGHT' (49). The semi-legendary saint of South Wales presides over the region's contemporary heroes, the Welsh soldiers and workers, but a greater force than Saint Cadoc is the British Army with its militarization of the political space (the left and right of a nationalist spectrum recruited and made uniform by the barked orders of an English sergeant at arms).

These propagandized emotions and beliefs relate alarmingly to the poetics of the project: Roberts's own styles, modernist, neo-Romantic, Welsh, documentary, match in their braidedness the propaganda styles of the war: for the war turns in the mind as a cultural environment, and draws the imagination towards the uniformities of all representations in wartime: the uniforms of those in the services suggesting the cultural control of ideas and enforced consensus aimed at by state propaganda. Those uniformities strike the mind as machine-made and factory-processed, Roberts argues. What might seem positive, the very variousness of the modes of control and persuasion that inhabit the mind in wartime, is in truth a sign that all citizens are informationally locked into the grids and cubes of a propaganda multiplex – Soviet, Italian, German, British. Propaganda might also be taken partly to be shaping the poetic form: Roberts's use of repetition and recurrent patterning could be taken to be animated by propaganda's use of 'repetition with variations', its symbols by the 'deliberate constructed symbolism' of totalitarian propaganda, its celebration of 'new hearts and hearths' against the 'money-goaders' (46) coloured by prestige suggestion. What transcends the propagandized totality is questionable, but one might see some resistant energy in the Gothic and apocalyptic styles that are also a running feature of the long poem's braided textures.

The war dead and love's counter-propaganda in the fourth dimension

While registering the totalizing absorbent power of the war's propaganda over the mind and material reality of the Welsh, the poem also tracks the Gothic imagination at war, a death-haunted elegiac lament that reaches out to the war dead, especially in air and at sea: 'Go down there further and see the lucid / Plane-of-night, strained with piteous men // Drowned in water-swills of crossing waves' (51). This Gothic death poetry points the way to a more overtly apocalyptic writing, perhaps the only style capable of capturing the spectacle and affect of mass death: 'Atonement of blood: seaflooded red' (50). The style here is patterned consciously on New Apocalypse poetics. The poets gathered together within the anthologies *The New Apocalypse* (1939), *The White Horseman* (1941) *The Crown and the Sickle* (1943, edited by J. F. Hendry and Henry Treece), had developed the style under the influence of Dylan Thomas, and before him of D. H. Lawrence, whose book *Apocalypse* (1931) had given the movement its name. Roberts's counter-machinic modes allude culturally to the *New Apocalypse* group: their 1938 manifesto argued for use of myth to help free minds from 'machine and mechanistic thinking' and reintegrate the personality in 'the Machine Age'.[26] Hendry's prefatory essay to *The New Apocalypse*, 'Writers and Apocalypse', advocated an organic mode of writing in opposition to abstract and mechanistic forces: 'the war for justice to man, to prevent his becoming an object as in abstract art or the Totalitarian State.'[27] Lawrence's analysis of the Book of Revelation in *Apocalypse* is alluded to as well: the poem's staging of the dragon, as Welsh emblem, weaponized aircraft and myth, plays on Lawrence's analysis of the red dragon of Revelation as a cosmic force and as a 'fluid, rapid, invincible, even clairvoyant potency',[28] a libidinal surge that Roberts identifies with her male protagonist, the gunner. The union of the seamstress-artist female and the gunner in the fantasy sequence of Part V modernizes Lawrence's account of the encounter of the pregnant 'great woman goddess' and the great red dragon 'Kosmodynamos' in the twelfth chapter of Revelation.[29]

The fifth section of *Gods with Stainless Ears* is prepared for by the nationalist rhetoric of the second, where a prophetic voice calls to the Welsh: 'We must upprise O my people', identified with an ecstatic illumination, an upshining, outshining 'the day's sun' (53). The February 1941 Swansea Blitz troubles the coming together of the lovers in Part III, a separation which worsens with the loss of a child in Part IV; but this loss brings the female poet in touch with the mourners of the war dead, another level of sympathy with the people: 'O my people here / With labour illused and minds deranged . . .' (63). This sudden access to this larger sympathy through 'lamentations of grief' redefines heroics as the people in endurance ('*Here are your Heroes*'), and points to the possibility of transcendence above the fray: 'While high up, swallowsoft . . . / Marine butterflies flood out the whole estuary' (63). This appeal to a new heroism of endurance and war-transcendent emotions (the high atmosphere flooded by butterflies blue as the seas) conjoins epic history and lyric's natural and erotic bonds in ways that (at this stage wishfully and sentimentally) seek to escape propaganda's appropriation of history-in-the-making as source of sloganeering, and integration propaganda's whipping up of crisis-emotionality to secure assent. The labour and mental suffering of the people provide a rival epic base while the marine butterflies sketch a Romantic sublime based on lyric and libidinal joy and love.

In Part V, the lovers come together and begin to rise above the warring world, their 'love in harmony on cloud in fourth dimensional state'.[30] The spacetime zone is drawn from Lawrence, who saw the temporality of pagan mythology as cyclical: 'One cycle finished, we can drop or rise to another level, and be in a new world at once.'[31] The lovers in Roberts's poem rise by 'steel escalator' from an icy world into the clouds, 'a trauma stratus' full of birds, then higher still to a 'far outer belt' where sail 'ketch and kestrel' alongside 'fighting propellor, / Swastika wings and grey rubber rafts' (65–6). Beyond this belt a final zone of 'clarity / Of *Peace*' a space where poetry is free of the war, a lyric space that dreams of a timeless zone beyond the war's propagandized epic: 'Sweet white air varied as syllables' (66). In this timeless zone, the woman sees a vision of herself and her gunner lover working together, he with his 'glazed chart' with 'pricked lines and projected / Latitudes' (66), she with her Singer sewing machine, 'Chromium wheel and black structure' (67), as she sews soldier shirts. The brief vision does not last, however, for though they wrap their 'own mystery' around them (67), they are 'compelled to descend' by the money-goaders, by 'the State'. The anarchist vision is therefore compromised, not least by the fact both lovers are working for the war effort as gunner and army seamstress, and are imbricated in the machines their timeless minds had sought to transcend, the chart with its projections, the chromium and black sewing machine. The steel escalator and vision of warplanes in the higher zones of the sky also convey the collusive machinic trap the lovers find themselves psychically and artistically caught up within. At the height of the timeless, fourth-dimensional space of peace, the two lovers have become air-machines, the planes with stainless-steel 'ears' of the war machine.

The fall and libidinal release

Their fall to earth is spectacular, and contains some of Roberts's most extraordinary poetry. What the descent reveals is how tainted their love and art is by war propaganda: they note as they fall that the god of this upper zone is bureaucratic with 'angel secretaries with / Paper wings' running things, their paper 'dyed mauve-scarlet / With chemical rings', their speech 'blue behind aniline minds' (67). They are industrial processes, commodity chemical creatures, their wings signs of their deep-dyed collusion. The lovers fall past them 'like old minesweepers' through storms, '*our own God / Within us*' (67), lines that reveal their war-metallic nature and purpose, and how far their absorption of war propaganda has gone – the God is propaganda, and inhabits their bodies with slogans like this. They fall through freezing air, ice on their wings like 'spangled / Mirrors': 'Continuous as *newsreel*, / Quadrillion cells spotting the air' (68). The snow turns into newsreel images as they fall, sign of propaganda, as if constructing all creation as state-representation. As they fall, a nightmare landscape is revealed as follows, the natural world inscribed by the god propaganda with 'Strokes of mapping pens' (68), recalling the 'pricked lines' of the gunner's projections. An industrial vision is revealed: 'Network of rails: pylons and steel installations / The only landmarks of our territory' (68). The modernist panorama envisioned by the Auden group is all there is, the whole earth a 'bleak telegraphic planet', intimating the ways writing is also machined and networked. Down they fall, 'gunner and black // Madonna with heart of tin' (68), accompanied by nightmare crows and curlews mocking their flight. They enter a hostile zone, 'a surreal, post-apocalyptic landscape', local culture 'erased by an all-powerful military-industrial complex', as Andrew Webb puts it.[32] The space resembles a mental home for poets, where a strange figure, the gunner defeated, scrawls his poems, 'Distrained... mallowfrail' (69) – signalling both the dispossession imposed by the war State, and power's scorn for romantic poets as flowery and weak. And yet, though the lovers have fallen, their wings clipped by the war's intensities and propaganda's divine powers to control and derange minds, the poem ends with an image of liberation:

> Catoptric on waterice he of deep love
> Frees dragon from the glacier glade
> Sights death fading into chilblain ears. (69)

'Catoptric' means mirror-like: these are the mirrors the ice left on their wings when they fell to earth. He has become a mirror-creature, as if made by the wintry propaganda that structures the discursive world, the icy environment that brought the lovers down.[33] Yet, within the confines of the lines, there can be found a weird lyricism in the recurrences, a weave and web that is more intricate and loving than the repetition with variations of the propagandist. The grapheme 'ic' in 'catoptric' re-emerges in 'waterice' and 'glacier' and 'chilblain', and takes on sonic form in 'Sights'. The 'he'-'deep'-'Frees' rhyming matches the triple a-grapheme repetition 'dragon'-'glacier'-'glade' finding lovely cadential conclusion in 'chilblain ears'. The rhythm weaves a stress-pattern that extends that sequence of a-graphemes, 'Catoptric'-'waterice'-'dragon'-'glacier'-'glade' revisioned as the four *a*'s of the very last line: 'death'-'fading'-'chilblain'-'ears'. Alongside the gamey play 'on'-'dragon'-'chilblain' and the alliterative effects, we can hear and see the phonemes and graphemes of 'dragon' disseminated along the lines, a lyric-epic force freed from verbal context within the single word:

> Catoptric **on** waterice he **of** deep love
> Frees **dragon** from the **glacier glade**
> Sights **death fading into** chilblain **ears**.[34]

The textures of the verse are semi-comic, even cartoonish, with the hero freeing the dragon from the icy lake presented as a mad poet seeing his vision of a dragon in the icy mirror turn into his own chilblained face with freezing ears. Yet it comes together. The poem acknowledges how far Wales has been co-opted and transformed by the war effort, including its bards. The air is the war's, all planes warplanes; the dragon of Wales is a machine co-opted to the lies of war propaganda; the poet condemned to either a propaganda role or to marginalized insanity; the war machine is running things with its scientism that infects both lyric and epic poem ('Catoptric' an example). Yet still, here, the gunner finds a means of expressing his deep love, of Wales, of his lover, of this glade, of true poetry, in this gesture of new mythmaking, a counter-propaganda that takes the form of this apocalyptic release of libidinal energy beyond the reach of the war machine, and within the timeless zone beyond the deaths of war as history. The god of war culture, propaganda as militarized language and ideology, cannot touch this dragon in its flight towards his lover (the true scribe), a flight that has as its response the very poem that we are reading, a love letter beyond censorship and propaganda's icy lethal grasp.

In *Gods with Stainless Ears* Lynette Roberts weaves together a counter-propagandist epic lyric that defends the capacity of creative poetry as love-making bond and regenerative sociality, despite the recruitment of culture and nature by the god of this world, propaganda. The dangers propaganda posed to the art of poetry are acute given the special incorporation of language and poetics into the repertoire of war propaganda, the use of repetition, symbol and emotional charge charted by Bartlett in his study of totalitarian modes of persuasion. The machinic processes of industrial warfare may be shown to be shaping the mechanical procedures of the long poem, particularly when designed to have both epic scope (control of history through nation-building and nation-defensive rhetoric) and lyric insinuation (courting the individual through desire and unconscious prompts). The fantasy flight of the lovers from the war's escalator, then their fall down to the post-apocalyptic frozen wastes of Wales-as-war-factory demonstrate the hold of propaganda on the souls of the lovers. Yet in the same movement, and through the very recruited rhetoric of the propagandized epic lyric, Roberts snatches the grace of a true anarchist love song from the freezing zone of war culture and establishes a lively, punchy and sinuous mode of resistance and solidarity that binds lovers, the Welsh and the readership into subversive community. The poem is the most searching analysis of propaganda on the mind at war, at the same time as registering the Welsh resistance to propaganda by the loving imagination. The 'dragon' that spreads through the icy space of the last lines of the poem moves like the mists Roberts noted in her landscape in the middle of the war, intimating peace:

> The peace and mist rising from this stream here in this meadow in the middle of the war, during the most successful month of the robot machine. Near a tree,

quiet and grey as those growing in Southern France, filled with the joyous notes and movements of birds. A peace permeating sky, grass, and leaf.[35]

Notes

1. Jacques Ellul, *Propaganda: The Formation of Men's Attitudes*, trans. Konrad Kellen and Jean Lerner (New York, NY: Vintage Books, 1965), 75–6.
2. F. C. Bartlett, *Political Propaganda* (Cambridge: Cambridge University Press, 1940), ix.
3. Ibid., 1.
4. Ibid., 9, 17.
5. Ibid., 19, 30.
6. Ibid., 43.
7. Ibid., 42.
8. Ibid., 66.
9. Ibid., 69.
10. Ibid., 45–6. For studies of British Second World War propaganda, see Charles Cruickshank, *The Fourth Arm: Psychological Warfare, 1938–45* (London: Davis-Poynter, 1977); Michael Balfour, *Propaganda in War 1939–45: Organisations, Policies and Publics in Britain and Germany* (London: Routledge & Kegan Paul, 1978); James Chapman, *The British at War: Cinema, State and Propaganda, 1939–1945* (London: I.B. Tauris, 1998); Philip M. Taylor, *Munitions of the Mind: A History of Propaganda*, 3rd ed. (Manchester: Manchester University Press, 2003); Edward Corse, *A Battle for Neutral Europe: British Cultural Propaganda during the Second World War* (London: Bloomsbury, 2012).
11. Bartlett, *Political Propaganda*, 133.
12. Ibid., 114.
13. Ibid., 140.
14. Ibid., 142–3.
15. Ibid., 139.
16. After the war Roberts developed schizophrenia in 1956, became a Jehovah's Witness, and after the rejection of her 1951 volume *The Fifth Pillar of Song* by Faber appears to have renounced poetry until her death in 1995. See Patrick McGuinness, 'Introduction', in Lynette Roberts, *Collected Poems*, ed. Patrick McGuiness (Manchester: Carcanet, 2005), xviii–xix.
17. Roberts had some insider knowledge of propaganda and the secret state: she was engaged at one time to Merlin Minshall, who worked under Ian Fleming in Naval Intelligence and served as a secret agent during the war; from the Apocalypse poetry scene she also knew Kathleen Raine, who went on to work for the Political Warfare Executive towards the end of the war. See Patrick McGuinness, 'Machine-

age Mabinogion "A Quite Extraordinary Affair": The Impetuous Life and Free-Ranging Work of Lynette Roberts', *Times Literary Supplement*, 6 November 2009, 14.

18 Roberts, 'Preface', *Gods with Stainless Ears, Collected Poems*, 43. Further citations to this edition are given in the text.

19 Lynette Roberts, 'A Carmarthenshire Diary', *Diaries, Letters and Recollections*, ed. Patrick McGuiness (Manchester: Carcanet, 2008), 20. There was a lot of evidence to back this up, from Mass-Observation and the BBC's own research: 'As Mass-Observers and Listener Researchers discovered again and again, respondents often made a point of telling them when they detected tendentiousness in a film, a radio programme or a newspaper article. With remarks like: "you got too much propaganda stuck down your throat", "propaganda, pure and simple, don't you think?", "they're overdoing the propaganda – it's not necessary"' (Robert Mackay, *Half the Battle: Civilian Morale in Britain during the Second World War* (Manchester: Manchester University Press, 2002), 181).

20 John Reith, the first Director-General of the BBC from 1927 to 1938 and briefly Minister of Information under Neville Chamberlain in 1940, wrote in 1949 that news provided the 'shock troops of propaganda' (John Reith, *Into the Wind* (London: Hodder & Stoughton, 1949), 354).

21 Roberts, 'Argument' preceding Part I of *Gods with Stainless Ears, Collected Poems*, 44.

22 For the history of the commandeering of land in Wales by the War Office (10 per cent by 1945) and how this is represented in the poem, see Andrew Webb, '"What Changes Break Before Us": Semi-Peripheral Modernity in Lynette Roberts's Poetry and Prose', in *Locating Lynette Roberts: 'Always Observant and Slightly Obscure'*, ed. Siriol McAvoy (Cardiff: University of Wales Press, 2019), 91.

23 See David Simpson, 'The Barry Merchant Navy Seamen In World War 2', Barry Merchant Seamen website (2007), (http://www.barrymerchantseamen.org.uk/articles/BMSww2part1.html [accessed 27 November 2023]). For general background on Wales's experience of the Second World War, see Stuart Broomfield, *Wales at War: The Experience of the Second World War in Wales* (Stroud: The History Press, 2009).

24 The concept of moulding as engineering public opinion is an important part of Edward Bernays' argument in *Propaganda* (1928): 'Those who manipulate this unseen mechanism of society constitute an invisible government which is the true ruling power of our country. We are governed, our minds are molded, our tastes formed, our ideas suggested, largely by men we have never heard of' (Edward Bernays, *Propaganda* (New York, NY: Horace Liveright, 1928), 9).

25 See, for example, MO's report *Home Propaganda: A Report Prepared by Mass Observation for the Advertising Service Guild* (London: Advertising Service Guild, 1941).

26 Manifesto quoted in Francis Scarfe, *Auden and After* (London: Routledge and Sons, 1942), 155. Roberts also identified industrialism itself with English culture, as

Maroula Joannou argues in her reading of *Gods with Stainless Ears* in the 'My Ain Folk' chapter of *Women's Writing, Englishness and National and Cultural Identity: The Mobile Woman and the Migrant Voice, 1938–1962* (Basingstoke: Palgrave Macmillan, 2012), 108–33.

27 J. F. Hendry, 'Writers and Apocalypse', *The New Apocalypse* (London: Fortune Press, 1939), 11.
28 D. H. Lawrence, *Apocalypse*, (1931) (New York, NY: Viking Press, 1960), 144.
29 Lawrence, *Apocalypse*, 136, 149.
30 Roberts, 'Argument' preceding Part V of *Gods with Stainless Ears*, *Collected Poems*, 64.
31 Lawrence, *Apocalypse*, 87.
32 Webb, 'What Changes Break Before Us', 69.
33 One of the coldest winters Wales has ever had was in 1940, with a temperature of −23° recorded at Rhayader in Radnorshire. Roberts noted the hunger of the birds during the freezing spell and wrote a poem about them as displaced persons: 'They were no longer birds but / Beings searching after food, spirits of flesh' ('Displaced Persons', *Collected Poems*, 91). She noted the resemblance of starving evacuees to hungry birds in a diary entry for 26 June 1940: 'I wrote a poem about the "Displaced Persons" in Europe, likening them to birds without winter food and dying of starvation' (Roberts, *Diaries, Letters and Recollections*, 25). The transformation of the lovers into birds, and the suffering registered in the wintry landscape by the gunner emerges from this memory and the connection drawn to the DPs of Europe.
34 Bold lettering signals the 'dragon' phoneme and grapheme repetitions.
35 Roberts, diary entry for 2 August 1942, *Diaries, Letters and Recollections*, 53.

11

'Dialectical tight-rope acts of self-deception'
Arthur Koestler's anti-communist propaganda
Annabel Williams

In his speculative Cold War novel *The Age of Longing* (1951), the British-Hungarian writer Arthur Koestler created an archetypal exponent of Soviet cultural propaganda: Leo Nikolayevich Leontiev, 'Hero of Culture and Joy of the People'. In his published writings, Leontiev's 'word decided who among the rank and file should be pulped and who printed on Japan paper'; in his public addresses, he can switch between two contradictory versions of a speech moments before its delivery, in accordance with the Party's changing political line.[1] But Leontiev is no mindless apparatchik; he is one of the 'Old Party Guard', and the task of generating inconsistent propaganda wears him down:

> The trouble was that it was not enough to translate the text of his speech into the ritual terminology, the rigid, Byzantine, catechismal style required for home consumption. He had to produce an entirely different text with an almost opposite message which, however, did not show any direct, open contradiction to the original [. . .].[2]

Most alarmingly for Leontiev, there is a possibility that his constant, wearying state of cognitive dissonance could make him actually believe what he writes. The consequence of his 'fatigue of the synapses' is writer's block.

Koestler's portrayal of this jaded propagandist, his cynical techniques and his fears, brings into focus the writer's own preoccupations of the period, at a time when he was also engaged as a cold warrior producing influential propaganda for branches of the British and American intelligence services. Probably the most notorious apostate communist of his day, Koestler had staged his major, public disavowal of Stalinism in the novel *Darkness at Noon* (1940), whose protagonist – Nikolai Rubashov, a prominent Soviet leader – becomes the latest casualty of Stalin's purges and, isolated in his cell, undergoes a dramatic psychological crisis as he tries to square his conscience with the Communist Party's twisted ethical system. Five years later, Koestler's book of essays *The Yogi and the Commissar* (1945) – an influential anti-communist polemic – traced his journey from conversion to communism in 1930s Berlin to his disillusionment with the reality of Stalinism. Now, in *The Age of Longing* – Koestler's first novel to appear after the Second World War – he grappled with the question of how far, and why, he had believed his own pre-conversion writings in support of Stalinist policy and doctrine. In his 1954 autobiography *The Invisible Writing*, Koestler reflected on his work composing broadsheets and leaflets for his cell of the Communist Party of Germany (KPD) in the 1930s, and his psychological 'portrait of the artist as a comrade' has notable similarities to Leontiev. In the autobiography, Koestler admits that his 'language and reasoning became reconditioned to the Party's jargon [. . .] [but] when it came to writing, [he] encountered an unconscious resistance'.[3] He was unable to produce articles for the Party press, and the limits to his facility for doublethink had a direct, inhibitory effect on his abilities as a propagandist.

Much of Koestler's mid-century polemics and propaganda have a self-referential quality, dwelling on issues of rationality, scepticism and credulity. Writing in 1949, Koestler described the hyper-rationalism of Soviet doctrine as a kind of mental acrobatics: its outrageous distortions of logic required its followers to perform 'dialectical tight-rope acts of self-deception'.[4] His account of his own balancing act and subsequent crashing to earth was published in *The God that Failed* (1949), which brought together essays by six intellectuals 'who had lost their dialectical balance'.[5] As Koestler argued, he was well placed to lay bare the workings of the communist convert's mind: 'Having experienced the almost unlimited possibilities of mental acrobatism on that tight-rope stretched across one's conscience, I know how much stretching it takes to make that elastic rope snap.'[6]

In this chapter, I examine the ways in which Koestler interrogated and repurposed propaganda techniques he had developed as a member of the KPD – from 1931 to 1938 – after a reversal of his political commitments took him over to the anti-communist cause. With particular attention to Koestler's (ostensibly) pro-communist travelogue *Red Days and White Nights* (1934), his later autobiographical retelling of that period in *The Invisible Writing* (1954), and his stridently anti-communist novel *The Age of Longing*, I chart the tortuous path of Koestler's career from his membership of the KPD to his role in the anti-communist Congress for Cultural Freedom (CCF). Considering the role irrationality played in the reception and creation of propaganda in the early years of the Cold War, I ask why – despite Koestler's sensitivity to political irrationalism – he was accused of anti-rationalist demagoguery in the 1950s both by fellow travellers and by some on the conservative right. Koestler's fiction, I argue, counterbalanced some of the lingering effects of the dialectical tight-rope expressed in his overt propaganda. Dramatizing minds in the grip of cognitive dissonance, Koestler's work reveals a preoccupation with the psychological toll of wartime propaganda – a concern that endured from his early work for the KPD and into his time as a leading public anti-communist at the CCF.

Thinking in contradictions

Koestler's first foray as a propagandist came in 1932 when he was commissioned by a branch of Comintern, the 'International Organisation of Revolutionary Writers', to compose a travelogue on his journey through the Soviet Union.[7] Thus, in 1932, he set out from Berlin for Kharkiv, then the capital of Soviet Ukraine, and proceeded to travel through European Russia, before crossing the Caucasus and finally reaching the Soviet states of Central Asia. In European Russia, Koestler travelled east from Moscow to Yaroslavl and Nizhny Novgorod, then back to Moscow; the cities' modern infrastructure – among them a synthetic rubber factory and car plant – enabled Koestler to rhapsodize over the economic productivity and potential of the region, and the virtues of Stalin's economic policies. In the Caucasus, he travelled across the three Autonomous Soviet Republics of Georgia, Armenia and Azerbaijan, and in Central Asia he visited cities and collective farms in the Soviet Republics of Turkmenistan and Uzbekistan.

Comintern's involvement in the project was kept secret, as was Koestler's membership of the KPD, whose officials decided he would be most effective as a propagandist if he maintained the pretence that he was a bourgeois news-correspondent. The book was to be shaped by the conceit that Koestler began his journey with an anti-communist bias, but had been won over after witnessing the successes of Stalin's first Five-Year plan. Thus it was to be titled, disingenuously, *Russia Through Bourgeois Eyes*. Evidently, though, Koestler was rather too convincing in his disguise as a liberal correspondent, because party apparatchiks were troubled by the final manuscript, which (according to Koestler, as he looked back in the 1950s) they labelled 'too frivolous and lighthearted' in style.[8] Excerpts from expurgated material that Koestler later reprinted in *The Invisible Writing* indicate where communist censors' hackles would have risen over his frivolity and sentimentality. In the Caucasus, where Koestler neglected to visit a single factory or collective farm, a 'curious holiday spirit' came over him, and his concerns with economic growth were supplanted by the romance of local colour: 'Our eyes still dazzled by the crystalline glare of the glaciers, we crowded into the semi-obscure taproom of an inn where men in tall fur-caps and with silver cartridge-belts were moving through a mist of charcoal smoke and mutton smell [. . .].'[9] Such lyrical passages were dropped from the final version of the book, which was cut to less than half the original length, and turned down for publication in the Russian, Georgian and Armenian editions, despite Koestler having already been given a generous advance on the book. The only edition to be printed was published in 1934 by the Ukrainian State Publishing House in Kharkiv, as *Von weissen Nächten und roten Tagen* (*Red Days and White Nights*), and was directed at German-speaking national minorities living in the region. From Comintern's perspective, Koestler's account of his Soviet tour was a failure.

The journey was to have fresh value as propaganda twenty years later, however, when it was retold in *The Invisible Writing*. It is striking, in the later revisiting of his travels, how much space Koestler gives to reprinting passages that had been expurgated from *Red Days and White Nights*; this was not simply because he was concerned to give a fuller, more accurate account of the journey, but because it best allowed him to lay bare the workings of censorship and self-censorship through which he could then scrutinize the cynical mechanics of Soviet thought and policy. As he demonstrated in 1954, Koestler's original travelogue was not just censored by party officials – he also went to serious lengths to censor his own observations, in subjecting his thought processes to a rigorous application of the Marxist dialectic. In *The Invisible Writing*, Koestler calls this the 'automatic sorting machine' in his head, which allowed him to dismiss negative impressions of the USSR as the 'heritage of the past', but perceive positive impressions as the 'seeds of the future'.[10] The trouble with *Red Days* for Comintern was that Koestler's prose was just too self-conscious about the processes of this sorting machine, which strained to keep up with the imperative to transform patent economic failures and misery into success. The effect is seen in one revealing passage composed shortly after Koestler's arrival in Kharkiv, which was unsurprisingly cut from *Red Days* and reinstated in *The Invisible Writing*:

> Let us not deceive ourselves: this writer did not stand up very well to the test of the first few days. He splashed about rather helplessly in the bottomless porridge of impressions which he had found instead of the neat and tidy contours of socialist life anticipated in his imagination [. . .] Foreign newspapers

are unobtainable, telegrams travel slower than the trains, a telephone call takes longer than a journey in the tram.

Yet in the centre of this sleepy village [. . .] there is a square with two modern skyscrapers; and next to it the new telephone exchange all in steel and glass; and there is a new model hospital, and the new tractor factory [. . .]

It looks like a film which, through a mistake, has been twice exposed by the photographer: once in the past and once in the future. [. . .]

Only slowly does the newcomer learn to think in contradictions; to distinguish, underneath a chaotic surface, the shape of things to come; to realise that in Sovietland the present is a fiction, a quivering membrane stretched between the past and the future.[11]

Koestler's gesture towards recognizing Soviet progress, identifying such symbols of modernity as the telephone exchange, tractor factory and skyscraper, is undermined in advance by an impression of generalized backwardness, and the sluggish pace by which any form of information travelled. Further, his metaphor of a twice-exposed film, and his declaration of the need to 'think in contradictions', is dangerously candid in pointing to Koestler's elective self-deception. The discomfort of cognitive dissonance – the grating inconsistencies between what he believed and what he wrote – manifestly inhibited the effectiveness of Koestler's propaganda for the Party. In 1954, though, he could write with freedom about the dark mire beneath the 'chaotic surface' of life in 'Sovietland'. He had actually arrived in Ukraine during the catastrophic famine known as the Holodomor, which killed as many as 10 million, and which has been classified by the European Parliament as genocide against the Ukrainian people by Stalin's regime.[12] Koestler later admitted his shock at seeing the desperation of Ukrainians who approached his train with starving babies in their arms, but he was told that these families were 'kulaks who had resisted the collectivization of the land'; for the purposes of the 1930s travelogue, he almost managed to convince himself that the appalling conditions were the legacy of a bourgeois past.[13]

It is important to note here that Koestler's own 'enlightened', post-KPD account of his motivations and actions must itself be taken with a dose of scepticism. As James Smith has demonstrated through his research into the British secret service files kept on Koestler, he was quite capable of manipulating even intelligence agencies in the retelling of his life story, and his 'evasions and inventions [. . .] form part of a wider pattern [. . .] [of his] canny manipulations of the secret world in order to further his own interests'.[14] Smith notes an 'almost pathological desire to integrate himself into secret causes', which expressed itself in his habit of courting multiple covert agencies despite having 'so publicly traded on a reputation as an opponent to those secret mechanisms of communist power'.[15]

Nevertheless, Koestler's manifest political volte-face, which began in 1938 with his exit from the Communist Party, led him in the early 1950s to exploit the mechanisms of his professed self-deception, making of it an exceptional weapon in the literary arsenal of anti-communist propaganda. Indeed, much of his fiction and non-fiction political writing of the period interrogated the continuing attraction of Soviet ideology to left-wing intellectuals – those whom he considered to remain in thrall to the 'automatic sorting machine'. Koestler generally explains the attitudes of these fellow travellers in pseudo-psychological terms as a kind of psychosis induced by excessive schooling in the revolutionary dialectic.[16] When it came to Soviet propaganda, Koestler seemed less concerned by the content of the communication than by the epistemology underpinning it – that is, how its adherents were trained to suppress critical thinking, and how it exploited the mind's capacity for irrationality.

Koestler's concerns about the 'closed circuit' of Soviet thought may be illuminated by way of Jamie Cohen-Cole's investigation into how the notion of the 'open mind' was politicized by Cold War-era intellectuals and policy makers. Where the open mind of the ideal American citizen was 'tolerant, broad, flexible, realistic, [and] unprejudiced', the closed mind – characterizing the 'subjects of totalitarian states' – was 'rigid, narrow, conformist, intolerant, ideological, and prejudiced'.[17] As Cohen-Cole goes on to explain, 'the lauding of mental attributes [. . .] was a partisan endeavour, even if it did not always travel under an explicit banner of political activity'.[18] Seen in this light, Koestler's juxtaposition of open-minded autonomy and Soviet, or fellow travelling, closed-minded conformity served to advance the discourse of the Western bloc's political elite, and 'helped to form the definition of rationality, creativity, and right thinking in mid-twentieth-century America'.[19] By presenting excerpts from *Red Days* alongside his critical commentary in *The Invisible Writing*, Koestler displayed for his readers the rigid Soviet epistemology alongside 'right thinking' anti-communist reasoning.[20]

Medicine men

As this chapter has begun to show, while earlier examples of Koestler's propaganda played upon his own and his audience's capacity for self-deception, his later work sought to understand and expose the mental vagaries that enabled such deception. His work for the KPD may not have been so successful as his later efforts to excoriate the Soviet regime, but his years in the party did provide a robust education in the art of how to communicate to advance political interests. Most important to this education was Koestler's mentoring by Willi Münzenberg, the KPD's de facto chief propagandist in Weimar Berlin, and then Paris from 1933 to 1936.

It had been Münzenberg's prodigious skill in executing covert propaganda campaigns that shaped Koestler's utopian perception of Soviet progress before his disturbing encounter with the reality in Ukraine. As Michael Scammell points out, the young Koestler's idea of the Soviet Union was 'formed by images of gigantic construction projects in Münzenberg's propaganda magazines, and by pictures of jolly workers transforming the country into an industrial paradise'.[21] Since its founding in Weimar Berlin in 1921, Münzenberg's powerful organization, the *International Arbeiter-Hilfe* (the IAH, or International Workers' Aid), financed a plethora of propagandist texts and artworks, including internationally successful films by Sergei Eisenstein and Vsevolod Pudovkin, whose *Battleship Potemkin* (1925) and *Storm over Asia* (1928) respectively were 'among the most powerful emotional experiences of [Koestler's] past'.[22] In 1954, Koestler detailed what he considered to be some of Münzenberg's innovations in the field of mass propaganda: the camouflaged 'front' organization, which gives a public face to a system of covert influence and funding; the discovery and mobilization of the liberal sympathizer; and the indirect propaganda value of the charitable appeal, which inspired solidarity from its contributors.[23] While broadly confirming Koestler's assessment of the scope of Münzenberg's propaganda empire, Sean McMeekin's account of the 'Red Millionaire' – which is unclouded by Koestler's residual respect – debunks the myth of his entrepreneurial genius: '[e]very business [Münzenberg] touched hemorrhaged [*sic*] red ink', to the extent that 'the Kremlin could barely keep up with servicing his debts'.[24] His prowess in the dark arts of propaganda, on the other hand, is undisputed: Münzenberg was 'a perpetrator of some of the most colossal lies of the modern age'.[25]

During Hitler's rise to power, Münzenberg directed Comintern's propaganda headquarters in Berlin, then Paris, in the guise of the 'World Committee Against War and Fascism'. As we shall see, various of Münzenberg's methods were repurposed in the anti-communist crusade in the late 1940s and early 1950s, when Koestler drew on his former mentor's example as he worked to counter the Soviets' ideological seduction of liberal intellectuals. Münzenberg gave Koestler his first assignments in Paris after the Reichstag fire in 1933 forced the KPD into exile from Germany. By this time, Koestler's faith in the utopian future of the Soviet Union was severely shaken, but the rise of Hitler and his fascist threat brought a new impetus to Koestler's need to believe in the communist cause – at least insofar as it then advocated anti-fascism and anti-imperialism. As a 'minor participant in the great propaganda battle between Berlin and Moscow', Koestler watched Münzenberg compete with Joseph Goebbels, the Nazi Minister of Propaganda, to use the burning of the German Parliament to win popular opinion on the international front.[26] Each aimed to convince the world that the other had set fire to the Reichstag. Tellingly, Koestler characterized the two as 'rival medicine men', which in his vocabulary was a way of highlighting their shared magnetism as public speakers. Drawing on a somewhat derogatory definition of the indigenous medicine man – the spiritual leader with supposed access to supernatural powers – Koestler characterized the propaganda tycoons as having renounced the strict use of truth in favour of their intense emotional appeal.[27] In Koestler's words, 'The world thought that it was witnessing a classic struggle between truth and falsehood, guilt and innocence. In reality both parties were guilty, though not of the crimes of which they accused each other.'[28]

By most accounts, Münzenberg won the battle for international hearts and minds over the fallout from the Reichstag fire, and his success can be attributed in part to his *Brown Book of the Reichstag Fire and Hitler Terror* (1933). The *Brown Book* used information gathered by Comintern to document the persecution of Jews, and to present a (partial, and partly fabricated) story of the burning of the Reichstag. Koestler was employed by Münzenberg to work in the KPD's Anti-fascist Archive, which collected the pamphlets, newspaper cuttings and other documents that went into the creation of a second *Brown Book*. With his privileged inside perspective on the medicine man's techniques, and particularly the *Brown Book*'s blending of comprehensive facts with 'guesswork and brazen bluff', Koestler acquired an important lesson: 'in the field of propaganda the half-truth was a weapon superior to the truth.'[29] This explained his other major insight from his time with Münzenberg: where it comes to propaganda, 'a democracy must always be at a disadvantage against a totalitarian opponent', since the former is less willing and able to deal in lies than the latter.[30] There will be more to say on this in a moment.

Münzenberg set an example for Koestler not only through the kinds of propaganda he produced but also in his relative aloofness from the finer points of communist doctrine: he was an activist, not a theoretician. According to an approving Koestler, 'the wrangles about the dialectically correct interpretation of the [Party] line left [Münzenberg] cold and contemptuous.'[31] McMeekin agrees with Koestler on this point, though his account of Münzenberg benefits from its greater objectivity: 'Münzenberg [. . .] believed wholeheartedly in the cause, [but he] had no qualms about employing ideologically dubious means to further Communist ends.'[32] In any case, Münzenberg was proof to Koestler that the propagandist need not succumb to the kinds of tortuous mental funambulism – the 'tight-rope acts of self-deception' – that their work might seek to inspire in their audience. Thus, tellingly, Koestler's 'ideologically dubious' position in the 1950s resembled Münzenberg's in the 1930s. Where Koestler now generated propagandist texts that contributed to the Western bloc's definition of the conformist 'closed mind' of the fellow-travelling intelligentsia, Münzenberg had once used similar means to characterize the same fellow-travelling liberals as being progressive in outlook. As Stephen Koch puts it, Münzenberg 'wanted to instil the feeling [. . .] that seriously to criticize or challenge Soviet policy was the unfailing mark of a bad, bigoted, and probably stupid person, while support was equally infallible proof of a forward-looking mind [. . .]'.[33] In the late 1940s and early 1950s, Koestler presented his unease at fellow-travelling self-deception using the language of psychoanalysis; he argued that 'the self-contradictory, split pattern of communist propaganda induces an equally split, schizophrenic mentality in those who are exposed to it'.[34] According to Koestler, the trouble with the typical communist mind was not so much that it was irrational but that it suffered from an excess of rigid rationalism.[35] Up to a point, this gave the communist movement an advantage over its more liberal counterparts: the Marxist schema provided a 'methodical approach to social phenomena more precise and "concrete" than that of *bourgeois* sociologists'.[36] On the other hand, the schema effected an 'abstract, schematic, and oversimplified way of thinking which [. . .] was often staggeringly naïve'.[37]

Koestler took this argument further in a 1953 article for the Anglo-American literary magazine *Encounter*, where he coined the concept of 'political neuroses'. He describes the erosion of political behaviour through psychological forces, which may be explained by the fact that the twentieth-century citizen is a 'political neurotic':

> Into the neurotic's distorted universe no facts are admitted which may upset its inner consistency. Arguments cannot penetrate the buffers of casuistry, the semantic shock-absorbers, the emotional defences. The inner censor – in the full psychiatric sense of the word – that protects the patient's illusions against the intrusion of reality, is incomparably more effective than any totalitarian state censorship. The political neurotic carries his private Iron Curtain inside his skull.[38]

The description is close to Koestler's account of his own 'inner censor' when he arrived in Soviet Ukraine in 1932. We might remember here Cohen-Cole's emphasis on the political orientation of definitions of the liberal versus the totalitarian mind in the period. On the other hand, Koestler is clear that it is not just the subject of the totalitarian state that succumbs to gross irrationality; with his customary flair for hyperbole, Koestler describes the human mind as 'basically schizophrenic', and he posits that the 'dogmatic belief in the political rationality of the individual is the ultimate reason why democracies are always on the defensive against totalitarian opponents'.[39] We may wonder whether Koestler's words were part of a democratic campaign that was truly 'on the defensive', however, when we consider that the magazine in which they appear was being covertly funded by the CIA as part of its campaign of cultural propaganda.[40]

The Congress for Cultural Freedom

Koestler cemented his reputation as the intelligentsia's public face of anti-communism at the first conference of the CCF in 1950. The Congress comprised a body of international writers, scholars and scientists and, like *Encounter* which the CCF sponsored, it was covertly funded by the CIA to disseminate anti-communist propaganda. A key goal was to dismantle the attraction that Marxism and communism had for many progressive European intellectuals. Koestler drafted the Congress's manifesto, and at the opening session he addressed a crowd of 15,000 in West Berlin – a location with considerable symbolic value, as a beleaguered outpost a hundred miles behind the Iron Curtain. It had personal significance for Koestler too, as the city where he had been recruited into Comintern. With left-wing fellow travellers in mind, Koestler described the conference as 'an attempt to dispel the intellectual confusion created by the totalitarian campaigns under the slogan of peace'.[41] His polemical language was calculated to banish the kinds of political equivocation, and the appetite for neutrality, that had taken Neville Chamberlain to Munich twelve years earlier.

Koestler's manifesto is suffused with the principle that a nation's state of peace is dependent on its citizens' freedoms, which critically include freedom of thought. As he begins, 'We hold it to be self-evident that intellectual freedom is one of the inalienable rights of man [. . .] The citizen of the totalitarian state is expected and forced not only to abstain from crime but to conform in all his thoughts and actions to a prescribed pattern.'⁴² Here, again, is the discourse of the 'intolerant, ideological, and prejudiced' mind identified by Cohen-Cole. There is a time 'to speak in relative clauses', Koestler declared in the conference's opening session, but what was needed to combat totalitarianism now was 'simple and direct language'.⁴³ Quoting the Bible, he delivered what was to become a catchphrase of the conference: 'Let your communication be, Yea, yea, Nay, nay; for whatsoever is more than these, comes from evil.'⁴⁴ Unlike the jaded Leontiev described earlier, Koestler's commitment to the principles of this manifesto ran deep. The diary he kept during the conference registers his preoccupation with the kind of citizen who 'conform[s] in all his thoughts and actions to a prescribed pattern', when he describes an encounter with a young communist during the delegates' visit to the Soviet sector of East Berlin: 'he is a nice little robot-brain [. . .] Complete conditioning in Brave New World sense. His answer to all arguments about free opinion etc "Yes but we don't need it, we are in a period of transition"'.⁴⁵ For some at the CCF, though, there was a problem with Koestler's oratory, which appeared to be charged with the same demagoguery as the Soviet peace conferences he so stridently denounced. Writing of the United States' 'massive ideological mobilization' in the Cold War, Nicholas Cull explains that where counter-propaganda was to be effective, the 'credibility of a message often hinged [. . .] on the nature of the messenger'.⁴⁶ Even as Koestler drew upon his intimate knowledge of Soviet casuistry, he was regarded by some as an unreliable messenger, partly because he had 'never surrendered his dialectical materialism'.⁴⁷ Richard Crossman, the friend with whom Koestler worked on *The God that Failed*, himself admitted that Koestler's life would 'always be lived inside [that] dialectic', which '[reflected] a searing inner struggle [that was] the mainspring of his creative work'.⁴⁸ Indeed, Koestler himself admitted that he 'retained a residue of the Marxian method of approach as a valuable asset'.⁴⁹

Distrustful observers of Koestler, which included the openly hostile historian Hugh Trevor-Roper, considered the ex-communist to be irreparably tainted by his old instruction in the revolutionary dialectic, his totalitarian inclinations seemingly now attracting him to the other ideological extreme of McCarthyism.⁵⁰ But Koestler's didacticism on behalf of the CCF should be understood not simply as a character trait but, quite as significantly, as a calculated reaction to the failures of Allied propaganda during the Second World War. In an essay first published in 1944 in the *New York Times Magazine*, Koestler decried how British and American citizens lacked awareness of the atrocities committed by Nazis against the Jews of Europe. The Ministry of Information (MOI) and the BBC 'lamentably failed to imbue the people with anything approaching a full awareness of [. . .] the grandeur and horror of the time into which they were born'.⁵¹ And the 'limitations of enlightenment by propaganda' must be explained once again, Koestler wrote, by human psychology: a 'state of split consciousness' renders the mind incapable of connecting the horrors of the Holocaust with 'the realities of [its] normal plane of existence'.⁵² If a democracy's propaganda failed as a tool to enlighten, then should the state instead use it to exploit its citizens' 'political neuroses' in the greater interest of peace? Koestler's unpublished papers of the years immediately following the Second World War indicate a thinker grappling with the question of what form his Cassandra cries against the Soviets should take, and his answer varied considerably in a short space of time.

In 1945–6, Koestler corresponded with George Orwell and Bertrand Russell on the subject of founding a new (though ultimately unrealized) League for the Rights of Man. This body would aim to defuse suspicion between the Western Powers and the USSR through mutual commitment to broadcasting factual material, and to the free exchange of ideas between the blocs. In January of that year, Orwell shared a draft petition with Koestler which distilled their deliberations so far. The petition's aim was to convince the British government of 'the necessity to include the psychological factor in their power-calculations [. . .] More precisely: that "psychological disarmament" should be an object of international negotiations'.⁵³ There was some disagreement with Russell, who had reservations about the wording of the 'psychological disarmament' clause, but – as Koestler replied to the philosopher – this was 'the fundament of the whole draft'.⁵⁴ At this point, the employment of counter-propaganda against the Soviet Union seemed far from Koestler's mind. By 1948, though, Koestler was spending time in the United States with key figures behind its anti-communist foreign policy, with whom he discussed the 'need for psychological warfare'.⁵⁵ Among these were the neoconservative James Burnham, who had worked for the CIA's predecessor – the Office of Strategic Services (OSS) – and who introduced Koestler to William J. Donovan, the OSS's former director. Münzenberg's disciple had effectively become a consultant on propagandist techniques to the American intelligence services.

Koestler's apparent vacillation between psychological disarmament and psychological mobilization in the 1940s and 1950s can be traced back to his apprenticeship with Münzenberg, when he had learnt to become sceptical regarding the West's chances of waging 'psychological warfare' against opponents like Stalin, for to wage effective psychological war the West would have to 'abandon precisely those principles and values in the name of which it fights'.⁵⁶ Frances Stonor Saunders presents the CIA's stance on this quandary in terms of an outright ethical failure: 'by its covert governance [. . .] [the CIA] was effectively acting in breach of the very declaration of rights it had paid for. To promote freedom of expression, the Agency had first to buy it, then to restrict it.'[57] Unlike the CIA, it seemed that Koestler lacked clarity and consistency over the question of how best to wage this war – another indication of his own 'split consciousness' – and he was forced to resign from the CCF within a year.[58] Koestler had another tool, however, with which to expose the dangers of the dialectical tight-rope laid out by Soviet doctrine: his fiction.

The Age of Longing

Koestler's novels enabled him to deal with the ethical issues around psychological war with a nuance that was impossible at the CCF. He used his fiction of the period to make an appeal to pseudo-reasoning fellow travellers by casting very direct light on their capacity for self-deception, dramatizing the mind's collusion with propaganda. In *The Age of Longing*, Jules Commanche, a French hero of the resistance modelled partly on André Malraux, becomes a mouthpiece for Koestler in outlining the fundamental irrationality of the political psyche. Using Freudian terms, he declares that 'the political instinct-life of people [. . .] is irrational and impervious to reasoned argument. [It] has its primitive, savage id, and its lofty super-ego; its mechanisms for the repression of facts, its inner censor which prevents, more effectively than a State censorship, any unpalatable information from reaching the neurotic's consciousness [. . .]'.[59] All of which explains why 'the so-called moderate Left with its purely rational appeal has failed'.[60]

Koestler's answer to this perceived failure was, in *The Age of Longing*, to present a series of differently conditioned minds partaking in their own psychological war. The novel is set in Paris a few years beyond Koestler's present day, and centres on an unlikely romance between a young American woman whose father is a diplomat, and a 'Commonwealth' spy (the USSR is here thinly camouflaged as the 'Freedomloving Commonwealth') who has been compiling a list of French intellectuals to be executed after an imminent Soviet invasion of France. The American, Hydie, befriends a group of intellectuals who are the few to recognize the threat. To convince Hydie of the danger, they take her to what they label a 'witches sabbath': a parody of the kind of Cominform-sponsored peace Congress which Koestler attacked in his own CCF conference speech. Among the Congress' speakers is a caricature of Jean-Paul Sartre, a Professor Pontieux, on whom Marxist doctrine has acted like a drug, with the effect that 'he can prove everything he believes, and he believes everything he can prove'.[61] It is at this Congress that we first encounter Leontiev – the cultural propagandist par excellence – who chooses between two antithetical versions of a speech that turns out to directly contradict the previous speakers. The party line has changed in the course of the Congress, and Professor Pontieux is seen to be 'mentally recapitulating his speech to check whether Leontiev's point of view could be fitted into it'.[62] Thus, Koestler satirizes the 'automatic sorting machine' in action.

The repercussions of giving in to such doublethink are made plain in the novel's epilogue, though Koestler was persuaded to drop this before the book was published. Initially, he had framed the central narrative with the conceit that it was written in imitation of an author, namely himself – A. Koestler – now dead after the collapse of the civilization being described, and now that the novel as an art-form is extinct: 'a product whose limitations of consciousness and expression were inherent in its form'. The excised epilogue tells how

> K's novel is supposed to have been written at a time when the catastrophe could still be prevented [. . .] Though [. . .] destiny's challenge is always couched in direct and elementary terms, it needs a prophet whose language is yea and nay, to meet it in an equally simple manner. But pre-Pubertarian man thought in elusive relative clauses, and the tribe of clever imbeciles who could prove everything they believed and believe everything they could prove, had sapped his powers of distinguishing between good and evil.[63]

We have seen from Koestler's CCF speeches his contemporaneous experiment in adopting the prophet's direct language of 'yea and nay'. It is ironic, then, that Koestler's expulsion from the CCF came partly on the advice of James Burnham, who suspected him of divided loyalties, and who found the evidence for this in *The Age of Longing*. In the novel, Burnham declared, 'Bolsheviks are rationally condemned, but imaginatively displayed as firm, purposeful and sexually dynamic' . . . Koestler's 'implicit audience' was still 'the Left'.[64]

Remarkably, the same qualities in Koestler's writing had led him into trouble with the KPD some twenty years earlier. His first (unpublished) novel, which he developed out of another of Münzenberg's propagandist assignments, earned the disapproval of party bureaucrats for its 'bourgeois individual psychology'.[65] In both texts, the psychological portraits of his Soviet characters led Koestler, paradoxically, to combat the tendency of Soviet propaganda to '[leave] out the human detail'.[66] It was as if Koestler's fiction inexorably betrayed the disillusionment he experienced over generating propaganda for both ideological camps; his 'split consciousness' surfaced to complicate the vision of each cause's revolutionary or moral promises with the reality of their compromises and betrayals. Though after leaving the CCF Koestler continued to write polemics on areas such as nuclear disarmament and the abolition of the UK's death penalty, his writing was never again so squarely in the service of any political cause. Koestler understood better than most how it felt to sway on the dialectical tight-rope, but his ability to recreate this in his fiction presented a stronger case, in his eyes, for dispensing with the techniques of mass propaganda altogether than with furthering it for the anti-communist crusade.

Notes

1. Arthur Koestler, *The Age of Longing* (London: Collins, 1951), 88.
2. Ibid., 147.
3. Arthur Koestler, *The Invisible Writing* (1954; London: Vintage, 2019), 38.
4. Arthur Koestler, 'The Initiates', in *The God that Failed* (New York, NY: Harper, 1949), 71.
5. Ibid., 101. The volume was edited by Richard Crossman, the British Labour politician and veteran of the Second World War-era British Political Warfare Executive and the Allies' Psychological Warfare Division.
6. Ibid., 72.
7. Comintern, the 'Communist International', was the Soviet-dominated association of national communist parties, which advocated world communism. It was succeeded by Cominform in 1947.
8. Koestler, *The Invisible Writing*, 187.
9. Ibid., 95.
10. Ibid., 66.
11. Ibid., 65–6.
12. 'Holodomor: Parliament recognizes Soviet starvation of Ukrainians as genocide', European Parliament press release, 15 December 2022 (see: https://www.europarl.europa.eu/news/en/press-room/20221209IPR64427/holodomor-parliament-recognises-soviet-starvation-of-ukrainians-as-genocide [accessed 15 November 2023]). The resolution draws explicit parallels between the famine of the 1930s and contemporary Russian aggression against Ukraine.
13. Koestler, 'The Initiates', 60.
14. James Smith, *British Writers and MI5 Surveillance, 1930–1960* (Cambridge: Cambridge University Press, 2013), 134.
15. Ibid., 142, 141.
16. Koestler's interests in psychology predated the crystallization of his anti-communist thought; while a student of mechanical engineering at the Technische Hochschule

in Vienna, Koestler came to read Freud, Alfred Adler, Wilhelm Stekel and Carl Jung, on areas of psychiatry, experimental psychology and the psychology of art.
17 Jamie Cohen-Cole, *The Open Mind: Cold War Politics and the Sciences of Human Nature* (Chicago, IL and London: University of Chicago Press, 2014), 4.
18 Ibid., 60.
19 Ibid., 62. Other non-fiction to advance this broad campaign include texts published by the Congress for Cultural Freedom, such as *World Technology and Human Destiny* (1963, ed. by Raymond Aron, George Kennan and Robert Oppenheimer), and Richard Löwenthal's *World Communism: The Disintegration of a Secular Faith* (1964). Among the novels that contributed to a Western bloc discourse polarising conformist Soviet thought and liberal autonomy were Doris Lessing's *The Golden Notebook* (1962), published six years after she left the British Communist Party.
20 Through the machinations of the CCF, Koestler's and others' efforts in print were loosely paralleled in the visual arts by abstract expressionism. As Cohen-Cole explains, the CCF sponsored exhibitions of artists like Jackson Pollock, who 'seemed to highlight the freedoms of the American way of life' – its abstract aesthetics being very far from the politics of class that preoccupied Soviet Realism (Cohen-Cole, *The Open Mind*, 58).
21 Michael Scammell, *Koestler: The Indispensable Intellectual* (London: Faber, 2010), 88.
22 Arthur Koestler, *Arrow in the Blue* (1952; London: Vintage, 2005), 332.
23 Unlike Koestler, Münzenberg passed up the opportunity to describe his own methods in his own words. As Sean McMeekin points out, his 1937 book *Propaganda as a Weapon* gives no meaningful insight into his propaganda techniques, and instead focuses on Hitler's and Goebbels's methods. Furthermore, in McMeekin's words, Münzenberg's book is 'politically opaque', which may be accounted for by Münzenberg's ideological slipperiness . Sean McMeekin, *The Red Millionaire: A Political Biography of Willi Münzenberg* (New Haven, CT: Yale University Press), 287.
24 McMeekin, *The Red Millionaire*, 2.
25 Ibid., 306.
26 Koestler, *The Invisible Writing*, 237.
27 Ibid.
28 Ibid.
29 Ibid., 249.
30 Ibid., 243, 249.
31 Ibid., 251.
32 McMeekin, *The Red Millionaire*, 3.
33 Stephen Koch, *Double Lives: Stalin, Willi Münzenberg and the Seduction of the Intellectuals* (London: HarperCollins, 1994), 13.

34 Koestler, *Arrow in the Blue*, 335.
35 On Koestler's Cold War reaction to Soviet rationalism – and how for him 'mathematics became a means of breaking with a philosophy that had come to seem too narrowly rationalistic' – see Matthew Taunton, 'Two and Two Make Five', in *Red Britain: The Russian Revolution in Mid-Century Culture* (Oxford: Oxford University Press, 2019), 60–112.
36 Koestler, *Arrow in the Blue*, 336.
37 Ibid., 337.
38 Arthur Koestler, 'A Guide to Political Neuroses', *Encounter*, November 1953, 26.
39 Arthur Koestler, 'Anatomy of a Myth', in *The Yogi and the Commissar*, 121; Koestler, 'A Guide to Political Neuroses', 25.
40 The discovery in 1967 of this source of funding notoriously led Stephen Spender, the magazine's founder and literary editor, to resign.
41 Arthur Koestler, 'The Right to Say No', in *The Trail of the Dinosaur* (London: Vintage, 1994), 112.
42 Arthur Koestler, 'Manifesto of the Congress for Cultural Freedom', in *The Trail of the Dinosaur*, 112–13.
43 Arthur Koestler, 'Two Methods of Action', in *The Trail of the Dinosaur*, 118.
44 Ibid., 116.
45 Arthur Koestler's Berlin diary, June 1950, Special Collections of Edinburgh University Library, Arthur Koestler Papers, MS2306/4/28.
46 Nicholas Cull, 'Counter-propaganda: Cases from US Public Diplomacy and Beyond', in *Propaganda and Conflict*, ed. Mark Connelly, Jo Fox, Ulf Schmidt, and Stefan Goebel (London: Bloomsbury, 2019), 275.
47 'Herr Grimme', quoted in Frances Stonor Saunders, *Who Paid the Piper?: The CIA and the Cultural Cold War* (London: Granta, 1999), 80.
48 Richard Crossman, 'Introduction', in *The God that Failed*, 18.
49 Koestler, *Arrow in the Blue*, 337.
50 Duncan White, *Cold Warriors* (London: Little, Brown, 2019), 280.
51 Arthur Koestler, 'On Disbelieving Atrocities', in *The Yogi and the Commissar*, 96. Koestler knew all too well of the widespread ignorance, and in some cases the outright disbelief, in Britain of the transportation of Jews in Europe. During the Second World War he lectured British troops on the subject and wrote anti-Nazi propaganda scripts for the MOI.
52 Koestler, 'On Disbelieving Atrocities', 97–8.
53 George Orwell, Draft for a Petition, typescript, Arthur Koestler Papers, MS2345/2/54.
54 Arthur Koestler to Bertrand Russell, 6 May 1946, Arthur Koestler Papers, MS2345/2/90.

55 Mamaine Koestler's US diary, holograph manuscript, 18 March 1948, Arthur Koestler Papers, MS2306/4/49.
56 Koestler, *The Invisible Writing*, 249.
57 Saunders, *Who Paid the Piper?*, 90.
58 According to Saunders, the reason for Koestler's eventual marginalization by the CCF was his inability to keep a moderate tone. Michael Josselson, who now ran the CCF for the CIA, had come to decide that restraint was needed to win over the unconvinced. See Saunders, *Who Paid the Piper?*, 90.
59 Koestler, *The Age of Longing*, 322.
60 Ibid., 323.
61 Ibid., 81.
62 Ibid., 90.
63 'Epigraph' to *The Age of Longing*, typescript, 1951, Papers of Arthur Koestler, MS 2317/1.
64 James Burnham, quoted in Michael Scammell, *Koestler*, 385.
65 Koestler, *The Invisible Writing*, 286.
66 Arthur Koestler, 'Soviet Myth and Reality', in *The Yogi and the Commissar*, 144.

12

Psychological warfare in Thomas Pynchon's *Gravity's Rainbow*

Kirk Robert Graham

A mad scientist scrambles through the ruins of a blitzed-out London flat, dodging loose bricks and broken bedposts, on the hunt for a dog who will, upon capture, be baptized with a corny Russian name in keeping with certain Pavlovian proclivities, when, just as he rounds on his quarry, the scientist's foot becomes wedged in – of all things – a toilet bowl that went unnoticed amid the debris. Meanwhile, across town, an enterprising and mellifluous BBC radio journalist becomes enamoured of an intelligence report about some Herero-Germans two generations removed from German South West Africa who may have found themselves working, tangentially at least, for the Nazi war machine, and so, while broadcasting one night to Germany, our journalist ad libs a report of the kind that would make any colonizer's skin crawl. And what luck! – by some strange machination, the journalist happens to precisely anticipate a link between the Herero-Germans and the secretive V2 rocket programme, thanks, no doubt, to his preternatural understanding of the German mind. The mad scientist and the canny newshound are connected by a psychological warfare department thrown up by circumstance which brings together all manner of oddballs and boffins from vaudevillians and cut-throats to statisticians and even occultists well-practised in the Ouija board. Such is the weirdness of Thomas Pynchon's *Gravity's Rainbow* (1973), a novel which, at its heart, remains one of the most veracious historical fictions of the twentieth century.[1]

This chapter will explore the place of wartime subversive propaganda in *Gravity's Rainbow*, both as subject and as a model for literary invention. *Gravity's Rainbow* is about a lot of things. A simple plot summary might begin with the character of Tyrone Slothrop, an American intelligence officer stationed in London in the final months of the Second World War. Having been experimented on by a notorious behavioural psychologist as a child, it appears Slothrop is now conditioned to be able to anticipate where incoming German V2 rockets will strike. His abilities soon come to the attention of the authorities (identified as a nebulous elite called 'The Firm', or more simply 'they'); their byzantine efforts to exploit him, and his efforts to keep out of their clutches while seeking the truth about his own making, drive the narrative. Written by an author who is morally and intellectually sensitive to the horrors of modernity – horrors that, Pynchon reminds us, did not end with the collapse of the Third Reich – *Gravity's Rainbow* is a frenetic reflection on the legacies of the Second World War and the unsettling activities cynically undertaken by government and business in the name of peace.

So, where does propaganda fit in?[2] *Gravity's Rainbow* directly and indirectly reflects the working practices, operations and campaigns of genuine Second World War propaganda organizations. The text is divided into four parts; the first part, entitled 'Beyond the Zero', is set in and around London over several months in late 1944 and is heavily populated by shadowy and nefarious Allied political warfare departments whose activities set the story in motion. Some of these organizations are historically real, others fictional, often embedded within another or overlapping in duties and in personnel, which ultimately makes for a disorienting tangle of acronyms and initialisms that is only a slight satirical inflation of the historical reality. The Political Warfare Executive (PWE) is one such war department, a British manufacturer of subversive propaganda which, in the text, also happens to oversee an esoteric group of researchers who develop an interest in the protagonist, Slothrop. Outside of the text, the PWE was formally established in 1941 as a consolidation of other organizations that had been mobilized since Britain's 1939 declaration of war. Ostensibly the fraternal counterpart to the sabotage- and espionage-oriented Special Operations Executive (SOE), the PWE was responsible for all foreign propaganda targeted at enemy and occupied Europe. This included (in the nomenclature of the day) 'white' operations broadcasting openly and attributed to Britain such as the BBC European Service, as well as 'black' operations which disguised their British origins to underpin subversive strategies. The PWE's black operations were extensive: these propagandists fielded more than forty clandestine radio stations in a variety of languages, printed countless newspapers, leaflets and other print media, and, in concert with SOE and other departments, established a 'whisper' network to spread malicious rumours. A black radio station called 'Gustav Siegfried Eins', or GS1, is representative of their output. Broadcasting in German on short wave from 1941 to 1943, GS1 was hosted by a fictional character called 'der Chef', a blustering Prussian officer. This PWE creation was fiercely patriotic and loyal to Hitler but was perpetually outraged by the depravity of the SS and the corruption of the Nazi Party and would go into extraordinary detail to describe the latest SS perversions reported to him by his fictitious network of anti-Nazi officers (in reality such detail was furnished by intelligence reports, phonebooks, street maps, aerial photographs and newspaper clippings). GS1 illustrates the PWE's mission to hasten war's end by slowly and methodically promoting divisions in German society and undermining enemy morale. For a writer like Pynchon, ever preoccupied with clandestine networks, red herrings and *sub rosa* ne'er-do-wells, the PWE must have had a certain allure.

Despite its playfulness and anarchic resistance to linear narrative conventions, *Gravity's Rainbow* is, as Steven Weisenburger writes, 'painstakingly written from the standpoint of historical accuracy'.[3] The historical sources for Pynchon's texts have long been the subject of fascination, a fascination inflated no doubt by his reclusive habits as much as by his brilliance.[4] Of course, scholarship on Pynchon's historical research has tended to focus on rocketry (and industrial science in general), which is hardly surprising given the text's thematic interrogation of the Space Age as both an expression of human ingenuity and the repulsive amorality of the military-industrial complex. Given rocketry's predominance, the integral place of the propaganda war in *Gravity's Rainbow* has been somewhat neglected.

It is difficult to make concrete assertions regarding Pynchon's historical sources. A researcher will have more luck turning up the yellowed pages of a 'Most Secret' MI5 file than they will any notebook in Pynchon's hand. Nevertheless, *Gravity's Rainbow* provides ample textual evidence that Pynchon was well-informed about wartime propaganda, so much so that a number of narrative devices even bear the greasy imprint of psychological warfare strategies. This is particularly impressive from the perspective of a historian because, at the time the novel went to print in 1973, the PWE was still an obscure British war department whose files wouldn't be declassified until 1975. Yet Pynchon strolls unnervingly close to historical accounts published later that same decade, even though his source material must necessarily have been far less tangible. Further to this, Pynchon's idiosyncratic approach to historical fiction shares some uncanny similarities with PWE morale subversion strategies, suggesting that Pynchon may have taken inspiration from the propaganda war in more ways than one.

Propagandists at the end of the rainbow

While Pynchon's historical fiction is notorious for strange digressions and absurd fantasies, this feature is always underpinned by what Khachig Tololyan calls its 'scrupulously accurate historical context'.[5] Readers have spent decades speculating about the sources which inspired his texts; *Gravity's Rainbow* has attracted attention for the astonishing detail with which Pynchon explores rocketry, Pavlovian psychology and even 1930s pop culture as evidence of the influence of particular texts on the creation of the novel.[6] For example, David Seed points out the importance of texts such as historic Baedekers and maps in Pynchon's construction of past places (both physical and psychological), as well as philosopher Marshall McLuhan's *Understanding Media: The Extensions of Man* (1964), a work of media theory about interconnection in a media-saturated society which influenced Pynchon's 1966 novel *The Crying of Lot 49*. For Seed, Pynchon's texts can be read as 'a montage of historical material gathered from diverse sources'.[7] More than a parlour game, exploring a text's intertextuality can enrich readings while frustrating totalizing interpretations.

The significance of the PWE in *Gravity's Rainbow* and the manner in which it has been depicted suggests further sources may be added to the jumble. The PWE hovers in the background of the first section of the novel, bound ephemerally to the protagonist and to the scientist-bureaucrats who hope to utilize this aberration. In his first scene, Slothrop, fretting half-heartedly over paperwork, reveals via free indirect discourse that he had that very morning received orders telling him to report to a certain hospital. The orders included a note 'requesting his reassignment "as part of the P.W.E. Testing Programme." Testing? P.W.E. is Political Warfare Executive, he looked that up'.[8] The PWE takes on an important narrative role right from the start; even if Slothrop is largely ignorant of his condition, this ominous aside suggests that he is already on the radar for psychological warfare researchers, foreshadowing his later flight. Of course, the inner workings and motivations of the secretive PWE are only ever viewed tangentially. Having winked at such murky goings-on throughout the opening chapters, the text then plays at encyclopaedia by dumping on the unwitting reader a list of war departments nested or entwined, the duties of which seem impossible to untangle from each other:

> P.W.E. laps over onto the Ministry of Information, the BBC European Service, the Special Operations Executive, the Ministry of Economic Warfare, and the F.O. Political Intelligence Department at Fitzmaurice House. Among others. When the Americans came in, their OSS, OWI, and Army Psychological Warfare Department had also to be coordinated with. Presently there arose the joint, SHAEF Psychological Warfare Division (PWD), reporting direct to Eisenhower, and to hold it all together a London Propaganda Coordinating Council, which has no real power at all.[9]

Here, we see the text identifying a historically accurate catalogue of war departments involved in the propaganda war between 1941 and 1944, almost as if the text were advertising its historical veracity.[10] But then, the departmental Russian dolls continue. Burly SOE agent Pirate Prentice, whose experiences also indicate some discomfiting encounters with psychological experimentation, riffs at one point on a PWE sub-branch called 'The White Visitation [. . .] which houses a catchall agency known as PISCES – Psychological Intelligence Schemes for Expediting Surrender. Whose surrender is not made clear'.[11] And within PISCES, we find scientist Edward Pointsman's Abreaction Research Facility or ARF, concerned primarily with Pavlovianism (necessitating the collection of stray dogs). It becomes apparent from Pointsman's complaints that PWE holds the purse-strings for all of these mazy off-shoots.[12] Providing further continuity between these organizations and many others besides, the reader encounters traces of 'the Firm', a shadowy network of 'political and financial power' that critic Hanjo Berressem identifies as 'Pynchon's metaphor for the political and technocratic apparatus of our time'.[13] While names like ARF and ACHTUNG (Allied Clearing House, Technical Units, Northern Germany) sing with absurdist menace, the line between authorial invention and historical reality is lost in maximalism and the point at which the author's research ends and play begins becomes harder to identify. The multitude of organizations name-checked in the first act of the novel – all 'colonies of that Mother City mapped wherever the enterprise is systematic death'[14] – are profoundly disorienting for the reader and protagonist alike, establishing at once the insignificance of scurrying individuals and the threat of bureaucratic machinery operating just out of sight.

The PWE was very much real; however, as Tololyan observes, '[o]f the bureaucracies of war that play a major role in *Gravity's Rainbow*, those devoted to psychological warfare are the least known about to historians, and hence to Pynchon'.[15] Like many such war departments, something of the PWE's wartime secrecy was preserved into the post-war period.[16] In Britain, the PWE's archive was intended to remain classified for fifty years, but, along with the records of many other war departments, this was reduced to thirty years following public disclosures about the codebreaking operation *Ultra*. Still, vestiges of secrecy lingered: the PWE's official history, written by prominent Bloomsbury Group writer David Garnett during demobilization in 1945–6, was locked away and only published in 2002; MI5 files about key personnel including exiled German communists and even a runaway Waffen-SS officer later indicted for war crimes were only released in the mid-2000s. Yet, in the decades after the war, despite the veil of secrecy that governments had draped over their wartime activities, enough had been published about psychological warfare for a writer like Pynchon to set his plot in motion.

While some readers speculate about the range of classified documents Pynchon may have accessed during his brief career as a technical writer in the defence industry, by the mid-1960s, a writer of sufficient imagination could piece together enough historical detail at a well-stocked public library. Memoirs and other accounts by propagandists had been floating around since the 1940s. Tololyan makes a compelling case for Paul Linebarger's *Psychological Warfare* (1948) as one of Pynchon's source texts.[17] Linebarger was a key figure in American psychological warfare owing to his involvement in the Office of War Information, a government propaganda agency; his book derives directly from this experience, although it also provides a potted history of psychological warfare from antiquity to the present. Curiously, however, he offers scant detail on the organization or activities of British propaganda operations. My reading suggests Pynchon may have cast his net further afield.

In fact, by the mid-1960s, there were several other sources about this secretive organization in circulation. Elizabeth P. Macdonald was not British but American and was quick to capitalize on the silence of her British colleagues when she published her romp of a war memoir, *Undercover Girl*, in 1947.[18] She had been recruited into OSS Morale Operations during the war and, as part of her training, had learned about PWE's clandestine radio campaigns thanks to the close Anglo-American collaboration in the months ahead of D-Day.[19] At the same time, former OSS researchers who had been seconded to PWE operations were openly publishing data collected during the war in academic journals, covering such topics as the nature of the German mind and the successes and failures of anti-Nazi re-education programmes.[20] A more holistic approach was taken by Daniel Lerner in 1949 with *Sykewar: Psychological Warfare against Germany, D-Day to VE-Day*.[21] Lerner himself worked as an intelligence officer for the Psychological Warfare Division of SHAEF and used his insider knowledge to produce an 'objective' analysis and history covering the organization, personalities and operations of American and British propagandists during the war. His is an admirable military history that complements Linebarger's work, but focuses primarily on PWD/SHAEF operations and, while he has a great deal of insight into 'white' operations, Lerner has less to say about 'black' operations.

Given its coordinating role at the heart of the Allies' European psychological warfare activities, the image of the PWE glimpsed sideways in American accounts is certainly that of a shadowy organization with a lot of fingers in a lot of pies. We might hope, then, that British accounts clear up this mess. Unfortunately, Robert

Bruce Lockhart's memoir, *Comes the Reckoning* (1949), did not help matters. Unlike Linebarger, MacDonald or Lerner, former spy and society gadabout Lockhart was certainly well-informed about every aspect of PWE operations as the department's Director-General; however, bound by Britain's Official Secrets Act, his memoir, written in the style he refined as gossip columnist for the *Evening Standard*, demonstrates his phenomenal capacity for name-dropping but is frustratingly light on detail. A novelist could have made much of these sources to conjure a shadowy menace to Slothrop and his anarchic confederates. As far as likely sources for *Gravity's Rainbow*, however, there is one other text which stands out as a contender.

Black Wing, *Black Boomerang*

Pynchon is clearly well-versed in the structural intricacies of Allied subversive propaganda organizations in Britain, but a close look at how these organizations and their activities are depicted hints further at the source material. *Gravity's Rainbow* introduces the character of Myron Grunton as a journalist working for the BBC and broadcasting regular reports to Germany, whose instincts lead him down the path of subversive propaganda. The reader learns that Grunton has come up with a cunning plan to play on German fears and neuroses. However, before the Americans joined the war, he was hobbled by British penny-pinching:

> He's had to keep putting his plan off, at first only a voice alone, lacking the data he really needed, no support, trying to get at the German soul from whatever came to hand, P/W interrogations, Foreign Office Handbooks, the brothers Grimm, tourist memories of his own . . . But at last the Americans came in, and the arrangement known as SHAEF, and an amazing amount of money.[22]

Grunton's plan, which comes to be known as 'Operation Black Wing', was supposedly spun from General Eisenhower's 'strategy of truth' in which disinformation and morale subversion depended above all on some kernel of verifiable fact which represented 'a hook on the war's pocked execution-wall to hang the story from'.[23] The intended effect was twofold: convince the audience to believe the lie, or convince the audience to doubt everything. Inspired by an intelligence report about 'real Africans, Hereros, ex-colonials from South-West Africa' that are somehow involved in the V2 rocket program, journalist Myron Grunton *ad libs* a commentary on European colonial paternalism live on air. Black Wing blooms, mushroom-like, absorbing new bodies and talents. Soon 'foreign morale data' begins dribbling back to London, providing keen insights into the enemy mind and the effectiveness – 'an American heresy' – of the propaganda operation.

In 1962, British journalist Denis 'Tom' Sefton Delmer published *Black Boomerang*, the second volume of his autobiography, which focused on his time as a wartime journalist and propagandist. Delmer had a storied career. He spent his formative years in Berlin as the son of an Australian-born English professor and became fluent in German, even acquiring the hard-edged and fatalistic sense of humour known as the *Berliner Schnauze*. He found work in the British popular press and became a Berlin correspondent during the final years of the Weimar Republic. During the campaign for the 1932 presidential election, Delmer accompanied Hitler on his airborne tour of Germany. He even developed enough of a rapport with the Nazis to share the company of Hitler's inner circle on the night of the Reichstag fire. Soon, however, the goodwill he had earned with the Nazis dissipated. When Britain and Germany went to war, his expertise made him a natural fit for the BBC, where he would broadcast prompt replies to German speeches and propaganda announcements, sometimes hastily improvised. By 1941, he had been invited into clandestine operations, quickly rising to become the PWE chief of 'black' propaganda directed at enemy and enemy-occupied Europe.

Black Boomerang is a salacious account of Britain's propaganda war written by a key insider and in the tone of a bawdy story from the popular press. Delmer deliberately plays up the humour and vulgarity of the British strategy, relishing his team's 'genius' for trickery and deceit. True to his journalistic roots, stories of sex and scandal feature prominently in Delmer's account of the PWE's efforts to undermine the German war effort; in his memoir, he even claims that a close study of Magnus Hirschfeld's research into 'sexual aberrations' added colour to some of his radio operations – 'der Chef', mentioned earlier, was Delmer's invention.[24] Delmer's memoir is a humorous, if sometimes self-serving, account of the propaganda war that places the PWE and British 'black' propaganda at the centre of the history of psychological warfare.

While evidence is circumstantial, there are parallels between Delmer's memoir and *Gravity's Rainbow* that are difficult to overlook. Obviously, the name of Grunton's Operation, 'Black Wing', may well have been derived from *Black Boomerang*. And we could speculate that Sefton Delmer's already quite Pynchonian sounding name has been rendered into the unappetizing Myron Grunton, a change that preserves the metre of the original. The affinities run even deeper, however.

The propaganda strategy detailed in *Gravity's Rainbow* – using intelligence gathered from a wide range of sources to make predictions about German motives and intentions, and then play on them through broadcast and other propaganda media – is also described at length and with a prankster's delight by Delmer in *Black Boomerang*. Delmer recalls, for example, an incident in which a captured Luftwaffe pilot announced during interrogation that there was no point keeping secrets from the British because they knew everything anyway – he gave the case of a top secret conference about an attempt to break through a British naval blockade of the Gironde estuary and make it to Japan, which Delmer's clandestine radio station *Deutsche Kurzwellensender Atlantik* had subsequently broadcast verbatim over the air. 'It was incredible too', wrote Delmer, 'for it was just not true'.[25] What had actually happened was that British naval intelligence had observed some changes in fleet movements in the area, made an educated guess about German plans, and informed Delmer. 'So just to play on the crews' nerves and show them that their secret was a secret no longer', writes Delmer, 'we decided to pay them the honour of a special musical serenade' which involved 'a cacophonous jumble of Japanese and Chinese records'.[26] Readers may well draw parallels between the PWE's use of music as an extension of its subversive strategy and Pynchon's penchant for including (often vulgar, always silly) lyrics, verse and rhyme throughout his fiction. However, what draws my attention here is the combination of intelligence and speculation at the inception of the idea, as well as the creation of a line of propaganda not to deceive, but mainly to unnerve the listener.

The PWE's approach to 'black' propaganda, developed with Delmer's guidance from 1941, is transfigured by Pynchon into figments such as the *Schwarzkommando*, a paramilitary unit which, within the strange causal logic of the text, began life as a highly elaborate black operation before becoming infected by the uncanny reality of war. Grunton took scanty evidence of something happening in Germany and invented a story about these Black Germans. The characters of the novel soon discover that this absurd story about the Herero-German *Schwarzkommando* somehow attached to the Nazi rocket programme is quite true, making Grunton's initial invention all the more stunning while also vindicating the 'strategy of truth'. The 'Zone Hereros' take on a whole range of symbolic and historical significance connecting Nazi ideology with the many genocides of European colonialism from which fascism derived inspiration and method. Operation 'Black Wing' is not direct evidence that Pynchon made a study of *Black Boomerang*, but it does affirm that his historical research into wartime propaganda was as rigorous as his study of rocketry.

'Conditioned stimulus = x'

The reader's first impressions of *Gravity's Rainbow*'s protagonist, Tyrone Slothrop, come indirectly when a company man is sent to secretly photograph a map Slothrop has hung above his desk covered in coloured star-shaped stickers accompanied by names – '. . . Alice, Delores, Shirley, a couple of Sallys . . .' – a London Lothario's firmament.[27] Slothrop began charting his complicated social life months before, but, thanks to some unusual correlations, this activity has since attracted the attention of 'the Firm'. There is nothing especially unusual about his behaviour except that each coupling occurs precisely where a German V2 rocket happens to strike hours or days later. The explanation is both straightforward and maddeningly nonsensical. The reader learns that when Slothrop was a young boy, he was exploited as a test subject by Pavlovian psychologist Laszlo Jamf. Years later, German rocket scientists have utilized 'Imipolex G', a new plastic developed by Jamf shortly before the war, an 'aromatic heterocyclic polymer' which functions as an insulator for a mechanism in the V2. As Pynchon's metaphysics of rocketry play havoc with cause and effect, it appears that Slothrop is conditioned to experience sexual arousal thanks to the stimulus Imipolex G *before* the rockets arrive and, as a result, his libido, cartographically plotted, can determine the location of incoming strikes.

The Pavlovian plot device in *Gravity's Rainbow* is itself a nod to the war as a key moment during which new advances in the science of psychology were unevenly incorporated into the vast apparatus of social control. Here, the PWE again played an important role in the development of what ultimately became a pillar of the propaganda war. Delmer was disparaging about the value of professional psychological research in PWE operations, much preferring to trust his own journalistic and creative instincts; his memoir mentions the contributions of Cambridge psychopathologist J. T. MacCurdy to a long-run malingering campaign intended to drive a wedge between German workers and soldiers and the authorities, but overlooks the substantial contributions of other psychologists, particularly in the later years of the war.[28] While it is not explicitly stated in *Black Boomerang* or the other texts that emerged in the post-war period, this prevailing scepticism towards psychology is certainly reflected in *Gravity's Rainbow*, even as a major part of the plot revolves around psychological conditioning. The novel's psychologists, such as the Pavlovian acolyte Edward Pointsman and his PWE sub-sub-branch ARF, exist at the fringes of the war effort, forced to subsist on a meagre budget, at least until they can demonstrate their practical utility.

Despite Delmer's hesitation, the peculiar requirements of propaganda and morale subversion ultimately opened new avenues for the science of psychology to serve the state. Interestingly, however, developments here were contingent not only on those requirements, but also on their cultural and political context. In America, the New Deal had raised the profile of psychology, and especially iterations of social psychology. As a result, expertise with a psychological inflection was, in fact, quite welcome at the Research and Analysis branch of the American Office of Strategic Services (or the OSS, the precursor to the CIA), which tended to express a neo-Freudian outlook associated with the Frankfurt School. The Ivy League universities from which the OSS chief William J. Donovan recruited personnel to his new spy organizations had become home to a significant number of German professors from a variety of disciplines who were exiled by the Nazis because of their political views, methodologies or ethnicity. Whereas the New Deal had paved the way for the development of psychology in America, this new science had far less cultural cachet in Britain. Without obvious practical applications, British propagandists were reluctant to invest time and resources into the psychological sciences. Ultimately, Britain's Ministry of Information (MOI) did undertake psychological research to help steer propaganda directed at the British population, which was oriented towards behaviourist social psychology. But the PWE remained opposed, continually avoiding the advice or recommendations of psychologists of all stripes; only when American and British political warfare collaborations intensified in the lead up to D-Day did some of the neo-Freudian insights gain traction at the PWE.[29]

Histories tracing the influence of psychology on wartime propaganda and intelligence organizations were, for a long time, quite thin on the ground. In this instance, rather than using insider accounts and historical research, Pynchon was likely influenced by an array of very real psychological research that informed the operations of PWE, the OSS and other Allied war departments. Much of this research was buried in government archives, but quite a few notable studies such as Walter C. Langer's *The Mind of Adolf Hitler*, and Erik H. Erikson's work on developmental psychology in the context of Nazi Germany were published and read with great curiosity (both men were recruited by the OSS).[30] Of course, during the war, such studies were really only adopted by strategists and policy makers when they affirmed preconceived ideas; Langer's study, for example, was well known in certain circles, but was ignored because it did not help intelligence officers anticipate Hitler's plans.[31] However, Pavlovianism was not a methodology adopted by the Allies. There are several likely reasons why

Pynchon wrote Pavlovianism into the plot. First, as conditioned responses go, this one is hysterically funny; second, it creates a MacGuffin out of the stimulus 'Imipolex G' and provides Slothrop with an object to pursue and a mystery to unravel as he journeys through the ruins of war-torn Europe; third, psychological conditioning had cultural currency in the years *after* the war, thanks in part to the villainous CIA and programmes such as MKUltra, as well as Cold War propaganda about the communist 'brain-washing' of American POWs in Korea.

In the late 1960s, few readily available sources existed which documented the actual contributions of psychology to the war effort, but there was certainly evidence enough to support a tenuous connection between propaganda organizations like the PWE and some kind of ungentlemanly psychological research which anticipated later Cold War developments. With fewer source texts available to draw upon, Pynchon's inventiveness takes him some distance from the territory more recently mapped out by historical research. And yet, even as Pynchon implements what is effectively an anachronism as a key plot device, he hits on a truth about PWE and the propaganda war which few historians have thought to examine: *Gravity's Rainbow* explores the key role that wartime Allied propaganda organizations played as conduits by which the social and psychological sciences entered into the service of the state to become a pillar of post-war technocracy.

The 'P' word

Throughout *Gravity's Rainbow*, the reader is exposed to a dizzying array of verifiable historical and scientific facts, often in the form of digressions, which lend an impressive sense of authenticity and historical rigour to a narrative that nevertheless falls short of convincing the reader, for example, that the Allies discovered how to train giant octopuses to conduct coastal assaults on young women in the manner of a Japanese *Shunga* painting.[32] While many contemporary writers of historical fiction similarly aspire to verisimilitude, it would be difficult to imagine an author like Hilary Mantel inventing a dubiously named sub-branch of the Lord Chamberlain's office in order to explore a tantalizing theory about the popularity of the name 'Thomas' in Tudor England. Pynchon's handling of the genre certainly hangs on the tropes of historical fiction but there is something unusual in his method.

In a 2003 essay on George Orwell's *Nineteen Eight-Four*, Pynchon presents a critique of the function and effect of information systems, which is worth quoting at length:

Every day public opinion is the target of rewritten history, official amnesia and outright lying, all of which is benevolently termed 'spin,' as if it were no more harmful than a ride on a merry-go-round. We know better than what they tell us, yet hope otherwise. We believe and doubt at the same time – it seems a condition of political thought in a modern superstate to be permanently of at least two minds on most issues. Needless to say, this is of inestimable use to those in power who wish to remain there, preferably forever.[33]

For Pynchon, history is always already the subject of 'spin', a condition which fosters a state of impotence. *Gravity's Rainbow* appears to reproduce this through its encyclopaedic tsunami of information. However, the paranoid Pynchonian narrative voice, embracing the relentless subjectivity of heteroglossia rather than the seeming 'objectivity' of officialdom, does not permit *belief* to persist for long. Doubt – or, rather, paranoia – is the remedy for impotence.

An exceptional feature of Pynchon's historical fiction in full flourish throughout *Gravity's Rainbow*, the inclusion of so much historical and scientific detail has been addressed by numerous scholars; Tololyan, for example, traces the plotting of narrative events against real-world happenings with 'cartographic' accuracy.[34] Pynchon's ceaseless deployment of verifiable detail – from the comprehensive list of war departments associated with subversive propaganda noted earlier to the meticulous detailing of US military movements across Europe in the weeks after the fall of Berlin – holds up a fun-house mirror to the PWE strategy of truth which meant to neutralize its audiences' defences and make it easier to smuggle in more subversive material.

Subsequently, the playfulness with which *Gravity's Rainbow* handles 'facts' generates some curious effects. As an example, we might consider the Pavlovian plot device at the centre of the narrative. Seed argues that *Gravity's Rainbow* is consistently hostile 'towards deterministic explanations of human behaviour' such as Pavlov's writings, peppered throughout the novel, and 'which always occur with absurd or negative connotations'.[35] Interestingly, Seed identifies a corollary undercurrent of Freudianism which unfolds in the text as a pessimistic view of collective repression. The Pavlovian plot device, then, does not simply entertain, nor is it merely an anachronistic attempt to develop historical veracity – for a novelist who has made a study of wartime subversive propaganda, it has propaganda value. The text squares off against determinism but does so by constructing a narrative that draws on deterministic ideas and then prods and pokes the reader into a scepticism seemingly of their own accord.

I suggest that Pynchon's approach to historical fiction may have been shaped by the propagandists' 'strategy of truth' which is attributed to Eisenhower in the text, but which was in fact pioneered by the subversive propagandists of the PWE under Sefton Delmer's leadership. Indeed, as a literary subject, the PWE was ready-made for a writer who is sceptical of both authority and the consensus view of reality. More than that, the novel's cavalier attitude to 'fact' raises questions about how we should think about the past as a subject of art and historical inquiry. As Berressem writes, Pynchon is committed to 'show[ing] the complexity of history, the fictional character of all forms of historiography, and the ways in which history is hijacked and falsely factualized by the powers that be'.[36] An exemplary postmodern text, the encyclopaedic quality of *Gravity's Rainbow* systematically diminishes the reader's belief that a definitive history might exist.

Not only does *Gravity's Rainbow* raise questions about our recent past, but it also interrogates how our world has been constructed and legitimated through the lens of history. In its metahistorical moments, the text offers a revealing commentary on history itself, often via characters who exist at the margins of polite society. For example, Katje Borgesius, a Dutch woman brutalized and exploited first by the Nazis and then by the Allies, is deeply cynical: 'The mass nature of wartime death is useful in many ways . . . It provides raw material to be recorded into History, so that children may be taught History as sequences of violence . . . and be more prepared for the adult world.'[37] Meanwhile, the ghost of German industrialist Walther Rathenau appears during a séance – speaking literally from outside of history – to declare that '[a]ll talk of cause and effect is secular history, and secular history is a diversionary tactic. Useful to you, gentlemen, but no longer so to us here'. For Pynchon, the kind of history that gets anything like a nod from the authorities is 'at best a conspiracy, not always among gentlemen, to defraud'.[38]

The mode of historiography native to liberalism – that of a progressive story of humanity's advancement from primitive barbarism to enlightenment – lends history a sense of predictability and coherence. It places evil in the past and insists on its existence in the present only as an aberration or an atavistic remnant of ancient horror. In post-war German culture, *Stunde Null* or zero hour marks the moment at which the Second World War ended, a moment that represents a supposedly radical break with the past and the beginnings of a new non-Nazi Germany. The 'zero' is also a key leitmotif in *Gravity's Rainbow*, a novel that riffs on the failure to destroy Nazism, as well as the Allied conspiracies that actually preserved and perpetuated elements of fascism in the post-war period. Instead of a narrative in which history progresses steadily from past to present, the paranoid Pynchonian historical consciousness evokes a sense of history that has *failed* to pass, of a past which is lingering on and haunting the present, evident in the 1960s with the rapid expansion of the intelligence community's power during the early Cold War. Indeed, the relatively sympathetic character of Roger Mexico, statistician and occasional assistant to Edward Pointsman, even denies the belief (understandably widespread in the Spring of 1945) that the war had ended: 'It's another bit of propaganda', he says, 'Something the P.W.E. planted.'[39] As Kylie Regan notes, Mexico recognizes the implications of the 'postwar' world as well as his complicity in its creation; 'Pynchon's depiction of Allied intelligence', she writes, 'is an extended meditation on the fundamental violence in which intelligence agencies engage'.[40] This alternative mode of history is, for the paranoid Pynchonian, the only way to make sense of the present. Only according to History with a capital H did fascism meet its end. But the perverse engines which led to its creation – capitalism, colonialism and racism – were never destroyed, only mutated to suit the post-war climate. And so, while a spasm of liberal idealism grips the world around him, Pynchon instead sees vestiges of fascism enduring in government tyranny and Wall Street graft, in the profiteering of the military-industrial complex and in the amorality of an increasingly media-saturated society.[41]

Zero hour

We might well ask why Pynchon chose the PWE as a subject at all when he could easily have written about the OSS or even the MOI, both of which had the virtue of being relatively well-documented and familiar to the public by the late 1960s. But it might well be that the PWE's secrecy was itself the allure: the little information that was publicly available thanks to a small handful of memoirs and academic texts promised a rich vein to be mined, especially for a writer with a taste for deceit, silliness, salaciousness and song. There is evidence throughout *Gravity's Rainbow* of a canny and intuitive knowledge of the working practices of the Allies' European propaganda operations, from small but significant details about the interrelationships between departments involved in psychological warfare, to important elements of the plot such as Grunton's invention of the *Schwarzkommando*, and even Slothrop's Pavlovian conditioning. Writing at the end of the 1960s, Thomas Pynchon was clearly well-informed about an area of history that even professional historians had yet to explore in any depth.

It is likely that the ongoing role of subversive propaganda throughout the Cold War provided a whip hand for a writer whose comprehension of media and communication underpins his endeavour. From Pynchon's formative years through to the moment *Gravity's Rainbow* was published, British and American governments were engaged in subversive efforts, from outright international conflicts such as the wars in Korea and Vietnam to more 'domestic' but equally bloody affairs such as the anti-communist mass killings in Indonesia or the British response to the Mau Mau uprising in Kenya. Once a reader is attuned to the rhythms of 'black' propaganda, Pynchon's decision to focus on this obscure war department makes far more sense. Certainly, *Gravity's Rainbow* is a testament to the way that wartime propaganda and the clandestine world that produced it have entered the wider cultural climate.

My reading of *Gravity's Rainbow* suggests that Pynchon latched onto the PWE because it was a suitable vehicle for his own narrative ambitions. The unexpected realization, however, is that the PWE's own approach to propaganda appears to have rubbed off on the text's stylistic ambitions too. Rather than simply depicting the PWE and its confederate organizations as literary subjects, *Gravity's Rainbow* actually flirts with the techniques developed by Allied propagandists such as Sefton Delmer to bury a subversive idea in as much comforting 'truth' and theatrical artifice as possible. In the case of *Gravity's Rainbow*, that subversive idea is the enlightenment of the paranoid. This encyclopaedic doorstop of a novel is a prankish expression of the method and intent of wartime subversive propaganda turned not against the conveniently uniformed enemy of the recent past, but rather, against contemporary, ambiguous and equally nefarious accretions of power. *Gravity's Rainbow* is a paranoid history that, above all, compels doubt regarding those larger historical narratives which are always, in some way, narratives of convenience and comfort.

Beyond the zero, beyond *Stunde Null*, *Gravity's Rainbow* is deeply concerned not with the historical rupture of the Holocaust, the rocket and the bomb, but with the discomfiting continuities between pre-war and post-war. Pynchon reminds us again and again that we have good reason to be sceptical about any kind of history that has been embraced by authority. 'They' are a presence on every page and 'their' reach is inescapable. But, as Pynchon reminds us, there is hope: 'they' might be in control, but, occasionally, they also get their feet stuck in toilet bowls.

Notes

1 The edition of *Gravity's Rainbow* cited throughout this essay is the 2006 Penguin Classics Deluxe Edition.

2   A note on terminology: 'psychological warfare' denotes actions which lead to a planned psychological reaction in another people; 'Political warfare' is a broader term that encompasses almost any action against any enemy short of utilizing military power. While there is considerable overlap in these terms, during the Second World War the British favoured usage of 'Political Warfare' while Americans spoke of 'Psychological Warfare'. Propaganda, and especially subversive propaganda, is a primary tool in either case.

3   Steven Weisenburger, 'The End of History? Thomas Pynchon and the Uses of the Past', *Twentieth Century Literature* 25, no. 1 (1979): 55.

4   While Pynchon is certainly not the only literary recluse of recent decades, his propensity to write about conspiracy and paranoia has fostered a cottage-industry of conspiracies about himself, evident, for example, in the 2002 documentary *A Journey into the Mind of P.* (See *Thomas Pynchon: A Journey into the Mind of P.* [Film] Directed by Donatello Dubini and Fosco Dubini (Germany: Dubini Filmproduktion, 2002)).

5   Khachig Tololyan, 'War as Background in *Gravity's Rainbow*', in *Approaches to Gravity's Rainbow*, ed. Charles Clerc (Columbus, OH: Ohio State UP, 1983), 32.

6   See, for example, Umberto Rossi, 'The Harmless Yank Hobby: Maps, Games, Missiles and Sundry Paranoias in *Time Out of Joint* and *Gravity's Rainbow*', *Pynchon Notes* 52–53 (2003): 106–23; Mark Quinn, 'Seeing the Wood for the Trees: Levels of Reading and Intertextual Mythmaking in Thomas Pynchon's *Gravity's Rainbow*', *Pynchon Notes* 56–57 (2009): 192–211. Leaving aside the more disciplined avenues of literary criticism, there are entire online communities of dedicated (and conspiratorial) Pynchonians developing highly creative, nuanced and insightful readings of his texts and their place in the world.

7   David Seed, 'Pynchon's Intertexts', in *The Cambridge Companion to Thomas Pynchon*, ed. Inger H. Dalsgaard, Luc Herman and Brian McHale (Cambridge: Cambridge University Press, 2012), 112.

8   Thomas Pynchon, *Gravity's Rainbow* (New York, NY: Penguin, 2006), 21.

9   Pynchon, *Gravity's Rainbow*, 78.

10 A few pages later the text also mentions 'the Electra House group' – Electra House being a predecessor agency of the PWE (Pynchon, *Gravity's Rainbow*, 82).

11 Pynchon, *Gravity's Rainbow*, 34–5.

12 Ibid., 53.

13 Hanjo Berressem, 'A Short Note on Pynchon's Sources for "The Firm"', *Pynchon Notes* 15 (1984): 77.

14 Pynchon, *Gravity's Rainbow*, 78.

15 Tololyan, 'War as Background in *Gravity's Rainbow*', 58.

16 Secret wartime activities in Britain were subject to the Official Secrets Act, a gag order to maintain state security and preserve the dignity of people who had been reduced to disreputable activities by the war.

17 Tololyan, 'War as Background in *Gravity's Rainbow*', 58–9; see Paul M. A. Linebarger, *Psychological Warfare* (Washington, DC: Infantry Journal Press, 1948).
18 Elizabeth P. Macdonald, *Undercover Girl* (New York, NY: Macmillan, 1947).
19 The Office of Strategic Services (OSS) was an American wartime intelligence agency which also maintained involvement in propaganda and other subversive activities; as such, the OSS and the PWE maintained close contacts and collaborations. 'Morale Operations' had a similar function to the PWE.
20 Edward Shils and Morris Janowitz, for example, published a fascinating paper on Wehrmacht morale; Shils was a key figure in Anglo-American psychological research among German POWs in the final months of the war: Shils and Janowitz, 'Cohesion and Disintegration in the Wehrmacht in World War II', *Public Opinion Quarterly* 12, no. 2 (1948): 280–315.
21 Daniel Lerner, *Sykewar: Psychological Warfare against Germany, D-Day to VE-Day* (New York: George W. Stewart, 1949).
22 Pynchon, *Gravity's Rainbow*, 75–6; among the PWE's many other wartime concerns, the department was also responsible for producing the 'Foreign Office Handbooks' that appeared in the backpack of every British soldier bound for Europe.
23 Pynchon, *Gravity's Rainbow*, 76.
24 Delmer, *Black Boomerang*, 65–6.
25 Ibid., 100.
26 Ibid. Readers will perhaps be reminded of the many comic songs and short verses that pepper Pynchon's novels, adding an ironic commentary to the action.
27 Pynchon, *Gravity's Rainbow*, 19.
28 Delmer, *Black Boomerang*, 130.
29 See Kirk Robert Graham, *British Subversive Propaganda during the Second World War: Germany, National Socialism and the Political Warfare Executive* (Cham: Palgrave Macmillan, 2021), specifically chapter four, 'Germany on the Couch: The Role of Psychology and the Social Sciences in the Development of Subversive Propaganda', 105–43.
30 Walter C. Langer, *The Mind of Adolf Hitler: The Secret Wartime Report* (New York, NY: Basic Books, 1972) and Erik H. Erikson, 'Hitler's Imagery and German Youth', *Psychiatry* 5, no. 4 (1942): 475–93.
31 Ellen Herman, *The Romance of American Psychology: Political Culture in the Age of Experts* (Berkeley, CA: University of California Press, 1995), 43; Graham, *British Subversive Propaganda during the Second World War*, 116–19.
32 Pynchon, *Gravity's Rainbow*, 188–9.
33 Thomas Pynchon, 'The Road to 1984', *The Guardian*, 3 May 2003.
34 Tololyan, 'War as Background in *Gravity's Rainbow*', 33–40.
35 Seed, 'Pynchon's Intertexts', 115.
36 Hanjo Berressem, 'Coda: How to Read Pynchon', in *The Cambridge Companion to Thomas Pynchon*, 172.

37 Pynchon, *Gravity's Rainbow*, 108–9.
38 Ibid., 167.
39 Ibid., 640. The reader is introduced to the idea of a past haunting the present from the first page with an ironic epigraph to the first section of the novel attributed to SS- *Sturmbahnführer* and architect of the Apollo missions' Saturn V rocket, Wernher von Braun: 'Nature does not know extinction; all it knows is transformation' (Ibid., 1).
40 Kylie Regan, *Counterintelligence Literature: Cold War American Espionage and Postmodern Fiction* (PhD thesis, West Lafayette, IN, Purdue University, 2020), 88. Regan identifies *Gravity's Rainbow* as an example of 'Counterintelligence Literature', a subversive postmodern genre written in part 'to hinder the promotion of the burgeoning intelligence community' (76).
41 Coda: the 'Black Boomerang' referred to in the title of Delmer's memoir was an outcome of the propagandist's war work that, decades later, he came to regret. Having spent years sowing division and discord by rhetorically pitting 'ordinary' German servicemen and their heroic officers against the criminality and corruption of the SS and the Nazi Party, Delmer felt himself partly responsible for the 'clean Wehrmacht' myth that, in the post-war period, absolved the German armed forces of culpability for the Holocaust and other dreadful crimes (Delmer, *Black Boomerang*, 256).

13

Dramatizing secrecy and propaganda
Sir David Hare in conversation[1]

Guy Woodward

Written and directed by David Hare, the 1978 BBC television film *Licking Hitler* depicts the activities of a black propaganda unit housed in an English country house in the early stages of the Second World War. Under the leadership of the combustible and violent Archie Maclean (Bill Paterson) the unit establishes a fake German radio station. Purporting to be operating within Germany, the station broadcasts exchanges between two invented German army officers, played by prisoners of war, who detest Hitler and despise the corruption of the Nazi regime. This performance closely resembles *Gustav Siegfried Eins*, the black radio station devised by the Political Warfare Executive (PWE) propagandist and former *Daily Express* journalist Sefton Delmer in 1941, which broadcast nationalist rants by an invented Prussian army officer known as 'der Chef', who accused Nazi leaders of corruption and debauchery in an attempt to undermine German confidence in the regime.

Licking Hitler also confronts the troubled legacy of the war in Britain and has been described by Hare as a 'corrective' to popular and mythical depictions of the conflict.[2] The conclusion of the film reveals that the fictional unit's work continued until the end of the war, when all its records were destroyed; an impersonal voiceover tells us that '[m]any of the most brilliant men from the Propaganda and Intelligence Services went on to careers in public life, in Parliament, Fleet Street, the universities and the BBC'.[3] We see Maclean embark on a career as a successful film director, and other characters become a Labour MP and a successful novelist. The final words are delivered by Maclean's assistant Anna Seaton (Kate Nelligan), whose coercive and abusive relationship with her boss is depicted in the film. Seaton has endured a further series of distressing episodes in the decades which followed the war; in lines directed at Maclean she traces a national malaise back to the deceptions and self-deceptions committed during the conflict, observing that

> In retrospect what you sensed then has become blindingly clear to the rest of us: that whereas we knew exactly what we were fighting against, none of us had the whisper of an idea as to what we were fighting for. Over the years I have been watching the steady impoverishment of the people's ideals, their loss of faith, the lying, the daily inveterate lying, the thirty-year-old deep corrosive national habit of lying, and I have remembered you.[4]

This is a theme heard again in Hare's stage play *Plenty* (1978), in which former Special Operations Executive agent Susan Traherne (also played by Kate Nelligan in the first production) observes that '[w]hen you start talking longingly about the war ... some deception usually follows'.[5]

When first broadcast in the *Play for Today* slot on BBC One on 10 January 1978, *Licking Hitler* was seen by an audience of 6.5 million and won the BAFTA for Best Single Play in 1979.[6] Sadly it is commercially unavailable at present and has not been repeated on British television for several years. This is a shame, given the critical acclaim which the film has received, and its importance in both raising awareness of British black propaganda campaigns and in revising wartime myths which currently appear resurgent. The following conversation explores the legacies of *Licking Hitler* in our contemporary age of disinformation.

* * *

Guy Woodward
I'd like to begin with the genesis of the film – what was your understanding of British wartime propaganda before you began work on *Licking Hitler*?

David Hare
I was born in 1947 – two years after the end of the Second World War – and cinema-going as a child and adolescent involved seeing a great many British films which recreated the war. I don't think it's just retrospectively that we see these films as ridiculous – as adolescents we tended not to believe what we were seeing. The heroics as they were represented after the war were, if you like, a compensation. Power was drifting away, the British Empire was being dismantled and Britain found itself broke. The surface of life in post-war Britain was incredibly impoverished and down-at-heel, and the mythmaking of these films sought to compensate for that.

Winston Churchill was given one of the most lucrative publishing contracts of all time to write his six-volume 1,700,000-word history of the Second World War, and he consciously and unapologetically said that not only did he live through the Second World War, but he was going to write the Second World War his way and own history by writing history.[7] And as historians have since argued, that six-volume work puts little emphasis on the Russian front, it puts very little emphasis on the extermination of the Jews, so the central story is obviously the myth of Britain alone.

So let's say that, living in Britain in the 1950s and 1960s, I was not emotionally inclined to believe the myths of the Second World War – although, clearly, people spoke of it nostalgically as a time of common purpose. I'd certainly never heard of the PWE. I had a stroke of luck while I was researching in the Wiener Library, which is a research library dedicated to the Holocaust and Nazi Germany.[8] I'd been asked to write a film about Simon Wiesenthal, a well-known hunter of Nazi war criminals. I was researching at a desk when a man opposite in a three-piece tweed suit and glasses, wheezing with terrible asthma – for no reason at all, I hadn't said a word to him – said 'You do not know who I am'. I said 'No, I don't know who you are', and he said, 'I am Sefton Delmer and I have sat as close to Adolf Hitler as I am sitting to you.'

This obviously was his cabaret with which he loved entrancing strangers, but he lucked on the one stranger who was really interested in his cabaret, and started telling me about his life as a correspondent in Berlin for the *Daily Express* before the war – and then his extraordinary career during the war at the PWE, which he told me he'd written a book about.[9] So I immediately took the book out of the library and went home and read it in complete disbelief. These high jinks! I had been told that this was a moral and decent war which was impeccably conducted on our side; I had no idea that there were black propaganda operations, and I had no idea how ridiculously petty some of these operations were.

Black propaganda only works if you do not notice that it is directed at you; you have to believe that you're overhearing something which is not intended for your ears or that you're seeing something which is not intended for your eyes. In this respect, you might say, George Orwell's *Nineteen Eighty-Four* (1949) got things wrong in describing a world in which you are being bossed around, and know that you are being bossed around, because there are huge great signs telling you lies. Obviously, the theory of the PWE was that the lies are much more potent if you don't know that they are lies and are not aware that you are the object or the target of the propaganda, and so, if you appear to be overhearing something not intended for you, you are more likely to go running and telling others 'guess what

I've heard on the radio'. And one formula they came up with was a programme in which listeners would overhear two German soldiers speaking one to another about what was really going on in the Germany army.

Guy Woodward

I understand that researching the play you travelled around the country and interviewed various other people who had been involved in the PWE?

David Hare

I was very conscious in 1976 that we were losing touch with a piece of history and that if I didn't go around now and talk to these people, you know . . . Jeremy Isaacs's wonderful documentary series *The World at War* (1973) had aired a few years before and he had similarly gone round doing exactly what I was doing, trying to catch people in the late years of their lives, because we'd come to realize how valuable this kind of personal testimony is.

I certainly remember meeting internees who had acted in the radio broadcasts. The plight of German and Italian internees in the Second World War was never the subject of any of those brave cinema films and wasn't a subject about which you heard too much. They found themselves in this extraordinary situation which I tried to show in the film, where they were brought in, did this sort of radio play in their native language, had some drinks, had some food and then in the evening were sent back to their own camps to continue their imprisonment or confinement, whatever you call it. And so, they lived these extraordinary double lives: they were treated terribly well and valued when they came in to do their work and then treated as potential enemy aliens the rest of the time.

Guy Woodward

Were people happy, or proud, to discuss this work with you?

David Hare

I don't think proud is a word I would use. Take John Fennel in *Licking Hitler*, who is based on Richard Crossman [who headed the PWE's German section from 1941 to 1943] – his attitude was that we lied during the war, of course, we lied. You lie because you wish to mislead the enemy and it's a simple technique of war which is as old as warfare itself and, if you can mislead your enemy in any way, that's perfectly fair.[10] Crossman took this attitude into the Labour Government of 1964, and unlike some of his colleagues he refused to see the moral problem with using propaganda on behalf of the government cause that you're fighting for. I don't think lying troubles contemporary politicians as much – we have a prime minister [Boris Johnson] at the moment who has twice been dismissed from jobs for lying, and he doesn't seem to be able to see what the problem is.[11]

The most interesting reaction to the film came on a radio programme called *Critics' Forum* from the film critic of the *Sunday Times* Dilys Powell – along with C. A. Lejeune probably the most famous film critic of the twentieth century in Britain – [and who served during the war in the PWE's Greek Section]. Powell was furious with the film in a way that was almost irrational – all the other critics said it was marvellous, so enjoyed it, fascinating little corner of the war, we didn't know anything about it. But she was furious and said: I can't think why he's made a film about this; everybody knew this was going on, everybody hated it, everybody disapproved of it and it was a terrible thing and it's a thing to be ashamed of, and why do we have to bring it up now. And what was so interesting was that by 'everybody' she meant the establishment, she meant that people in the know knew about this.

You say six and a half million people watched it, but I don't believe ten of them knew about this particular piece of British history. I really don't think I've ever heard of anyone who said: 'oh yes, I knew about this'. The film hit the British public with the force of revelation because absolutely nobody had heard about this activity and people were very shocked and upset by it.

Powell suggested that everybody knew Sefton Delmer was a fruitcake – well, if everyone knew Sefton Delmer was a fruitcake, why was he allowed to do what he did for four years? And when people talk about Guy Burgess or Donald Maclean or Anthony Blunt, it's exactly the same thing – we hear that of course, we knew, of course, Burgess or Maclean was dodgy, of course we knew that. And you kind of go well, yes, because England was run as a cartel and it's still run as a cartel today: what everybody – in quotes – *knows* is not actually what everybody means, and that's why this story, I think, is so interesting.

Guy Woodward

I wonder if we could move on to talk a bit about the making of the film – was it always intended for television?

David Hare

Loads of people have asked me to make it into a stage play and I've always refused, and people have also asked me to make it as a feature film. But I didn't want that, I wanted it to be punchy, I wanted it to be sixty minutes long and leave viewers asking questions, which is why sixty minutes suited me absolutely fine.

Guy Woodward

I think it was made in seventeen days – and this was your first experience of directing?

David Hare

I had a very brilliant producer, David Rose, who went on to become the initiator of FilmFour. He called me and said I love your script I think it's absolutely fantastic, and I said, well, there are two things: first, it has to be made on film and in those days, a lot of drama was made in studios. And he said, but it's all interiors, why do you have to make it on film? and I said, because it has to resemble the films of the 1940s and I'm going to shoot it in the manner of films of the 1940s, the camera's barely going to move, and the stock is going to make it look as if it was a 1940s film, and everything I do is going to make it into a piece of propaganda – in inverted commas – it's a film that recreates what films were like. Secondly, I said, I want to direct it and he said, have you ever directed before on film? I said no, never, but I said I've watched a lot of films, and he said fine, you do it. And at the end of the first day I confessed to the cameraman and said, I have to tell you I have never actually shot a foot of film in my life before, and the cameraman just said, well, it didn't show.

Guy Woodward

What were you trying to do differently in *Licking Hitler*?

David Hare

By and large, aside from [the films] *Odette* (1950) and *Carve Her Name with Pride* (1958), the work of women in the Second World War had been a completely neglected area up until that point, but there followed a torrent of films in which women were the central characters. A couple of years later, Ian McEwan wrote a television play about the Enigma [codebreaking] operations [at Bletchley Park], for example, and there were many others.[12] You couldn't be a writer in the 1970s – I couldn't – without wanting to write from a feminist perspective, so I wanted to look at the way women were treated in the Second World War, thrust into really important roles and then expected to return to domestic roles at the end of the war. Over the past twenty or thirty years, there's been a huge amount of attention on the photographer Lee Miller for example, who had exactly this experience of joining the Eighth Army, being with them when they liberated Paris, moving on to Alsace, witnessing the fall of Berlin, having herself photographed in Hitler's bath, spending one more year in Germany as it tried to put itself together again, and then going back and having everyone tell her to return to being a housewife. The contrast between what women were asked to do in the Second World War, and what was then expected of them when they returned to Britain after the war was so dramatic.

But also, I was trying to overturn the great myths and to write something truthful about the Second World War. One of the most depressing things at present is that British cinema has returned to the Winston Churchill version of the war, as if none of us had ever done anything subversive. You know, I took Christopher Nolan's *Dunkirk* (2017) personally; it was a film that could have been made in 1950 in its politics and attitudes. And I thought, have you really not seen any of the radical work which was done about the Second World War? The same could be said of the simply laughable film about Churchill with Gary Oldman [*Darkest Hour* (2017)] which even invented a scene in which Churchill went down the tube to consult with straphangers about the progress of the Second World War, and what he should do, a scene as unlikely as it is possible for fiction to be. The tide has turned back in my lifetime, and any progress we ever made considering the questions of how we fought the Germans, and what we had to do to ourselves in order to fight the Germans, has been lost.

Whereas in France, you have this extraordinarily rich tradition of harrowing movies addressing the period – it's in France that you get *Night and Fog* (1956) by Alain Resnais, the first major documentary about the camps; you get Louis Malle making *Lacombe, Lucien* (1974) which is about collaboration and *Au revoir les enfants* (1987), a great film about the separation between 'pure' French and Jewish schoolboys. Then, in my view, greatest of all you have this extraordinary Jean-Pierre Melville picture *Army of Shadows* (1969) which shows how unbelievably cruel the work of the French resistance was – you see resistance fighters killing each other in order to prevent them falling into enemy hands. And when you see that film, you realize that the French are grown up about what happened to them between 1939 and 1945 in a way that the British refuse to be grown up about it. So, I feel that I've been wasting my time trying to persuade the world at large that there's more to the Second World War than schoolboy heroics.

Guy Woodward
You seem to be suggesting that things are getting worse.

David Hare
They are getting worse. And obviously any social historian is going to say that it's Brexit-inspired; of course it is, you know, you can see it. There's a sort of feeling of oh we've tried hard enough to explore this subject seriously, let's go back to wham-bam . . . I mean, *Dunkirk*? Sometimes I think I misremember it, it's so ridiculous. Is this meant to be at any level taken seriously as history? At what level are we meant to receive this? The desire to really look at what happened during the Second World War seems to have vanished completely just now.

Guy Woodward

Your mention of Brexit reminds me of *Plenty* (1978), which has quite a lot to say about Britain's relationship with Europe – it was written shortly after Britain's accession to the European Economic Community (EEC) in 1973. In *Plenty*, are you suggesting that the war changed Britain's relationship with Europe? In the final scene, Susan tells the French farmer that '[i]t may be [. . .] That things quickly change. We have grown up. We will improve our world'.

David Hare

I think there was a sense that Britain had tried for twenty years after the war to go it alone and all it had seen was diminishing power and diminishing wealth, and so we needed to throw ourselves in with an economic group which was far more prosperous than we were. I think Michael Frayn has said that he's mystified by the concentration in fiction on the Nazis, when the twenty or thirty years in Germany after the Second World War – when it escapes Nazism and forms a working democracy – are far more miraculous and fascinating than anything that happened during the war.[13] But you had a situation in this country in the 1970s when people wondered why Germany was doing everything right and we were doing everything wrong; the right-wing way of saying the same thing was to say that the Germans lost the war and they are rich, and we won the war, and we are poor. But there was a general sense that we had to join an economic group, which would bring us the prosperity that was so evident on the continent, and that was so clearly lacking in our country.

Guy Woodward

Something else that runs through both of those plays is spying and the secret services – you are not perhaps thought of as a spy writer, and yet since *Licking Hitler* and *Plenty*, your work has often grappled with the actions and legacies of the secret state. The Worricker trilogy (*Page Eight* (2011), *Turks & Caicos* (2014) and *Salting the Battlefield* (2014)), for example, depicts a rogue MI5 agent trying to act truthfully in the face of competing state interests. Is this area something you think about a lot?

David Hare

Yes – MI5 fascinates me. What drew me to MI5 as a subject was the realization that the arguments within MI5 were just as profound as the arguments outside it. To us, a secret organization is presented as monolithic, that has a single view. The leadership of MI6, for example, took a view on the Iraq invasion – Richard Dearlove [Chief of MI6 from 1999 to 2004] catastrophically claimed that there was evidence of weapons of mass destruction in Iraq. And when Tony Blair wanted that evidence from MI6, they presented it. MI5, rather interestingly, refused to go along with this, and refused to say that there was any evidence of weapons of mass destruction. When I spoke to people in MI5 about this, I asked if Blair was angry with them, and whether they stopped being invited to meetings, and they said it's much subtler than that, you just get subtly frozen out if you refuse to go along with the official policy.

And that was very interesting because, like the country, MI5 was divided about the Iraq invasion, and they were divided about collusion in torture and rendition. So, these issues that were argued about in the country at large were also being argued about within MI5 – only with much better-informed arguments and much more ferocious arguments. I wanted to represent the secret services as *us*, arguing in the way that *we* argue, rather than as a monolith with a single view; in fact, we can see that they have many, many views. That seemed to me an eloquent way of talking about all the really important things that were going on in my country in those years.

Guy Woodward
Many have identified disinformation as a threat to democracy at the moment – Anglophone liberals at least appear to feel transfixed or paralysed by phenomena like QAnon or anti-vaccination campaigns. Is this something that interests you?

David Hare
I'm most interested in the official side of this – I would love somebody to write a version of *Licking Hitler* about [British Army psychological warfare unit] the 77th Brigade.[14] We're talking as if [state-led] disinformation is a historical phenomenon but it's also a contemporary phenomenon. How many people know that four hundred people work in an army department called the 77th Brigade? If you try and find out what the 77th Brigade does, you will be told it is defensive; in other words, you will be told that it corrects online disinformation on the internet. And then you say, well ok, you correct online disinformation on the internet, but do you stray into spreading online disinformation? And they say, well, inevitably in any propaganda war, [British] propaganda is being put up against Russian propaganda and Chinese propaganda. I'm not for a second discounting these problems – Russian and Chinese propaganda are real problems, and any serious intelligence agency is going to try and deal with them. However, who in this country knows that we have four hundred people in an army propaganda unit working on disinformation?

I'm not a conspiracy theorist – when I watch the ten o'clock news, I tend to assume that what I'm being told is true; however, when I know that there are four hundred people who are paid by the army to tell me things which are not necessarily true . . . It looks to me like that what the 77th Brigade does is just a continuation of the PWE, and so, you see, *Licking Hitler* does not just describe a historical problem, it also describes a contemporary problem. How do you fight lies?

Guy Woodward
What is your ethical view of this? Do you think the ends justify the means? The conclusion of *Licking Hitler* suggests that establishment hypocrisy is in the dock, rather than black propaganda per se.

David Hare
A lot of the *Licking Hitler/Plenty* impulse came out of the fact that after the Second World War, it was believed that there was no such condition as post-traumatic stress disorder – people often came back from the war deeply damaged and, in my adolescence, a lot of people were behaving very strangely because they'd seen things which at the time it was thought should not be talked about. Nowadays, if you've been fighting in the war, there's a special camp in Cyprus that you go to in order to debrief, but also in order to make yourself feel better, to talk about the things that you've seen. And you pass through a process whereby you are assumed to have suffered some emotional impact from the events that you've witnessed. No such thing existed in the Second World War, and instead this ridiculous gang of actors – John Mills and Richard Attenborough and Jack Hawkins and all these people – pretended that you could fight a war without damaging yourself. I don't doubt that the Second World War was a great cause, but let's not lie to ourselves about the manner in which we fought it. And in some ways, we fought it by imitating our enemies, and the same is true of the propaganda war.

Within MI5, there was a very specific ethical problem, which is that in this country, since medieval times, or rather, you know, since the sixteenth and seventeenth centuries, torture and collusion in torture has been illegal. Now we know that when ministers stood up and said we had not colluded in torture, they were lying because we had colluded in torture. And those few whistle-blowers who dared to blow the whistle on our collusion in torture were quickly removed from post. And the damage that did really bothers me, because I think that the British should not collude in torture, that's what I believe. And also, I believe that, obviously, the intelligence that you gain through torture is completely useless and likely to be misleading, because frankly when you're – as people were in Uzbekistan – boiling people alive, with our collusion, then they will say anything.[15] Obviously if you're being boiled alive you'll say anything.

Guy Woodward

Something else we see at the conclusion of *Licking Hitler* is Archie Maclean becoming a successful film director, and I wonder if you see any connections and parallels between the art forms in which you work and the work of propagandists?

David Hare

I honestly don't know. I was with a film crew once filming on the Place de la Concorde [in Paris] and someone who worked in advertising said art is no different from advertising, that all an artist is doing is trying to sell their point of view, which is essentially no different from what an advertiser does. The whole film crew joined in this argument, which very nearly came to blows – the artistic side saying that what we do is not propaganda and the advertising side arguing that what *we* do is art, which is in a different category, and you know, the other half saying you're fooling yourself and that art is just a highbrow version of advertising.

Guy Woodward

The other thing that really interested me is the question of social class in the film – rather than a direct translation of Delmer, you make a very conscious decision to make Maclean a working-class Glaswegian with a tenement background. Why was that?

David Hare

I just wanted someone who loathed the establishment and was outside it, but was a genius at doing the work. Someone who was intruding on the establishment and didn't have any of the establishment's values, whereas Anna is obviously a posh girl who is completely riveted. A number of people objected that it was completely implausible that she was so posh that she actually didn't know how to make a cup of tea. But that detail was taken from Jessica Mitford, who ran away with Esmond Romilly to the Spanish Civil War and when they got there, he said, can you make me a cup of tea, and Jessica Mitford, who was only nineteen at the time said, I have no idea how, I always have people to make it for me.

Guy Woodward

Why is it so hard to get hold of *Licking Hitler* today?

David Hare

It was shown on Channel 4 many years ago. Michael Grade [Chief Executive of Channel 4 from 1988 to 1997] loved the film, and wanted it to be the first BBC-made programme ever to be shown on Channel 4. But then he scheduled it opposite the [1990] World Cup final![16] I said, Michael, I really appreciate the gesture, it's really kind of you, but I don't think many people are likely to notice that it's on.

I was told it was going to be shown on BBC 4 last year [2020] – there was a wonderful documentary made to commemorate *Play for Today*, and to accompany this they were going to show the best plays from the archive. I was told *Licking Hitler* was going to be one of them, but it never appeared.[17] I don't think the 77th Brigade intervened. Look, the BBC is like all liberal organizations, it is incredibly careless of the people who love it most, you know, it loves kicking its friends, and anyone who's ever been a friend to the BBC . . . well, I've had the experience of being kicked.

Guy Woodward

In conclusion, I wonder if you have any plans to return to these areas – either to propaganda or to the secret state?

David Hare

I sort of promised myself no more Second World War, because it was so rich and it was such a wonderful time in my life, at the age of thirty to go out and talk to people about what they'd been through was so fascinating to me – to hear the truth, instead of hearing the fiction that had prevailed for so long. When I look back on my life, it's one of the most satisfying things I've ever done.

But the question of why untruth is so embedded now in British public life, I don't think I'll ever tire of that subject. When I caught Covid, I wrote a play called *Beat the Devil* (2021) which has also been adapted into a film showing on Sky Arts. It's about my experiences with Covid. Throughout Covid, the whole country knew that the government failed on PPE, was late closing the country down, made a series of crashing errors, test and trace didn't work. If the whole country knows it, why can't you say it? Why not just admit it so that we can all move on?

What is this belief that if you're in politics you can never tell the truth? It's exactly the same with this incident over the weekend – you know, Marcus Rashford has been perfectly willing to say, I'm sorry I took a lousy penalty, but Priti Patel can't say 'look, it was really stupid of me to condemn players taking the knee' – that was plainly a catastrophic thing to do, it's encouraged racism and encouraged all the ugly scenes that we've seen since, why can't she say that?[18] Rashford can say what he says, why can't she say that? The whole country knows it's true, but she doesn't say it, and so I don't really understand this belief of politicians that you have to lie on all occasions, why is it necessary? Why don't you just say yeah, I made a stupid mistake, I'm sorry and we move on. If they were able to recognize their errors of judgement, it would be easier to restore the relationship between us and the people who rule us.

Notes

1 This interview took place online on 13 July 2021 as part of the conference *The Writer as Psychological Warrior: Intellectuals, Propaganda, and Modern Conflict* (Durham University, 12–16 July 2021).
2 'LFF Connects – David Hare | BFI London Film Festival 2018' (https://www.youtube.com/watch?v=7x-p7-BEOF4 [accessed 15 November 2023]).
3 David Hare, *Plays 1* (London: Faber and Faber, 1996), 367.
4 Hare, *Plays 1*, 370.
5 Hare, *Plays 1*, 412. A film adaptation of the play starring Meryl Streep was released in 1985.
6 Alan Burton and Tom May provide this figure with reference to BBC archival materials. They note that 6.5 million was a 40.3 per cent audience share, against 26.6 per cent for BBC Two 'whose main programming in opposition was a *Man Alive* documentary about dieting in young girls – and 33.1 per cent for ITV, which showed *Hello! Central State Puppet Theatre of the Soviet Union* and the news' (Alan Burton and Tom May, '"Treading on Sacred Turf": History, Femininity and the Secret War in the Plays for Today *Licking Hitler, The Imitation Game* and *Rainy Day Women*', *Journal of British Cinema and Television* 19, no. 3 (July 2022): 349–50; 'Television in 1979', http://awards.bafta.org/award/1979/television [accessed 15 November 2023].
7 David Reynolds notes that when 'locked in wartime controversy' Churchill was known to say 'I shall leave it to history, but remember that I shall be one of the historians' (David Reynolds, *In Command of History: Churchill Fighting and Writing the Second World War* (New York, NY: Random House, 2005), xix). Reynolds notes that Churchill's original contract for the US book and newspaper serialization rights to *The Second World War* (1948–53) was worth $2.23 million, which Reynolds estimated would have been the equivalent of anything between $18 million and $50 million at the time of writing in 2005 (Reynolds, *In Command of History*, 538).
8 At this point the Wiener Library occupied premises on Devonshire Street in Westminster; the library moved to its current location on Russell Square in Bloomsbury in 2011.

9   Sefton Delmer, *Black Boomerang: An Autobiography: Volume Two* (London: Secker & Warburg, 1962).

10 In public Crossman expressed rather different views, however: in a hostile review of Delmer's memoir *Black Boomerang* published in the *New Statesman* in 1962, he argued that '[l]ike strategic bombing [black propaganda] is nihilistic in purpose and solely destructive in effect' and suggested that British operations surpassed Nazi Germany's 'own level of lying, half-lying and news perversion' (quoted in Howe, *The Black Game*, 264, 265). Returning to the comparison in 1973, Crossman wrote that aside from the area bombing of German cities, 'subversive operations and black propaganda were the only aspects of war in which we achieved real pre-eminence. We trained a small army of gifted amateurs for all the dirtiest tricks from lying, bugging, forging and embezzlement to sheer murder – all, of course, in the cause of preserving the democratic way of life'. (Richard Crossman, 'Personal View', *The Times*, 16 May 1973, 18).

11 Boris Johnson's biographer Sonia Purnell writes that as a journalist he was sacked in 1988 by Charles Wilson, editor of *The Times*, for inventing a quotation in a published article (Sonia Purnell, *Just Boris: The Irresistible Rise of a Political Celebrity* (London: Aurum Press, 2011), 101). In 2004 Johnson was sacked as Shadow Minister for the Arts by the leader of the Conservative Party Michael Howard, after he had lied about an extra-marital affair with the *Spectator* columnist Petronella Wyatt (Purnell, *Just Boris*, 266).

12 Like *Licking Hitler*, McEwan's *The Imitation Game* was broadcast in the *Play for Today* slot, on 24 February 1980. It was directed by Richard Eyre.

13 Frayn's play *Democracy* (2003) addresses the 1974 exposure of West German Chancellor Willy Brandt's personal assistant Günter Guillaume as an agent for the East German intelligence service, the Stasi.

14 According to the British Army, the 77th Brigade is 'a hybrid unit of Regulars and Reservists with specialist skills to combat new forms of warfare in the information environment for the defence of the UK and its overseas territories' ('77th Brigade Information Operations' (https://www.army.mod.uk/who-we-are/formations-divisions-brigades/6th-united-kingdom-division/77-brigade/) [accessed 15 November 2023]). On its creation in 2015 the brigade was described as a 'a special force of Facebook warriors, skilled in psychological operations and use of social media to engage in unconventional warfare in the information age' (Ewen MacAskill, 'British Army Creates Team of Facebook Warriors', *The Guardian*, 31 January 2015 (https://www.theguardian.com/uk-news/2015/jan/31/british-army-facebook-warriors-77th-brigade [accessed 15 November 2023]).

15 This refers to revelations by Craig Murray, British Ambassador to Uzbekistan from 2002 to 2004, that the Uzbek security services were regularly torturing detainees; Murray suggested that intelligence being passed to the British and US intelligence agencies had been obtained by the use of torture, including immersion

in boiling liquids. See Craig Murray, *Murder in Samarkand: A British Ambassador's Controversial Defiance of Tyranny in the War on Terror* (Edinburgh and London: Mainstream Publishing, 2006). Murray's book was adapted by Hare as a radio play, broadcast on BBC Radio 4 on 20 February 2010.

16 The film was broadcast on Channel 4 on 8 July 1990 at 8.30 pm, as coverage of the men's World Cup final between West Germany and Argentina was being broadcast by both BBC One and ITV ('Sunday's Television & Radio', *The Times*, 7 July 1990, 27).

17 BBC Genome suggests that the film has only been repeated once by the BBC following its first broadcast on 10 January 1978, on 31 July 1979: https://genome.ch.bbc.co.uk/783718a2915c45a9b946d070f007ca63 [accessed 15 November 2023].

18 This conversation took place four days after the final of the delayed men's Euro 2020 football tournament, held at Wembley Stadium in London on 11 July 2021, in which Italy beat England in a penalty shootout. Rashford was one of three English players to miss a penalty in the shootout, and received racist abuse on social media in the aftermath of the defeat. In a post on Twitter he apologized for missing the penalty but said he refused to 'apologise for who I am and where I came from' (https://twitter.com/MarcusRashford/status/1414672529717964807/photo/3 [accessed 15 November 2023]). Shortly after the tournament began and during an interview with newly established right-wing news channel GB News, Conservative home secretary Priti Patel had dodged a question about whether England fans unhappy with the players' decision to kneel briefly before each match as an expression of anti-racism were justified in booing, saying, 'That's a choice for them quite frankly' (Jon Stone, 'Priti Patel Says Fans Have Right to Boo England Team for "Gesture Politics" of Taking the Knee', *Independent*, 14 June 2021, (https://www.independent.co.uk/news/uk/politics/priti-patel-taking-knee-boo-england-b1865409.html [accessed 15 November 2023]).

Select Bibliography

Anthony, Scott. *Public Relations and the Making of Modern Britain: Stephen Tallents and the Birth of a Progressive Media Profession*. Manchester: Manchester University Press, 2012.
Anthony, Scott. *The Story of Propaganda Film*. London: British Film Institute, 2024.
Atkinson, Harriet. *Showing Resistance: Propaganda and Modernist Exhibitions in Britain, 1933–53*. Manchester: Manchester University Press, 2024.
Balfour, Michael. *Propaganda in War, 1939–1945: Organisations, Policies and Publics in Britain and Germany*. London: Routledge & Kegan Paul, 1979.
Barnhisel, Greg. *Cold War Modernists: Art, Literature, and American Cultural Diplomacy*. New York, NY: Columbia University Press, 2015.
Bartlett, Frederic C. *Political Propaganda*. Cambridge: Cambridge University Press, 1940.
Berman, Jessica. 'Re-routing Community: Colonial Broadcasting and the Aesthetics of Relation'. In *Modernist Communities across Cultures and Media*, edited by Caroline Pollentier and Sarah Wilson, 251–69. Gainesville, FL: University Press of Florida, 2019.
Bowman, Jim. *Narratives of Cyprus: Modern Travel Writing and Cultural Encounters Since Lawrence Durrell*. London: I.B. Tauris, 2014.
Briggs, Asa. *The History of Broadcasting in the United Kingdom, Volume 2: The Golden Age of Wireless*. Oxford: Oxford University Press, 1965.
Briggs, Asa. *The History of Broadcasting in the United Kingdom, Volume 3: The War of Words*. Rev edn. Oxford: Oxford University Press, 1995.
Carney, Michael. *Britain in Pictures: A History and Bibliography*. London: Werner Shaw, 1995.
Chapman, James. *The British at War: Cinema, State and Propaganda, 1939–45*. London: I.B. Tauris, 1998.
Clark, Fife. *The Central Office of Information*. London: George Allen & Unwin, 1970.
Cohen, Debra Rae. 'Catchphrase Community: *ITMA* and Radiogenic Morale'. In *Modernist Communities Across Cultures and Media*, edited by Caroline Pollentier and Sarah Wilson, 234–50. Gainesville, FL: University Press of Florida, 2019.
Cohen-Cole, Jamie. *The Open Mind: Cold War Politics and the Sciences of Human Nature*. Chicago, IL and London: University of Chicago Press, 2014.
Cooke, Simon, and Natalie Ferris, eds. 'Special Issue: Women, Modernism, and Intelligence Work'. *Modernist Cultures* 16, no. 4 (2021).
Coombs, Douglas. *Spreading the Word: The Library Work of the British Council*. London: Mansell, 1988.
Cormac, Rory. 'British "Black" Productions: Forgeries, Front Groups, and Propaganda, 1951–1977'. *Journal of Cold War Studies* 24, no. 3 (2022): 4–42.

Corse, Edward. *A Battle for Neutral Europe: British Cultural Propaganda During the Second World War*. London: Bloomsbury Academic, 2013.

Crosby, Emily, and Linda Kaye, eds. *Projecting Britain: The Guide to British Cinemagazines*. London: British Universities Film & Video Council, 2008.

Davis, Thomas. *The Extinct Scene: Late Modernism and Everyday Life*. New York, NY: Columbia University Press, 2015.

Defty, Andrew. *Britain, America and Anti-Communist Propaganda, 1945–1953: The Information Research Department*. Abingdon: Routledge, 2004.

Dibbs, Martin. *Radio Fun and the BBC Variety Department, 1922–67: Comedy and Popular Music on Air*. Cham: Palgrave Macmillan, 2019.

Dinsman, Melissa. *Modernism at the Microphone: Radio, Propaganda, and Literary Aesthetics During World War II*. London: Bloomsbury Academic, 2015.

Doherty, Martin A. *Nazi Wireless Propaganda: Lord Haw-Haw and British Public Opinion in the Second World War*. Edinburgh: Edinburgh University Press, 2000.

Dolan, Josephine. 'The Voice that Cannot Be Heard: Radio/Broadcasting and "The Archive"'. *Radio Journal: International Studies in Broadcast & Audio Media* 1, no. 1 (2003): 63–72.

Donaldson, Frances. *The British Council: The First Fifty Years*. London: Cape, 1984.

Ellul, Jacques. *Propaganda: The Formation of Men's Attitudes*, trans. Konrad Kellen and Jean Lerner. New York, NY: Vintage Books, 1965.

Esty, Jed. *A Shrinking Island: Modernism and National Culture in England*. Princeton: Princeton University Press, 2004.

Fox, Jo. *Film Propaganda in Britain and Nazi Germany: World War II Cinema*. Oxford: Berg, 2007.

Fox, Jo. 'Confronting Lord Haw-Haw: Rumour and Britain's Wartime Anti-Lies Bureau'. *Journal of Modern History* 91, no. 1 (2019): 74–108.

Ganor, Sheer. 'Forbidden Words, Banished Voices: Jewish Refugees at the Service of BBC Propaganda to Wartime Germany'. *Journal of Contemporary History* 55, no. 1 (2020): 97–119.

Garnett, David. *The Secret History of PWE: The Political Warfare Executive, 1939–1945*. London: St. Ermin's Press, 2002.

Graham, Kirk Robert. *British Subversive Propaganda during the Second World War: Germany, National Socialism and the Political Warfare Executive*. Cham: Palgrave Macmillan, 2021.

Griffith, Glyne. *The BBC and the Development of Anglophone Caribbean Literature, 1943–1958*. Cham: Palgrave Macmillan, 2016.

Hadjiathanasiou, Maria. 'Colonial Rule, Cultural Relations and the British Council in Cyprus, 1935–55'. *The Journal of Imperial and Commonwealth History* 46, no. 6 (2018): 1096–124.

Hadjiathanasiou, Maria. *Propaganda and the Cyprus Revolt: Rebellion, Counter-Insurgency and the Media, 1955–59*. London: I.B. Tauris, 2020.

Hendy, David. *The BBC: A People's History*. London: Profile Books, 2022.

Holman, Valerie. 'Carefully Concealed Connections: The Ministry of Information and British Publishing, 1939–1946'. *Book History* 8 (2005): 197–226.

Irving, Henry. 'The Ministry of Information on the British Home Front'. In *Allied Communication to the Public During the Second World War: National and Transnational Networks*, edited by Simon Eliot and Marc Wiggam, 21–38. London: Bloomsbury Academic, 2019.

Joannou, Maroula. *Women's Writing, Englishness and National and Cultural Identity: The Mobile Woman and the Migrant Voice, 1938-1962*. Basingstoke: Palgrave Macmillan, 2012.

Johnston, Gordon, and Emma Robertson. *BBC World Service: Overseas Broadcasting, 1932-2018*. London: Palgrave Macmillan, 2019.

Kalliney, Peter. *Commonwealth of Letters: British Literary Culture and the Emergence of Postcolonial Aesthetics*. New York, NY: Oxford University Press, 2013.

Keane, Damien. *Ireland and the Problem of Information: Irish Writing, Radio, Late Modernist Communication*. University Park, PA: Penn State University Press, 2014.

Low, Gail. 'Professing the Common Wealth of Literature, Leeds 1957-1969'. *The Journal of Commonwealth Literature* 50, no. 3 (2015): 267–81.

MacKenzie, John M. *Propaganda and Empire: The Manipulation of British Public Opinion 1880-1960*. Manchester: Manchester University Press, 1984.

Morse, Daniel Ryan. *Radio Empire: The BBC's Eastern Service and the Emergence of the Global Anglophone Novel*. New York, NY: Columbia University Press, 2020.

Nicholas, Siân. *The Echo of War: Home Front Propaganda and the Wartime BBC, 1939-45*. Manchester: Manchester University Press, 1996.

Piette, Adam. *Imagination at War: British Fiction and Poetry, 1939-1945*. London: Papermac, 1995.

Plock, Vike Martina. *The BBC German Service during the Second World War: Broadcasting to the Enemy*. Cham: Palgrave Macmillan, 2021.

Potter, Rachel. 'International PEN: Writers, Free Expression, Organisations'. In *A History of 1930s British Literature*, edited by Benjamin Kohlmann and Matthew Taunton, 120–33. Cambridge: Cambridge University Press, 2019.

Potter, Rachel. 'Literature and Human Rights'. In *British Literature in Transition 1920-1940: Futility and Anarchy*, edited by Charles Ferrall and Dougal McNeill, 108–24. Cambridge: Cambridge University Press, 2018.

Potter, Simon. *Broadcasting Empire: The BBC and the British World, 1922-1970*. Oxford: Oxford University Press, 2012.

Potter, Simon. *Wireless Internationalism and Distant Listening: Britain, Propaganda, and the Invention of Global Radio, 1920-1939*. Oxford: Oxford University Press, 2020.

Potts, Jim. 'Truth Will Triumph: The British Council and Cultural Relations in Greece'. In *Greece and Britain Since 1945*, 2nd edn, edited by David Wills, 103–35. Newcastle upon Tyne: Cambridge Scholars Publishing, 2014.

Procter, James. 'Wireless Writing, the Second World War and the West Indian Literary Imagination'. In *British Literature in Transition 1940-60: Postwar*, edited by Gill Plain, 117–35. Cambridge: Cambridge University Press, 2019.

Renier, Olive, and Vladimir Rubinstein. *Assigned to Listen: The Evesham Experience 1939-43*. London: British Broadcasting Corporation, 1986.

Rice, Tom. *Films for the Colonies: Cinema and the Preservation of the British Empire*. Oakland, CA: University of California Press, 2019.

Rogers, Asha. *State Sponsored Literature: Britain and Cultural Diversity after 1945*. Oxford: Oxford University Press, 2020.

Saint-Amour, Paul K. *Tense Future: Modernism, Total War, Encyclopedic Form*. New York, NY: Oxford University Press, 2015.

Smith, James. *British Writers and MI5 Surveillance, 1930–1960*. Cambridge: Cambridge University Press, 2013.

Smith, James. 'Covert Legacies in Postwar British Fiction'. In *British Literature in Transition, 1940–1960*, edited by Gill Plain, 337–52. Cambridge: Cambridge University Press, 2019.

Stonebridge, Lyndsey. *Writing and Righting: Literature in the Age of Human Rights*. Oxford: Oxford University Press, 2021.

Stonor Saunders, Frances. *Who Paid the Piper? The CIA and the Cultural Cold War*. London: Granta, 1999.

Taunton, Matthew. *Red Britain: The Russian Revolution in Mid-Century Culture*. Oxford: Oxford University Press, 2019.

Taylor, Philip M. *Munitions of the Mind: A History of Propaganda from the Ancient World to the Present Day*. 3rd edn. Manchester: Manchester University Press, 2003.

Taylor, Philip M. *The Projection of Britain: British Overseas Publicity and Propaganda, 1919–1939*. Cambridge: Cambridge University Press, 1981.

Vaughan, James R. '"A Certain Idea of Britain": British Cultural Diplomacy in the Middle East, 1945–57'. *Contemporary British History* 19, no. 2 (2005): 151–68.

Webb, Alban. *London Calling: Britain, the BBC World Service and the Cold War*. London: Bloomsbury Academic, 2014.

Welch, David, ed. *Propaganda, Power and Persuasion: From World War 1 to Wikileaks*. London: I.B. Tauris, 2014.

Welch, David. *Persuading the People: British Propaganda in World War II Cinema*. London: British Library, 2016.

Welch, David. *Protecting the People: The Central Office of Information and the Reshaping of Post-War Britain, 1946–2011*. London: British Library, 2019.

White, Duncan. *Cold Warriors: Writers Who Waged the Literary Cold War*. London: Little, Brown, 2019.

Whittington, Ian. *Writing the Radio War: Literature, Politics and the BBC, 1939–1945*. Edinburgh: Edinburgh University Press, 2018.

Wilford, Hugh. *The CIA, the British Left and the Cold War: Calling the Tune?* London: Frank Cass, 2003.

Wollaeger, Mark. *Modernism, Media, and Propaganda: British Narrative from 1900 to 1945*. Princeton, NJ: Princeton University Press, 2006.

Index

77th Brigade   241–2, 244, 246 n.14

Aden   126, 130
Admiralty   35, 137
Adolf in Blunderland   19
Agate, James   23
Air Ministry   35
Akar, John   156
Albania   129
Ali, Ahmed   49
Allen, Edward   48–9, 55
Anand, Mulk Raj   49, 55
Annan, Lord Noel   148
Anson, Peter F
   British Sea-Fisherman   103
Anti-Imperialist League   67
Architectural Review   82, 94
Arlott, John   51–3, 55
Armenia, Soviet republic of   198
Army of Shadows   239
Artists International Association   86
Askey, Arthur   17, 19, 21
   'Run, Adolf, run'   19
Athens   128–30, 135
   British Institute in   129–30
Athens Radio   137
Attenborough, Richard   242
Au revoir les enfants   239
Auden Group, the   190
Auden, W. H.   53
   The Ascent of F6   107
Auger, C. P.   35, 45 n.9
Australia   115
Axis   41, 65, 126
   propaganda   38, 105, 130
Azerbaijan, Soviet republic of   198

Baghdad   130
Baillie-Stewart, Norman   18
Baldwin, James   154
Band Waggon   17, 21
Bankole Jones, John   10, 146, 150, 153–8

A Mother's Dilemma. An English Mother. An African Father. England 1936   154
Bankole Jones, Samuel   153
Barfoot, Rhian and Kieron Smith
   'Introduction: [A] Writer of Words and Nothing Else'   48
Barnhisel, Greg   4
Barrington, Jonah   17–18
Barthes, Roland   83
Bartlett, F. C.   179–81, 183, 186, 192
   political propaganda   10, 179–81
Battleship Potemkin   202
Bauhaus   88, 97 n.33
Bayer, Herbert   88
BBC Handbook 1940   35–6, 38, 46 n.22
Beachcroft, T. O.   165
Belgium   42–3
Beneš, Edvard   67
Benjamin, Walter   98 n.37, 99 n.48
Bennett, Arnold   71
Bentley, Phyllis   67, 69, 71, 166–7
   The Brontë Sisters   166
Beowulf   168
Berlin   26, 67, 74, 88, 197, 198, 202, 203, 205–6, 221, 226, 235, 238
Berlin, Isaiah   148
Bernays, Edward
   Propaganda   194 n.24
Berressem, Hanjo   218, 227
Betjeman, John
   English Small Towns   112
Bird, Francis   92–3
Black Book of Carmarthen   185
Black, George   17
Black, Misha   84, 88, 94–5, 96 n.16
Blair, Tony   241
Blake, William   51, 52
Bletchley Park   238
Blitz
   London   65, 86–91, 97 n.25, 214
   myth of   20, 24
   Swansea   189

Bloomsbury Group   71, 218
Blunden, Edmund   162, 170–1
  John Keats   166
Blunt, Anthony   237
Boateng, Lord Paul   159 n.28
Bolivia   66
Book of Revelation   188–9
Book of Verse   9, 49–58
Bottrall, Ronald   176 n.54
Bowen, Elizabeth   10, 102, 119 n.13
Bowman, Jim   138
Bracken, Brendan   148
Bradbrook, M. C.
  T. S. Eliot   166, 170
Brains Trust   92
Brander, Laurence   167–70
  Tobias Smollett   167
Breuer, Marcel   88
Briggs, Asa   20, 36, 37
Brinitzer, Carl   74
British Book News   162, 164, 165
British Broadcasting Corporation
    (BBC)   1–3, 6–7, 9, 11, 17,
    19–23, 34, 35, 38–41, 48–50, 52,
    54, 56, 65, 68–78, 90, 102, 106,
    151, 152, 154–6, 165, 167, 181,
    206, 214, 220, 221, 233, 234, 244
  Austrian Service   71, 77
  Eastern Service   1, 49–58, 59 n.15
    List of Eastern Service
      Programmes   50
  Empire Service   34, 72
  European Service   7, 70, 73, 75, 215,
    217
  Forces Network   20
  French Service   41, 69, 74
  German Service   74
  Home Service   19, 49
  Monitoring Service   5, 9, 33–44, 75
  Overseas Service   34, 38, 151
  Variety Department   17, 19
  World Service   10, 151, 152, 156
British Council   2, 5, 8, 10, 125–32, 134,
    135, 138, 152, 161–72
  Books and Periodicals
    Committee   163, 164
  Editorial Panel   164, 167
  Education Department   164
  English Studies Advisory
    Committee   164
  establishment of offices in
    Mediterranean and the Middle
    East   126
  instigation to conduct cultural
    propaganda   161
  Literature Panel   165, 169, 171
  Writers and Their Work   2, 10, 162–72
    list of authors covered in early
      years   166–7
    sales figures comparisons for
      volumes   170
British Institute   126, 129–31, 135, 136
British Pathé   17
Brotherhood of Freedom   130–1
*Brown Book of the Reichstag Fire and
    Hitler Terror*   203
Browning, Robert   51
Brussels   43
Building Workers' Union Exhibition   88
Buitenhuis, Peter
  The Great War of Words   2–3
Bullock, Alan   76
Bullough, Geoffrey   164, 165
Burgess, Guy   237
Burnham, James   207, 209
Burns and Allen Show   22
Burton, Alan and Tom May
  "Treading on Sacred Turf"   245 n.6

Cairo   129, 130, 135, 165
Calling Sierra Leone   155
Cambridge University   180, 223
Cardiff, Maurice   127–9, 134–6, 138,
    140 n.27
Caribbean Voices   53
Carmichael, Stokely   154
Carve Her Name with Pride   238
Caughie, Pamela   25–6
Caversham (location of BBC Monitoring
    Service)   36
Cecil, Lord David
  The English Poets   113
Central Intelligence Agency (CIA)   4, 67,
    75, 172, 205, 207–8, 225
Central Office of Information (COI)   2,
    7, 10, 145–6, 148–53, 155, 157,
    158
  Films Division   149
  increase in film and TV budget and
    move to 'telemagazine'   148

list of 'cinemagazines' produced by 150
Central School of Arts and Crafts 182
Chamberlain, Neville 19, 72, 205
Channel 4 244
China 66, 69, 168, 170
 contemporary Chinese propaganda 241
Chitale, Venu 49
Churchill, Winston 19, 72, 89, 235, 239, 245 n.7
Cleverdon, Douglas 54
Cohen-Cole, Jamie 201, 205, 206, 211 n.20
Cold War 1–4, 7, 8, 10, 67, 75, 95, 147, 151, 155, 156, 161, 162, 196, 198, 201, 206, 225, 228
 Cultural Cold War 3–4, 10, 53, 67, 75, 149, 162, 172
Coleridge, Samuel Taylor 51
Collini, Stefan 8
Collins (publisher) 103, 108, 121 n.36
Colonial Film Unit 153
Colonial Office 115, 141 n.34, 151, 163
Comintern 198–9, 202, 203, 205, 210 n.7
Commonwealth 114–17, 145–6, 152, 164, 168–9
communism 53, 67, 130, 140 n.18, 149, 156, 166, 167, 185, 196–8, 201, 203–6, 225
Communist Party of Germany (KPD) 197, 198, 200–3, 209
Compton-Burnett, Ivy 167
Conan Doyle, Arthur 169
Congress for Cultural Freedom (CCF) 4, 67, 75, 167, 197–8, 205–10, 211 n.20, 213 n.58
Connolly, Cyril 49
Coombs, Douglas 161–3
Cooper, Lettice
 George Eliot 167
Cormac, Rory 14 n.27
Corse, Edward 163
Covid-19 pandemic 244
The Criterion 165
Critics' Forum 237
Crossman, Richard 206, 236, 246 n.10
 The God that Failed 53, 197, 206
Crown Film Unit 147
Cull, Nicholas 206

cultural diplomacy, *see also* propaganda
 distinction between propaganda and cultural diplomacy 8
Cultural Relations Department (CRD) 8
Cyprus 2, 10, 125–38
 Church of Cyprus 126, 133
 establishment of independent Republic of Cyprus in 1960 126
 Revolt (1955–9) 125–30, 132–8
 Sovereign Base Areas and Treaty Concerning the Establishment of the Republic of Cyprus (1960) 127
Cyprus Broadcasting Service 137
Cyprus Public Information Office 136
The Cyprus Review 136–7
Czechoslovakia 67, 68, 74

Daily Express 17, 21, 233, 235
Daily Telegraph 74
Darkest Hour 239
Darling, F. Fraser 102
Darlington, W. A.
 Sheridan 167
Davis, Thomas 117
Day Lewis, Cecil 50, 53, 54, 56, 91
De Gaulle, Charles 74
Dearlove, Richard 240–1
Debayo, Jumoke 152
Degenerate Art Exhibition (1937) 84, 96 n.13
Delaney, Terence 56–7
Delmer, Sefton 7, 221–3, 227, 229, 232 n.41, 233, 235, 237, 243
 Black Boomerang 221–3
Denning, Lord 155
Department EH 7, 230 n.10
Desani, G. V. 49
Deutschlandsender 43
Diamantis, Adamantios 136
Dibbs, Martin 20, 29 n.29
Dimitrakis, Panagiotis 128
Dinsman, Melissa 3
Display 87, 89, 94, 100 n.67
Dobrée, Bonamy 165, 168
 Kipling 167
Doherty, M. A. 18, 28 nn.17, 28
Dolan, Josephine 34, 44
Donaldson, Frances 163
Donovan, William J. 207, 224

Dorward, Alan
  Bertrand Russell 167
Drogheda, Earl of   147–9, 151
  Drogheda Report   148, 161, 172 n.5
Dublin   166
Dunkirk   1940 evacuation of   42
Dunkirk (2017 film)   239
Durrell, Lawrence   10, 127–31, 134–8, 140 n.27
  Bitter Lemons   137, 138
  Justine   136
Duschinsky, Richard   77, 78
Dyrenforth, James   19

Egbuna, Obi   152
Egypt   126, 130
Eisenhower, Dwight D.   217, 220, 226–7
Eisenstein, Sergei   202
Eliot, T. S.   49, 51, 162, 164, 165, 170, 182
Ellul, Jacques   6, 101, 119 n.2, 146, 157, 179–80, 186
Empire, British   10, 51, 57–8, 101, 103, 105, 107, 114–17, 125–8, 130, 164, 234, *see also* British Broadcasting Corporation Empire Service; Empire Marketing Board
Empire Marketing Board   116, 153
Empson, William   51
Encounter   204, 205
Erikson, Erik H.   224
Esslin, Martin   75, 77
Esty, Jed   104, 118
Ethiopia   34
Ethniki Organosis Kyprion Agoniston (EOKA)   125, 127, 132–5, 137
Evans, Harold   151, 154
Evans, Ifor   164
Evesham (location of BBC Monitoring Service)   36, 75

Faber and Faber   182
Fairchild, A. H. R.   170
fascism   18, 65, 67, 70, 71, 104, 105, 107, 116–18, 166, 180, 202–3, 222, 227, 228
Fausset, Hugh I'Anson   48
Fenwick, Trevor   83
Fielden, Lionel   53

Financial Times   147–8
First World War   2, 4, 6, 66, 167, 182
Foreign Broadcast Intelligence Service (USA)   45 n.13
Foreign Office (British)   7, 8, 34, 35, 68, 71, 73, 130, 132, 135, 149, 161, 163, 220, *see also* Information Research Department
  News Department   163
Forster, E. M.   49, 52, 71
Fox, Jo   19, 27 n.15, 28 n.17
France   8, 41–3, 68, 71, 74, 125, 164, 208, 239
Frayn, Michael   240
  Democracy   246 n.13
Free Europe's Forces   91
Free French   68, 69, 74
Freetown   154
Freud, Sigmund   53, 210–11 n.16
Freudian   208, 224, 226
From Our Own Correspondent   155
Fulford, Roger
  Osbert Sitwell   167

Gandhi, Mahatma   50
Ganor, Sheer   74
Garnett, David   12 n.17, 45 n.11, 218
Gascoyne, David   162
Gellner, Julius   74, 77
General Post Office (GPO)   71, 72, 83, 91
  Film Unit   153
Georgia, Soviet republic of   198
Germany   24, 25, 41, 42, 68, 69, 71, 74, 113, 114, 203, 214, 219–24, 227, 233, 235, 236, 238–40, *see also* Nazi Party/Nazism
  German colonies in Africa   117, 214
  invasion of Greece   129
  invasion of Soviet Union   185
  invasion of the Sudetenland   34, 73
  propaganda campaigns   20, 24, 36, 38, 41–3, 57, 83, 84, 88, 102, 105, 114, 116, 180–1, 186, 188
  V2 rocket programme in fiction   214–16, 223
Gillie, Darsie   74
Gitelman, Lisa   35
The God that Failed   53, 197, 206
Goebbels, Joseph   25, 203

Gogynfeirdd poems   187
Gombrich, Ernst   71, 75
Grade, Michael   244
Grandin, Thomas   44 n.3
Graves, Harold   27 n.12, 32
Graves, Robert   182
Gray, Milner   84, 96 n.16
Greece   125, 126, 129, 130, 133–7
Greene, Hugh Carleton   74
Griffith, Glyne   53
Grigson, Geoffrey
   Wild Flowers in Britain   104
Grivas, Georgios   134
Gropius, Walter   88

Halifax, Lord   163
Hall, John   149
Hall, Stuart   98 nn.41, 46
Hamilton, Mary Agnes   71
Handley, Tommy   19, 21–6, 28 nn.22, 28,
   29 n.41
Harding, E. A.   35–6
Harding, John   134
Hare, David   2, 233–45
   Beat the Devil   244
   Licking Hitler   2, 11, 233–44
   Page Eight   240
   Plenty   234, 240, 242
   Salting the Battlefield   240
   Turks & Caicos   240
Harman, Richard   86
Harrison, Austen   132
Harrisson, Tom   22, 29–30 nn.47–8
Haskell, Arnold
   Australia   114, 115
Haw-Haw, Lord, *see* Lord Haw Haw
Hawkins, Desmond   56
Hawkins, Jack   242
Hayman, Emily   69
Hendry, J. F. and Henry Treece
   editors of *The New Apocalypse, The
   White Horseman*, and *The
   Crown and the Sickle*   188
Hendy, David   72, 73, 75, 76
Herlitschka, Herberth   69
Hewland, E. D.   117–18
Highet, A. G.   83–4
Hill, Charles   150–1
Hilliard, Christopher   171

Hitler, Adolf   19–26, 71, 73, 77, 202, 203,
   215, 221, 224, 233, 235, 238
Hobson, Harold   18
Hodder & Stoughton   2
Holden, Inez
   It Was Different at the Time   24–5
Hollis, Christopher   166–7
   G. K. Chesterton   166
Holman, Valerie   101, 105
The Holocaust   206–7, 229, 235
Home Office   35, 76, 77
Hosain, Attia   49
How to Fight the Fire-Bomb   91
Howard University   154
Hunter, Rita   149
Huxley, Elspeth   116
   East Africa   116–17

India   1, 2, 9, 48–58, 69, 130, 162, 170
   Independence and Partition   52
Information Research Department (IRD)
   1, 4, 5, 7, 14 nn.27, 31, 150, 161,
   166, 172
Institute of Public Relations   153
International Organisation of
   Revolutionary Writers   198
International Press Exhibition   87
International Workers' Aid   202
Iraq   126, 130
   invasion of (2003)   240–1
Iriye, Akira   66
Isaacs, Jeremy   236
Italy   25, 34, 128, 164
   Propaganda techniques of   180–1,
   186, 188
It's That Man Again   2, 9, 17, 20–6,
   28 n.28, 30 n.59, 31 n.66

J. M. Dent (publisher)   54
Jaffe, Aaron   57
Jameson, Storm   2, 65, 67, 69, 71, 74, 75
   Europe to Let   74
Japan   82, 170
   propaganda by   57
Jebb, Gladwyn   141 n.34
Johnson, Boris   236, 246 n.11
Johnson, Laura   37
Johnson, Pamela Hansford
   I. Compton-Burnett   167

258　　　　　　　　　　Index

Johnston, Gordon and Emma Robertson
   *BBC World Service: Overseas
      Broadcasting 1932–2018*　151
Joint Broadcasting Committee　102
Joyce, James　40, 56–7, 106
Joyce, William, *see* Lord Haw-Haw

Kafka, Ben　35
Kalliney, Peter　4, 55, 173 n.9
Kaplan, Robert D.　125
Kathimerini　135
Katsimbalis, George　130, 135–6
Katz, Daniel　38
Kavanagh, Ted　23, 25, 31 n.66
Kaye, Linda　148
Keane, Damien　50
Keats, John　51, 170
'Keep Calm and Carry On' (poster)
   98 n.38
Kellner, Peter　154
Kenya　116
   Mau Mau uprising　229
Kester, Max　19
Kharkiv　199–200
King George VI　90
King Kong (musical)　152
Kirkpatrick, Ivone　75
Knight, Eric　91
Koch, Stephen　204
Koestler, Arthur　2, 4, 10, 67, 91, 196–210
   Age of Longing　196–7, 208–10
   contribution to *The God that
      Failed*　197
   Darkness at Noon　4, 196–7
   Invisible Writing　197–201
   Red Days and White Nights　197, 199, 201
   Yogi and the Commissar　197
Kokoschka, Oskar　84
Korean War　225, 229
Kreipe, Heinrich　129
Kris, Ernst　45 n.13
Kwapong, A. A.　155
Kyrenia　132, 135

La France Libre　69
Lacombe, Lucien　239
Lancaster, Osbert　129
Langer, Walter C.
   The Mind of Adolf Hitler　224

Lapithos　132
Larkin, Philip　61 n.52
Lawrence, D. H.　106, 188–9
   Apocalypse　188–9
League of Nations　67
Lean, Edward Tangye　33, 41–4
   Voices in the Darkness　41–4
Leavis, F. R.　167, 171
   'Mr. Pryce-Jones, The British Council
      and British Culture'　171
Leeper, Rex　161
Lehmann, John　53–4, 65, 71
Leigh Fermor, Patrick　125, 127–30, 133–6, 138, 140 n.27
Lejeune, Caroline　22, 237
Lerner, Daniel　219
   *Sykewar: Psychological Warfare
      against Germany, D-Day to
      VE-Day*　219
Lessing, Doris　169, 211 n.19
Leszczer, Jonas　77
Leszczer, Serafine　77
Letter from America　155
Life　18, 91
Lift Your Head, Comrade　91
Lindsay, Kenneth
   English Education　113
Linebarger, Paul　219
   Psychological Warfare　219
Lissitzky, El　87
Listener　25
'Listening Post'　38
Liverpool University Press　162, 171–2
Lloyd, Lord George　163
Lockhart, Robert Bruce　220
   Comes the Reckoning　220
London　7, 9, 36, 51, 52, 54, 72, 83, 86, 105, 152, 154, 156, 163, 165, 182
   hosts 1941 Pen Congress　65–70
   hosts European governments-in-exile
      during Second World War　35
   as location for morale boosting
      propaganda　86–93
   Thomas Pynchon's use of London as
      fictional setting　214–15, 221
London Can Take It　91
London Line　10, 145–6, 148–57
   different versions of　145–6, 153
London Pride　10, 82, 85–95

'London Pride' (song by Noel Coward) 96 n.24
Longmans, Green & Co 162, 165, 170
Lord Haw-Haw 9, 17–26, 28 n.28
    parodies of 17
Lord Haw-Haw of Zeesen 17
Louizos, Evangelos 136
Luxembourg 43

The Mabinogion 187
McCarthy, Desmond 67
McCarthyism 206
Macaulay, Rose 10, 18, 102, 108, 119 n.13
    Life Among the English 112
MacCurdy, J. T. 223
Macdonald, Elizabeth P. 219
    Undercover Girl 219
McEwan, Ian 238
    The Imitation Game 246 n.12
McKenna, Wayne 106
MacKenzie, John M. 133
Maclean, Donald 237
McLuhan, Marshall
    Understanding Media: *The Extensions of Man* 217
McMeekin, Sean 202–4, 211 n.23
Macmillan (publisher) 2
Macmillan, Harold 135, 151
MacNeice, Louis 10, 48, 52, 53, 91
Mahdi, Badamassie 152
Makarios III, Archbishop 126, 132, 135
Malaya Emergency 134
Malkki, Liisa H. 76–7
Malle, Louis 239
Malraux, André 208
Manchester Guardian 74
Mann, Erika 67, 69
Mann, Thomas 66
Mansell, Gerard 35
Mantel, Hilary 225
March of the Nation 91
Marwick, Arthur 156
Marx, Karl 53
    Marxism 53, 199, 204–6, 208
Masaryk, Jan 67
Masefield, John 163
Mass-Observation 22, 94, 114, 165, 186–7, 194 n.19

Matheson, Hilda 102, 105, 106, 114, 118
Mayhew, Christopher 150
Mazrui, Ali Al'amin 155
Melville, Jean-Pierre 239
Menand, Louis 8
Menon, Narayana 52, 55
Methuen (publisher) 2
Mexico 65, 66
MI5 218, 240–2
MI6, *see* Secret Intelligence Service
Miller, Henry 129, 130
Miller, Lee 238
Miller, Max 17
Millin, Sarah
    South Africa 117
Mills, John 242
Milton Bryan (site of PWE facility) 7
Ministry of Home Security 91
Ministry of Information (MOI) 2, 4–7, 10, 21–2, 35–7, 54, 71, 74, 91–2, 94, 101, 105, 125, 130, 148, 161, 167, 179–82, 186, 187, 206, 224, 228
    Britain in Pictures book series 2, 10, 101–18, 165
    table of selected books in series 109–11
    Exhibition Division 93
    exhibitions 82–95, 97 n.26
    home front photography team 93
    Photograph Library 87, 96 n.28
Mitford, Jessica 243
Modern Publicity in War 94
Moholy-Nagy, László 88, 97 nn.33, 44
Montis, Costas
    Closed Doors: An Answer to Bitter Lemons by Lawrence Durrell 137
Morgan, Charles 69
Morrison, Herbert 86
Morse, Daniel Ryan 3
Mosley, Oswald 18
Mukerjee, Ankhi 48
Münzenberg, Willi 202–4, 207, 209, 211 n.23
Murdoch, Iris 169
Murray, Craig 246 n.15
Murray, John Grey 133
My Word 155

Naipaul, V. S. 53
National Book Council 164, 165
National Theatre 54
Nazi Party/Nazism (Germany) 3, 9, 17,
    19, 24–5, 67, 71, 73, 75–6, 83,
    84, 115, 117, 180, 181, 186, 203,
    206, 214–16, 221, 222, 224, 227,
    232 n.41, 233, 235, 240
Neale, Hannah (née Bright-Taylor) 150,
    152
Nelligan, Kate 233, 234
Netherlands 43
Neumann, Robert 69
New Apocalypse poetics 188
New Criticism 51, 54, 60 n.19
New Directions 54
New Statesman 22, 102
New Towns for Old 91
New York Times 125
New York Times Magazine 206
Ngakane, Lionel 152
Ngũgĩ wa Thiong'o 152
Nicholas, Siân 19, 20
Nicosia 126, 135, 136
Nigeria 153
Night and Fog 239
Nolan, Christopher 239
Northcote House Publishers 171
Norway 67

Obote, Milton 155
O'Brien, Kate 102, 119 n.13
The Observer 22
O'Connor, Brigid and Stephan Roman
    'Building Bridges with Books: The
    British Council's Sixty-Year
    Record' 163–4
Odette 238
Odhams (publisher) 105
O'Duffy, Eoin 71
Office of Strategic Services (OSS) 207,
    217, 219, 224, 228, 230 n.19
    use of psychological science 224
Office of War Information (OWI) 217,
    219
Oldman, Gary 239
Orwell, George 1, 3, 4, 10, 43–4, 49,
    55–6, 91, 102, 108, 119 n.13,
    120 n.32, 207

Animal Farm 4
Nineteen Eighty-Four 225–6, 235
Orzoff, Andrea 67
Osborne, John 169
Otten, Karl 74
Oxford University 155, 168

Palestine (British Mandate) 126
Palmer, Richmond 126
Paris 74, 202, 208, 238, 243
Patel, Priti 244–5, 247 n.18
Paterson, Bill 233
Pavlovian psychology 217, 218, 223–6,
    228
Peace Pledge Union 67
Penguin (publisher) 92
Pereszlényi, Julius, *see* Esslin, Martin
Philip, André 74
Pick, Frank 83
Picture Post 91–2, 98 n.41
Piette, Adam 21–2, 29 n.40
Pile, Frederick 18
Play For Today 234, 244
Plock, Vike Martina 3, 76–7
Plumb, J. H.
    G. M. Trevelyan 167
Poets, Essayists and Novelists club
    (PEN) 2, 5, 9, 65–72, 74–8
    1938 Czechoslovakia Congress 67
    1941 London Congress 65–70, 77
Poland 67, 68
Political Warfare Executive (PWE) 5, 7,
    11, 12 n.16, 14 n.31, 35, 37, 39,
    45 n.11, 71, 74, 75, 78, 125, 129,
    161, 167, 215–29, 233–7, 242
    *Deutsche Kurzwellensender
    Atlantik* 222
    'Gustav Siegfried Eins'
    broadcasts 215, 233
Potter, Rachel 70
Potter, Simon 40, 133
Potts, Jim 129
Pound, Ezra 71
Powell, Dilys 237
Pratchett, Terry 175 n.41
Priestley, J. B. 3, 20, 69, 71, 72, 77, 78
    'Postscripts' 20
Prodromos 131
Proops, Marjorie 149

propaganda, *see also entries for agencies; individuals; locations; and works*
  appeals to 'Englishness' and/or 'Britishness'   101–2, 104–7, 114
  British appeal to Empire and colonies   10, 49–50, 72, 101, 114–17, 125–7, 138
  comparison of different national techniques   180–1, 183, 186, 188
  definitions of   5–9
  difference between political warfare and psychological warfare   230 n.2
  difference between propaganda and cultural diplomacy   8
  distinction between types   6, 13 n.23, 101, 119 n.2
    'Black'   6, 7, 215–16, 235
    'counter propaganda'   18, 20, 26, 28 n.27, 179, 182, 184, 206, 207
    'Grey'   7
    'Grey literature'   35, 45 n.9
    'indirect propaganda'   101, 103
    'White'   7, 101
  media
    books   101–18, 137–8, 161–72, 198–201, 203
    cinema and televisual   91, 145–53, 156–8
    exhibitions   82–95
    magazines   136–7, 205
    oral   128, 130–4
    photography   82–5, 88–93
    radio   17–26, 32–44, 48–58, 69–78, 114, 155, 180, 215, 222, 233
  reflections on propaganda in literature   179, 181–93, 196–210, 214–29, 233–9, 241–5
  refugees and   65–78
  use of psychological science in   224, 225
  Willi Münzenberg's innovations in   202–4
Pryce-Jones, Alan   171
Pudovkin, Vsevolod   202
Pynchon, Thomas   2, 11, 214–29
  The Crying of Lot 49   217
  Gravity's Rainbow   2, 11, 214–29

QAnon   241

Radio Fun   24, 26
Radio Luxembourg   23, 30 n.54
Raine, Kathleen   167, 193 n.17
  William Blake   167
Rao, Raja   57
Rashford, Marcus   244–5, 247 n.18
Read, Herbert   162, 167
  Byron   166–7
  The Red Book   187
Regan, Kylie   228
Reichstag fire (1933)   202–3, 221
Renier, Olive and Vladimir Rubinstein
  Assigned to Listen   37
Resnais, Alain   239
Reynolds, David   245 n.7
Rhodes, Cecil   117
Rhodes Hall (Oxford)   155
Rhys, Keidrych   182
Rice, Tom   153
Riefenstahl, Leni   147
Rilla, Walter   74
Roberts, Harry
  English Gardens   113–14
Roberts, Lynette   2, 10, 179, 181–93 nn.16–17, 195 n.33
  Gods with Stainless Ears   2, 10, 179, 181–93
  Poems   182, 184
Rogers, Asha   171
Rolo, Charles J.   18, 19
Romilly, Esmond   243
Rose, David   238
Rotheray, Brian   44 n.4
Roufos, Rodis   130
  The Bronze Age   137–8
Royal Court Theatre   152
Ruganda, John   152
Runciman, Steven   129
Russell, Bertrand   207
Russia   198, *see also* Soviet Union
  contemporary propaganda   241

Sabine, Noel
  The British Colonial Empire   115–16
Sackville-West, Edward   51, 53
Sackville-West, Vita   10, 53, 56, 102
Said, Edward   60 n.33

Saint-Amour, Paul 102
Sanoudakis, Antonis 136
Sartre, Jean-Paul 208
Saunders, Frances Stonor
   Who Paid the Piper? The CIA and the Cultural Cold War 3–4, 207–8, 213 n.58
Saurat, Denis 67
Schellenberg, T. R. 44 n.5
Schwartz, Joanna 77
Sconce, Jeffrey 26
Scott, Catharine Amy Dawson 66
Scott-Kilvert, Ian 169
Scrutiny 171
Second World War 1–10, *see also entries for agencies; individuals; and locations*
   development of a cadre of British 'soldier-aesthete' during wartime 125, 127–33
   growth of British Council during the war 163
   legacy of the war in literature and culture 179–93, 214–29, 233–45
   radio comedy propaganda in 17–26
   radio monitoring in 32–44
   refugee writers 65–78
   print propaganda 101–18
   wartime exhibitions 82–95
Secret Intelligence Service (MI6) 148, 240–1
Seed, David 217, 226
Seferis, George 130, 136
   'Salamis in Cyprus' 137
Selvon, Sam 53
SHAEF, Psychological Warfare Division (PWD/SHAEF) 217, 219
Shakespeare, William 52, 165, 167, 170
Shaw, Bernard 165–6, 170
Shelf Appeal 91, 93–4
Shelley, Percy Bysshe 51, 53
Sherrard, Philip 129
Shils, Edward and Morris Janowitz
   'Cohesion and Disintegration in the Wehrmacht in World War II' 231 n.20
Sierra Leone 2, 10, 153–6
   Sierra Leone Ministry of Information 156
   Sierra Leone News Agency 156

Sikorski, Władysław 67
Sinclair, Robert 91
Sisson C. J.
   Shakespeare 170–1
Sitwell, Edith 10
Słonimski, Antoni 69
Smith, James 71, 200–1
Smythe, F. S.
   British Mountaineers 107, 113
Snow, Charles 167
Solti, Georg 148
Soviet Union 54, 152, 166, 185, 196, 198–210, 235
   propaganda techniques of 4, 87, 180–1, 186, 188, 196, 201
Soyinka, Wole 152, 169
   'The Detainee' 152
   The Lion and the Jewel 152
Spanish Civil War 53, 243
Special Operations Executive (SOE) 75, 125, 128, 129, 135, 215, 218
Spectator 102, 135
Speier, Hans 45 n.13
Spender, Stephen 50, 53–4, 56, 71, 162
Spyridakis, Konstantinos 136
Squires, Claire 48
Stalin, Joseph 166, 196, 198, 200, 207
Stalinism 196–7
Starey, Gavin 91
Stark, Freya 2, 125, 127, 128, 130–4, 137, 138, 140 n.27, 141 n.34
   The Journey's Echo 131
Stephenson, Donald 58
Stevens, Siaka 156
Stonebridge, Lyndsey 70
Storm over Asia 202
Stuart, Campbell 7
Sudetenland (invasion of) 34, 73
Suez Crisis (1956) 148
Sumner, George 17
Sutherland, Efua 152
Swan, Michael
   Henry James 166
Swansea Blitz (February 1941) 189
Sweden 164
Swinnerton, Frank
   Arnold Bennett 166

Tagore, Rabindranath 66
Tallents, Stephen 96 n.10, 153

The Tatler 23
Taunton, Matthew   212 n.35
Taylor, Geoffrey
   Insect Life in Britain   112–13
Taylor, Philip M.   4, 6
Tennyson, Alfred   51, 113
Third Programme   50, 51, 152
Thomas, Adrian   84–5
Thomas, Dylan   2, 48–51, 53–8, 58 n.7,
      59 n.12, 61 nn.44, 48, 91, 182,
      186, 188
   Under Milk Wood   48, 54
Thomson, David   145
Thomson, Lord   150
The Times   68, 89, 90, 103
Times Literary Supplement   162, 170, 171
Tolkien, J. R. R.   168–9
   Lord of the Rings   168, 169
Tololyan, Khachig   216–19, 226
Tremayne, Penelope   129, 133
Trevor-Roper, Hugh   206
Turkey   126, 132, 133, 135
Turkmen Soviet Socialist Republic   198
Turner, Lyndsey   54
Turner, W. J.   102, 105–8, 112–14, 118
   English Ballet   106
   English Music   106–8, 112

Ukrainian Soviet Socialist Republic
      198–200, 202, 205
   German-speaking population   199
UNESCO   8
United States of America   1, 3, 18, 19, 22,
      29 n.44, 35, 38, 45 n.13, 54, 55,
      67–9, 77, 91, 147, 149, 152, 154,
      155, 172, 183, 196, 201, 206,
      207, 214, 217, 220, 224, 229
   accounts of British propaganda   219
   appeals to USA in British
      propaganda   1, 91
   tours of British propaganda in   94
Universal Declaration of Human Rights
      (1948)   70
Unwin, Stanley   163
Usill, Harley V.
   *The Story of the British People in
      Pictures*   105
USSR, *see* Soviet Union
Uzbekistan   243, 246 n.15
   Uzbek Soviet Socialist Republic   198

Vaughan, James   130–1
Vietnam War   229
Viswanathan, Gauri   50
Voice   53

Walcott, Derek   53
Wales   49, 57, 179, 182–9, 191–2
Wales (journal)   182
War Office   35
War Propaganda Bureau   2
Ward, A. C.   165
   Bernard Shaw   165–6
Warner, Oliver   166–7
   Joseph Conrad   166
Warner, Rex   102, 129, 130, 162
   E. M. Forster   166
Warner, Sylvia Townsend   167
   Jane Austen   167
Wehner, Carl   76, 77
Weidenfeld, George   75
Weisenburger, Steven   216
Welch, David   5–6
Wellesley, Dorothy   105, 113
   English Poets in Pictures   120 n.33
Wellington House   2–3
Wells, H. G.   66, 67, 69, 71, 75
Wentworth, Lady   102
West, Rebecca   25, 26, 66, 69
West, Richard   154
Western Brothers   17, 27 n.10
Wheeler, Charles   155
White, Antonia   19, 33, 39–41
   BBC at War   19, 39–41
   Frost in May   39
Whittington, Ian   3, 18, 28 nn.25, 28,
      71–2
Wiener Library   235, 245 n.8
Wiesenthal, Simon   235
Wilford, Hugh   4
Wilkinson, Ellen   86
Williams, Raymond   92, 121 n.34
Winant, John   68–9
Wollaeger, Mark   71
   *Modernism, Media, and
      Propaganda*   3
Women at War (exhibition)   91
Women's International League   67
Woodward, Guy   130–1
Woolf, Virginia   69, 71, 108, 170
Wordsworth, William   51, 170

Workers International Relief 67
The World at War 236
World Committee Against War and
    Fascism 202
World of Plenty 91
Worsley, Francis 21, 23, 24, 30 n.59

Yeats, W. B. 55, 71
Yemen 130
Yonge, Charles Maurice 102
Yugoslavia 41, 43, 130

www.ingramcontent.com/pod-product-compliance
Lightning Source LLC
Chambersburg PA
CBHW071813300426
44116CB00009B/1300